W9-CJT-163

A BASIC
RECIPE BOOK
FOR EPICURES

A BASIC RECIPE BOOK FOR EPICURES

21 BASIC RECIPES WITH DOZENS OF SPLENDID DISHES BASED ON THEM

Lillian Langseth-Christensen

FUNK & WAGNALLS
NEW YORK

Library of Congress Catalog Card Number: 68–31892

Published by Funk & Wagnalls, *A Division of* Reader's Digest Books, Inc.

PRINTED IN THE UNITED STATES OF AMERICA

FOR

Debbie AND *Lans*

Acknowledgments

I would like to express my thanks to the following organizations for allowing me to reproduce their charts (see pp. 180–187):

National Live Stock and Meat Board, Chicago, Illinois
Poultry and Egg National Board, Chicago, Illinois
The Fishery Council, New York, N.Y.

I want to thank Mrs. Betty Wodjenski for her interest and for her assistance in typing the manuscript.

Contents

Information

1. All measurements used in this book are level. Standard measuring spoons and cups are used throughout, except where food is so shaped that cup measurements would not be accurate. In those cases ounces and pounds are used.
2. A pinch means less than ⅛ teaspoon.
3. All flour, unless bread, cake, or corn flour is specified, is enriched, all-purpose flour.
4. All oil, unless olive oil is specified, is salad oil.
5. All sugar, unless otherwise specified, is granulated sugar.
6. All eggs used in the recipes should be Large or Extra Large, weighing from 24 to 27 ounces per dozen.
7. All recipes, unless otherwise specified, serve six.

A BASIC
RECIPE BOOK
FOR EPICURES

HOW TO USE THIS BOOK AND PROFIT FROM IT

This is not another book of isolated recipes to be thumbed through when you cannot think what to cook for dinner. It is a book that will show you how forever to avoid that predicament.

This book is based on a ground work of twenty-one instruction recipes and some seven hundred elaborations and embellishments upon them. They are the twenty-one basic recipes that underlie the thousands of simple or imaginative variations that constitute our cookery. The purpose of this book is to demonstrate that the basic recipes are the only ones that every good cook has to know and every young novice cook has to learn. All other recipes are descended from them and require the same preparation; they appear in lists or charts after each basic recipe.

The beginner should memorize the twenty-one basic recipes, more or less in the order in which they are listed; the experienced cook should simply brush up on them. A basic recipe is elementary in that it is not a combination of other recipes but consists only of its necessary ingredients. It in turn is used as a base for the countless descendant recipes.

Take mayonnaise, for example. An early chronicler with an eye for basic recipe cooking wrote, "Mayonnaise is a planet around which numerous satellites gravitate, the highway from which many paths diverge." That is only another way of saying what we illustrate so clearly on pages 118 to 127. There you will find an instruction recipe for basic mayonnaise, a second recipe for making it quickly in an electric blender, and forty-nine other variations. You can add almost anything to it—spices, herbs, condiments, citrus fruit juices, brandy, whipped cream, or gelatin. You can follow the great traditional variations which appear in the book or improvise with combinations of your own. You are off. Go down all those divergent paths that lead from the mayonnaise highway, and your menus, at least the cold ones, will never again be repetitious. You will have learned just one recipe, and hundreds of others will be yours gratis. It takes a little less than a minute to make mayonnaise in a blender and less than five to beat it in a bowl. If you prefer to buy it in a jar, this book is just as valid since all the variations apply to basic mayonnaise, no matter who made it.

Since all Occidental cookery depends completely on basic recipes, they should be learned with care and for keeps. Treat them with respect. They have been around for centuries and have become the ancestors that are the base of enormous family trees. They are the recipes upon which you will presently learn to improvise, they are the recipes which can and should be cooked ahead (the only exception is hollandaise, the other basic egg sauce), and they are the patient, stand-by recipes which will see you through all kitchen emergencies.

The list of basic recipes sounds like a French menu largely because most of them are French. The housewives of France have been cooking systematically with basic recipes for generations. They've always had their stockpots going for them, their jars of roux and béchamel, and their cache of tart paste. For them basic recipe cooking has been providential and economical, for us it has to save time and money and work. The basic recipes, like all rudimentary things, are fundamentally simple. You will learn to make a thin pancake and fill it with jam and serve it up in seconds. It doesn't have to be crêpes suzette every time . . . but it can be, at the drop of a little orange liqueur.

When the novice has caught up to the experienced cook and has learned the basic recipes, this book turns into a menu exploder. Just knowing how to make a few individual dishes, no matter how superb, does not make one a cook. It is the large repertoire, the endless variations, the knowledge and wisdom to cook ahead that really count.

This is a book with purpose: To teach the novice cook the basic "five finger exercises" of the kitchen; to show her that when the elementary groundwork has been mastered she can cook anything; to prove that it is possible to be a versatile gourmet cook without straining a muscle; to show the experienced cook that she has a far wider repertoire at her fingertips than she ever suspected.

Cooking, in a sense, is an endless series of variations on a surprisingly small number of basic themes. This book has isolated and simplified the themes and listed the best known and most useful variations. Most cooks do not realize that they know more than they think. They look upon each newly acquired dish as an isolated accomplishment and repeat it into infinity because they forget to consider the related dishes, the countless cousins on the same family tree.

The quickest way to change from a novice who shudders over entertaining and whose small repertoire collapses in an emergency into a versatile cook and calm hostess is to learn the twenty-one basic recipes (see page 4) and study their many descendants. The cook who, up to now, has been proud of her unrelated specialties cannot cope with unexpected guests. Unless she has all the necessary ingredients in the house and the time to prepare them, she has to take her guests to the nearest restaurant. She does not know that yesterday's leftover chicken is first cousin to poularde princesse (p. 62). All she has to do is take a few minutes to stir up a sauce suprême, page 54, open a can of artichoke bottoms and voilà! She has taken another leaf out of the secret book of French cooking. To top it all she whips the egg whites left over from the sauce suprême into a fantastic concoction from Salzburg called Salzburger nockerdln (page 264), which is much easier to eat than pronounce.

The two other advantages of basic recipe cooking are economy in time and money. The week's cooked-ahead supply of white sauce can reappear during the week in various unrelated dishes. The white sauce is the unrecognizable base of dishes as diverse as Sunday's cream soup, Monday's soufflé, Tuesday's fricassee, Wednesday's creamed eggs, Thursday's casserole, and Friday's fish gratinée. The tail end of the white sauce need not be thrown away. Stir it with softened gelatin and heavy cream and it becomes that beautiful white coating on Saturday's chicken Jeanette.

A more extreme example of basic recipe cooking is to learn to make that unassuming little choux paste cocktail puff and find it is identical to the mighty Croquembouche, showpiece of the master chef. All cooking is closely related, and it is just as easy to learn one hundred recipes as one. It also means the end of menu making (and eating) boredom.

It is, of course, not enough just to read the basic recipe and prepare it haphazardly. The recipe should be learned in all its ramifications down to the smallest, apparently insignificant, detail. There is no step in the preparation of a sound basic recipe that does not have a good reason behind it, usually a reason discovered by our betters. The family trees of variations that follow the basic recipes are only reminders that nothing need be the same, at least not for several weeks. If you can make one lovely creamy cream sauce, bake a tender tart shell, and fry a float-away fritter, you can do them all. After that use the charts under basic cooking processes and you can cook. Don't repeat your excellent hollandaise sauce forever: Change it into Sauce Maltaise for your next asparagus and into Sauce Choron or magenta for the next tender steak.

There are only twenty-one basic recipes, some of which, such as puff pastry, may never have to enter your life. You don't really have to know how to make noodles either, but most of the recipes are important. If you are in a hurry, you can be a good and versatile cook in weeks. There may be some failures at first. Our dog, who used to eat all my failures, had to eat twenty-four egg whites in one day before I learned to make that meringue confection from Vienna, the "Spanische Wind Torte," page 263.

THE TWENTY-ONE BASIC RECIPES

1 Chicken Stock
2 Beef Stock
3 Veal Stock
4 Fish Stock
5 White Sauce
6 Brown Sauce
7 Hollandaise Sauce
8 Mayonnaise Sauce
9 Aspic
10 Mousse
11 Fritters and Croquettes
12 Pancakes and Omelets

13 Strudel Paste
14 Noodle Paste
15 Short Paste
16 Flaky and Puff Pastry
17 Choux Paste
18 Cake Batters
19 Sugar Paste
20 Yeast Bread
21 Quick Bread

LESSON I

MENU MAKING

Cooking is no longer an art practiced by professionals alone. It is a necessity practiced by most women and many men, and they are wisely turning it into a pleasure.

It is not on cooking alone that a successful dinner depends, and it is not with cooking that the dinner begins. The meal has to be planned in advance and the menu should be made before, not during, the cooking. The whole thing should start with a pad and pencil, not with a kitchen spoon or a marketing cart.

The menu must consist not only of dishes and accompaniments that complement them, but the courses have to be planned to support and enhance each other. What good does the most beautiful fillet of beef do the guest who has been fed sweet-sour pork and pineapple balls with cocktails and is about to end his meal with marshmallow delight? Do not go into bankruptcy for caviar if you are going to follow it with deviled chicken and follow that with hot gingerbread.

Anyone who is interested in food can learn to cook, but menu making takes more than a set of directions. It requires imagination, talent, good taste, and a sense of harmony. We shall give you all the basic rules for good menu making and we try to show you how to develop the other factors.

While the best cook cannot produce a good dinner if she does not know how to make a good menu, the best menu maker cannot produce a good dinner unless she has a wide repertoire from which to choose. The purpose of this book is to widen the cook's repertoire with one swoop and thereby enable her to make beautiful, harmonious, and easily executed menus.

The rules and examples that follow are not the old basic rules which said that dinner had to include one vegetable that grew over the ground and one vegetable that grew under the ground (probably the period when peas and carrots were wed). They are the new basic rules that fit our new conditions: The fact that most homemakers and hostesses are also the cook and the fact that time has become shorter than it used to be. Finally the new rules bear in mind the happy circumstances that we have refrigerators and freezers and that in spite of our lack of time, our interest, understanding, and pleasure in good food and entertaining are increasing constantly.

There are two kinds of menus that have to be faced: those for daily home consumption and those for entertaining. The daily meals are, of course, the hardest since they must be adapted to growing children, active husbands, weight watching (whether for increase or decrease), and the budget. Pediatricians usually advise on children's diets, and mothers should remember to vary them as much as they possibly can so that they will not end up with a child who lives on peanut butter. Eating habits are acquired early and the brides who find they have husbands who eat steak and nothing but steak have only their mothers-in-law to blame.

Variety in daily menus should be in the food as well as in the preparation of it. Chicken need not always be fried, pies can be filled with any number of things besides apples. Boiled beef with horseradish sauce is a pleasant change from the standing rib roast.

Casseroles are all very well, but only when several days elapse between them. Leftovers should be used, of course—there are even some dishes we eat just for the sake of the leftovers—but they should not follow immediately upon the dish from which they sprang. When leg of lamb comes, let the shepherd's pie be at least two days behind.

Menu making is reminiscent of music: Even the terms are the same. The cook and the soprano need a large repertoire, the dinner and the opera are better for a prelude, and both need an intermission. Beautiful arias alone do not make an opera, and superb isolated dishes do not make a dinner. There has to be a score for the opera, a program for the concert, and a menu for dinner. There has to be a conductor and the scene has to be properly set. Both need harmony and melody and unobtrusive accompaniments. There has to be a sympathetic audience and, if the cook is to survive, there has to be applause.

BASIC RULES FOR MENU MAKING

With our changing entertaining habits the hostess can do almost anything she wants with her menus, provided she does not offend against the basic rules of good taste, reason, and health. It no longer matters whether there is a soup course, but it does matter, and any doctor will agree, that no one can eat a meal made up entirely of deep fat fried foods, cucumber salad, and ice cold beer.

1. Make your menu according to your abilities and the time you have available. Always bear in mind that there will be less time than you think.

2. Include dishes that come easily to you. Never try a new recipe on a guest.

3. Make menu, cooking schedule, and marketing list simultaneously and check staples. In addition to checking your staples and your marketing list when you make the menu, check your equipment. Have you enough double boilers to keep soup, sauce, and vegetables hot? Can you have hot canapés, a roast, and warm plates too? Will you blow a fuse if you use numerous small electric appliances?

4. Do not attempt to bake while you are cooking. If the menu is going to include anything home-baked, do it the day, or several days, before. Nothing disrupts the preparation of a dinner party and the hairdo more than getting bread, cookies, cakes, or pastries in and out of the oven.

5. Even when there is both time and help, at least one of the courses should be prepared and cooked ahead. All dinners are better for being prepared at leisure and for being prepared by a relaxed hostess. When there is no help and little time, it is essential that the majority of the dishes be prepared and cooked ahead. In making the menu, select only one course that has to be cooked the same day and choose that course carefully. It can be a roast that roasts by itself or a casserole that bakes by itself. If it is a slow-cooking dish, be sure it is one that does not require frequent basting or observation. Nothing is more disconcerting to a guest than the sound of a kitchen timer going off, or a hostess rushing off in mid-sentence.

If you do not choose a slow-cooking dish, then select a last-minute dish such as filet steaks or scallopini. Guests would rather lose the hostess for the last ten minutes before dinner than have her interrupt a pleasant cocktail hour with constant exits and entrances.

Warm-weather menus are easy to make, since almost everything can be prepared ahead and chilled. Cold-weather dishes when cooked ahead have to be reheated, and reheating is an art in itself. Make a menu that takes reheating into account. If part of it is oven heating and part of it is double-boiler heating, remember there are plates to heat, too.

Always prepare everything that is preparable the day, or days, before the party. Wash parsley, chop some of it, prepare salad greens, salad dressings, sauces, butter pats or balls, hardcooked eggs, garnishes. Store parsley and greens in air-tight plastic bags. Store everything else in covered containers. Place hardcooked eggs and butter in cold water.

6. Do not concern yourself with nutrition in making a dinner party menu (what if your guests do not have their minimum daily intake of Vitamin C), but do concern yourself with health. Even if your guests are vigorous and well, do not give them too many heavy foods or fatal combinations.

7. Don't give them ultra-exotic, far-fetched dishes. Snails, frogs' legs, total garlic sauces, and baby squid are only for those who love them.

8. Do not give men luncheon dishes. Most of them dislike molded salads.

9. Alternate cooking processes, alternate hot and cold dishes, alternate light and heavy dishes. Alternate colors, alternate sauced and unsauced dishes.

10. Watch carefully; you can easily end up with nothing but fruit or nothing but sauces.

Melon Wedges with Lime Juice
Duck with Orange Sauce
Cherries Jubilee

or

Asparagus Hollandaise
Vitello Tonnato
(Veal with Tunafish Sauce)
Profiteroles with Chocolate Sauce

Or you can suddenly discover your dinner is all one color, white.

Cream of Leek and Potato Soup
Chicken Jeanette
Cauliflower Salad
Vanilla Bavarian Cream with Meringues

Or a fried dinner.

Mushroom Fritters with Tartar Sauce
Viennese Fried Chicken
Shoestring Potatoes
Beignet Soufflé

Or an unintentional boiled dinner.

Cream of Mushroom Soup
Chicken in Spinach Sauce
Corn
Rice Ring with Stewed Peaches

Then there is the alcoholic dinner for teetotalers.

Green Turtle Soup with Sherry
Boeuf Bourguignonne
Crêpes Suzette

These are the sort of things you do not realize are happening until they have happened.

11. Take the golden middle road, not too little and not too much, not too fat and not too lean.

12. In spring and in fall be prepared to change the temperature of your dinner with the weather. Chilled soups can be heated, hot dishes can be chilled.

13. If it is an important dinner, have a dry run by trying it on your family. Rehearse, time yourself, know just when to put in the soufflé and when to light the candles.

14. Have the wit to abandon some traditional combinations and re-create some lovely old ones. There are hundreds of variations in this book that will give your guests the change they hoped for when they accepted your invitation.

WINES

How to Serve? Or with What to Serve?

1. Serve red wine at room temperature. Open the bottle several

hours before the wine is to be served. Serve red wines with red meat, game, gamebirds, roast lamb, and with cheese.

2. Chill rosé wines and serve them with red or white meat in spring or summer. Rosés are not cold-weather wines.

3. Serve chilled white wine with fish, poultry, white meats such as veal, and blanquettes or stews of lamb.

4. Chilled champagne may be served throughout a meal, or as a dessert wine.

5. Wine bowls, Sangria, and similar combinations are summer drinks. The general rules for white and red wines and what to serve them with holds good for bowls and for the Central European Bowlen too. Serve May wine with white meat, Sangria with red meat.

6. Dessert wines are served with desserts. Liqueurs and brandy are served with or after black coffee after dinner.

7. Cold beer is served with some pork dishes or stews, cheeses or dark meats, never with sweets or fruit.

HOW TO USE THE BASIC MENUS THAT FOLLOW

1. Select a menu that suits the occasion and your abilities.

2. The menu is only a token suggestion, worked out to spread work and not to overstrain cooking space and equipment. Do not hesitate to make substitutions from the lists of variations after basic recipes.

3. If the menu suggests cream of asparagus soup, any creamed vegetable soup can be substituted, provided the vegetable does not reappear on the menu in any other form.

4. Substitute any roast in a menu based on a roasted meat.

5. Substitute and add or subtract, but follow the general balance of the meal.

6. Do not substitute a heavy cream soup or rich dessert where a bouillon or sherbet is suggested, but do improvise and adapt to suit your preferences and your budget. Serve fish, cheese, eggs, and greens with cocktails before a meat dinner. Serve meatballs or sausages before a chicken or fish dinner.

7. Check wine list on pages 11 and 12 for substitute wines. If menu is changed from a red to a white meat, wine should be changed according to above suggestions.

7 BASIC DINNER PARTY MENUS FOR WINTER

I.

With Cocktails:
Cheese Wafers
Celery and Olives
Chicken Liver Pâté with Crackers

Hot Cream of Mushroom Soup
Oven-Dried Brioche Slices

Roast Saddle of Lamb
(takes 35 minutes on rotisserie without basting)
Purée of Green Peas
topped with
Browned Onion Slices
Mint Sauce
Potatoes in Casserole

Coffee Mousse
Sugar Cookies

Coffee

Serve a light red wine

SCHEDULE

Bake at any time and store in freezer:
- Cheese wafers
- Sugar cookies

One or two days before dinner:
- Make cream of mushroom soup
- Oven dry brioche slices
- Prepare chicken liver pâté
- Cook and purée green peas
- Prepare and chill coffee mousse

On day of dinner:
- Clean and crisp celery
- Prepare and bake potatoes in casserole
- Brown onions to garnish peas
- Roast saddle of lamb
- Make coffee

II. With Cocktails:
Carrot Sticks with Cream Cheese and Onion Dip
Anchovy and Egg Slices on Toast Rounds

Spinach Soufflé with Mushroom Sauce

Italian Broiled Chicken with Risotto
and
Mixed Green Salad

Zabaglione with Half Moons

Coffee

Serve a dry white wine

SCHEDULE
Bake at anytime and store in freezer:
- Half moons

One or two days before dinner:
- Hardcook eggs
- Mix cream cheese, onion juice, and mayonnaise
- Toast bread rounds
- Make soufflé base
- Make mushroom sauce
- Make salad dressing
- Prepare and chill zabaglione

On day of dinner:
- Clean and crisp salad greens
- Cut and crisp carrot sticks
- Add stiff egg whites and bake soufflé
- Broil chicken
- Cook risotto
- Make coffee

III. With Cocktails:
Crisp Cucumber Slices
Small Crabmeat Puffs
Fresh-Roasted Pistachio Nuts

Clear Bouillon with Madeira Wine
and Choux Paste "Peas"

Roasted Individual Birds:
Squab, Game Hens, or Baby Pheasant
Green Vegetable

Thin Noodles with Fried Breadcrumbs
Ligonberries

Celery Root Salad with Oregano Dressing

Orange Ice with Curaçao
Dry Wafers

Coffee

Serve red wine with squab or pheasant
Serve white wine with game hens

SCHEDULE
Bake at anytime and store in freezer:
- Dry wafers

One or two days before dinner:
- Toast bread rounds for crabmeat puffs
- Prepare choux paste "peas"
- Fry breadcrumbs and store in airtight container
- Cook and slice celery root, or use canned
- Make salad dressing
- Prepare crabmeat mixture for puffs

On day of dinner:
- Slice and season cucumbers
- Broil crabmeat puffs
- Roast birds, make brown sauce
- Boil vegetable and noodles
- Make coffee

IV. A GOOD FRENCH DINNER

Assorted hors d'oeuvre

Burgundian Beef Stew
or
Lamb Cassoulet

Green Bean Salad

Rum Baba

Coffee

Serve a heavier red wine with the stew than with the cassoulet

SCHEDULE
The day before:
Prepare everything
On day of dinner:
Heat stew or cassoulet and baba before serving.

V. A GOOD HUNGARIAN DINNER

Mushroom Fritters with Remoulade Sauce

Paprika Chicken
Parsley Potatoes
Celery Root and Cucumber Salads

Applesauce with Macaroon Crumb Topping

Coffee

Serve a white wine

SCHEDULE
The day before:
Prepare everything except mushrooms and potatoes.
On day of dinner:
Fry mushroom fritters at the last moment
Heat paprika chicken
Boil potatoes

VI.

With Cocktails:
Broiled Tomato and Bacon Puffs
Sliced Egg Roll with Hot Mustard Sauce
Crisp Celery

Tuna Fish and White Beans
Vinaigrette

Leg of Lamb
Potato Soufflé
Baby Carrots with Parsley

Pecan Pie
Rum-Flavored Whipped Cream

Coffee

Serve a light red wine

SCHEDULE

The day before:

Prepare mustard sauce, tuna fish and white beans, vinaigrette sauce. Clean and crisp celery. Marinate lamb. Bake pecan pie. Boil and mash potatoes.

The same day:

Heat egg rolls. Broil tomato and bacon puffs. Roast lamb, boil carrots, bake potato soufflé, and whip cream.

VII. A TRADITIONAL ROAST BEEF DINNER

Cream of Celery Soup
with
Toasted Cheese Crackers

Standing Rib Roast of Beef
Yorkshire Pudding
A Green Vegetable, in Season

Tomato Salad
topped with
Minced Onions and Parsley

Sherry Trifle

Coffee

SCHEDULE

The day before:

Prepare trifle, celery soup, and salad dressing.

The same day:

While roasting beef, bake Yorkshire pudding, heat soup, peel and slice tomatoes, and cook green vegetable. Toast cheese crackers.

7 SIT-DOWN DINNER PARTY MENUS FOR SUMMER

Everything except the fresh fruit can be prepared one day or several days before.

I. Cold Chlodnic served over Ice Cubes

Cold Poached Egg on Vegetable Salad under Aspic

Strawberries and Devonshire Cream

Coffee

Serve a dry white wine

II. Chilled Half Cantaloupe
filled with
Port Wine

Salmon in Aspic

Cucumber Salad with
Lemon Mayonnaise

Cold Rum Mousse

Coffee

Serve a dry white wine

III. Chilled Half Cantaloupe
filled with
Jellied Madrilene
garnished with
Sour Cream,
Lime Wedges,
and
Minced Parsley or Dill

Chicken Chaud-Froid
with
Cold Cauliflower Polonaise

Biscuit Tortoni

Coffee

Serve a dry white wine

IV. Chilled Cream of Cucumber Soup
garnished with
Whipped Cream and Finely Cut Chives

Vitello Tonnato
Potato Salad

Cold Sabayone with Grated Orange Rind

Coffee

Serve a dry white wine

V. Trout in Aspic with Caviar Mayonnaise

Caesar Salad

Peach Champagne
Thin Sugar Cookies

Coffee

VI. Asparagus Vinaigrette

Toasted Biscuits

Cold Roast Beef in Aspic

Tomatoes stuffed with Potato Salad

Freshly Grated Horseradish

Lemon Ice

Coffee

Serve Sangria or a rosé

VII. Chilled Avocado Soup

Crabmeat Mousse Ring
filled with
Cucumber Salad
Dill Mayonnaise

Raspberries Romanoff

Coffee

Serve a dry white wine

II. A SPRING, SUMMER, OR AUTUMN BUFFET

With Cocktails:
Broiled Chicken Livers
Cheese-Stuffed Celery and Endive
Mustard-Stuffed Eggs

Hot or Cold Cream of Pea Soup
with
Tomato Slices

Cold Ham or Tongue in Aspic

Hot Cauliflower, Almond, and Cheese Casserole

Salad of Romaine Lettuce
and
Chiffonade Dressing

Hot or Cold Apple Dumplings
Hard Sauce

Coffee

Serve a rosé, red wine, or beer

III. A SPRING OR AUTUMN BUFFET

With Cocktails:
Crabmeat Remick
Cheese Puffs
Beefsteak Tartar Balls
rolled in
Minced Parsley

Boula Gratinée

Vitello Tonnato

Broccoli Salad
Vinaigrette Sauce

Apricot Mousse
Hot Apricot Brandy Sauce

Coffee

Serve a white wine

IV. A FALL OR WINTER BUFFET

With Cocktails:
Shrimp with Horseradish and Cocktail Sauce
Cheddar and Wine Cheese with Crackers
Bowl of Crisp Watercress

Hot Chicken and Clam Broth
with
Salted Whipped Cream

Toasted Lebanese or Arab Bread

Hot Beef and Kidney Pies
Salad of Mixed Greens, Tomatoes, Hardcooked Eggs, Cucumbers
Roquefort Dressing

Frozen Rum Soufflé
Puff Pastry Disks

Coffee

Serve a red wine

V. A FALL OR WINTER BUFFET

With Cocktails:
Individual Shrimp Quiches

Cold Cream of Spinach Soup
with
Whipped Cream and Garlic Croutons

Hot Veal Stew with Onions and Mushrooms

Hot Bacon Biscuits

Mixed Green Salad with Italian Dressing

Deep-Dish Peach Pie with Whipped Ice Cream Sauce

Coffee

Serve a white wine

VI. A FALL OR WINTER BUFFET

With Cocktails:
Smörgasbord
with
Buttered Swedish Limpa Bread
and
Buttered Pumpernickle

Hot Baked Ham
in a
Short Crust Cover
Spiced Currant Jelly Sauce
and
Mustard Cream Sauce

Ratatouille, or Eggplant and Tomato Casserole

Coffee Mousse
Soft Ice Cream and Rum Sauce

Linzer Cookies

Coffee

Serve a rosé

SCHEDULE

Everything can be prepared one or two days before and reheated.

VII. A WINTER BUFFET

With Cocktails:
Hot Bacon Crackers
Cold Clams under Diced Aspic
Cold Sliced Eggs with Anchovies

Hot Turkey
carved and arranged around a mound of
Spiced Apples
Rich Brown Sauce Poured over the Turkey
and
Garnished with Smoked Tongue
and Truffles or Olives

Cold Cauliflower Vinaigrette

surrounded by
Mounds of Tomato, Zucchini, Asparagus, and Broccoli Salad

Cherries Jubilee

Coffee

Serve a dry white wine or gespritzter

SCHEDULE
Everything can be prepared the day before and reheated.

7 MENUS FOR MISCELLANEOUS PARTIES

I. A SUMMER DINNER PARTY

With Cocktails:
Thin Slices of Smoked Salmon
Rolled Around Horseradish Cream, Chilled, and Sliced
Stuffed Cherry Tomatoes
Iced Melon Wedges Marinated in Madeira

Soft Jellied Madrilene with Vegetables

Oven-Parched Toast Fingers

Cold Sliced Filet of Beef
Cold Béarnaise Sauce
Artichoke Bottoms
filled with
Purée of Chestnuts

Crisp Watercress with Brown Breadcrumb Dressing

Cold Vanilla Soufflé
with
Linzer Tarts

Coffee

Serve Sangria

II. A DINNER WHEN ASPARAGUS IS AT ITS BEST

With Cocktails:
Hot Ripe Olives
Cold Spiced Mushrooms and Rye Bread Slices

Hot Asparagus
with
Thin Prosciutto Ham Slices
and
Brown Butter and Crumb Sauce

Broiled Steak or Chops
Potatoes Anna

Watercress Salad

Macedoine of Cold Fruit
with
Grand Marnier

Coffee

Serve a red wine

SCHEDULE
Prepare on day before:
Spiced mushrooms
The rest of this dinner is prepared during the last two hours before it is served.

III. BETWEEN-SEASONS SUNDAY LUNCH

With Cocktails:
Liver Pâté with Chilled Green Grapes
Cheese Canapés

Hot Bouillon
with
Madeira Wine
Heated Brioche Slices
with
Garlic Butter Balls

Cold Chicken Mousse Ring
filled with
Vegetable Salad

Open Cherry Tart with
Almond-Flavored Whipped Cream

Coffee

Serve a chilled Moselle wine

SCHEDULE

Prepare one day or several days before:

- Pâté
- Bouillon
- Butter balls
- Chicken mousse
- Vegetable salad
- Cherry tart

Prepare same day:

- Cheese canapés
- Slice and heat frozen brioches
- Whipped cream
- Coffee

IV. LATE SUNDAY BREAKFAST

Iced Champagne

Tomato Juice

Nova Scotia or Mildest Smoked Salmon
with
Scrambled Eggs

Oven-Dried Rye Bread Slices
Small Popovers
Rosettes of Sweet Butter
Assorted Jams

Bowl of Fresh Fruit

Tea or Coffee

SCHEDULE

Prepare same day:

- Popovers
- Scrambled eggs

V. GALA LATE SUPPER

Champagne

Blini with Caviar, Drawn Butter, and Sour Cream

Chicken Jeanette
with
Macedoine of Vegetables
and
Mayonnaise

Curried Melba Toast Rolls

Coffee Bombe
Sweet Crescents

Coffee

SCHEDULE
The day before:
Prepare chicken, vegetables, mayonnaise, toast, bombe, and sweet crescents.
The same day:
Prepare blini at the table.

VI. A SPRING DINNER

Cebiche of a White Fish or Shrimp

Warm Chunks of Buttered Italian Bread

Chicken in Spanish Rice

Green Salad

Orange Mousse

Coffee

Serve a dry white wine

SCHEDULE
The day before:
Prepare orange mousse, green salad, and cebiche.
The same day:
Prepare chicken and rice
Warm bread before serving

VII. A COUNTRY DINNER IN AUTUMN

Guacamole
with
Parched Toast

Chicken Pie
under Cheese Crust

Mixed Salad

Chocolate Mousse

Coffee

Serve a dry white wine

COCKTAIL PARTIES

Suggestions for cocktail parties should be pared down to fit the occasion. For a large party, try to combine meat, fish, cheese, and eggs with cold crisp greens or fruit. At a Sunday cocktail party which may almost take the place of lunch, include hearty items such as spareribs or a quiche. For a large, standing cocktail party, remember that guests will have only one free hand, the other will be holding their drink. If they are smoking, they may have only two free fingers.

I. Hot cheese puffs
Hot meatballs rolled around Roquefort cheese
Broiled chicken livers wrapped in bacon
Cold spinach- and garlic-stuffed mushrooms, glazed with aspic
Cold shrimp pâté with crackers
Cold unhulled strawberries
Cold curried melon balls
Salted nuts, crisp greens, and hot ripe olives

II. Hot onion and mushroom quiche
Curried raw cauliflower
Shrimp in remoulade sauce
Iced fruit platter, melon balls or wedges, strawberries, apple slices, cold canned or fresh figs with walnut and chutney dip
Bologna sausage rounds with mustard cheese
Hot sardine puffs
Spiced pecans

III. Broiled shrimp
Guacamole with potato chips and lime wedges
Hot bacon crackers
Chilled cherry tomatoes
Curried parched nuts
Chilled seedless grapes
Tree-ripened olives

IV. Butterfly shrimps with orange chutney
Crisp cucumber slices sprinkled with black pepper and seasoning salt
Egg slices on black bread with anchovy butter
Crisp watercress sprigs

V. Sliced frankfurters in blankets with mustard dip
Crisp endive leaves stuffed with Roquefort
Cherry tomatoes
Corn crisps or freshly popped corn
Carrot sticks
Garlic almonds
Melon balls with Westphalian ham on cocktail picks

VI. Hot barbecued spareribs
Hot blini with tuna fish salad
Homebaked cheese wafers
Iced and crisped celery sandwiches
Scallions, fennel, and cucumber slices
Artichoke hearts vinaigrette on cocktail picks

VII. Warm profiteroles filled with cold anchovy butter
Chunks of cold lobster with brandied mayonnaise
Salted parched hazelnuts (filberts)

7 QUICK MENUS FOR THE HOSTESS WITHOUT TIME

These dinners are partly from the pantry shelf and partly out of the freezing compartment. They are not cooked ahead.

I.

Consommé Bellevue
(*Half and Half Chicken Consommé and Clam Juice*)
Topped with Whipped Cream

Heated Frozen Brioche Rolls
with
Cold Butter

Baked Ham Steaks
with
Sour Cherry Sauce
(*1 can drained sour cherries combined with 1 jar melted Red Currant Jelly*)
Frozen Sweet Potatoes
heated with
Brown Sugar
A Frozen Green Vegetable

Orange Sabayone
(*prepared immediately before serving*)
Coffee

Serve a chilled rosé

II.

Canned French Onion Soup
topped with
Slices of Toasted French Bread and Grated Parmesan Cheese

Broiled Salmon Steaks
with Parsley
Broiled Tomato and Onion Slices
Mousseline Sauce
Packaged Hashed Brown Potatoes in Casserole

Lettuce with prepared French Dressing

Canned Peaches or Bananas Flambé
(prepared at the table)
Coffee

Serve a dry white wine

III. Melon Wedges with Chutney and Lime Slices

Heated Frozen Croissants
with
Cold Butter

Broiled Steak, Individual Steaks, or Chops
Packaged Mashed Potatoes
baked with
Cheese and Breadcrumb Topping

A Frozen Green Vegetable

Brandied Prune Whip
made with
Jars of Strained Prunes (Baby Food)

Coffee

Serve a red wine

IV. Antipasto

Hot Italian Bread

Veal Scallopini Marsala
with
Freshly Boiled Pasta
and
Tomato Sauce
Grated Parmesan Cheese

Mixed Green Salad
with
Prepared Italian Dressing

Orange Sherbet with Curacao
with
Amaretti or Macaroons

Coffee

Serve an Italian red wine

V. Hearts of Palm or Artichoke Hearts Vinaigrette

Baked and Buttered Frozen Buttermilk Biscuits

Sautéed Frozen Trout Amandine
Frozen Potato Balls
with
Butter and Parsley
Quick Canned Corn and Tomato Casserole

Salzburger Nockerdln
(baked just before serving)

Coffee

Serve a dry white wine

VI. Hot Bouillon with Sherry

Heated Sesame Crackers

Beef Tongue with Mustard Sauce
(*Certain brands can be heated in their plastic wrapping and served at once*)
Horseradish Cream

Frozen Chopped Spinach
with
Hardcooked Eggs

Herbed Packaged Rice

Hot Compote with Liqueur
and
Sweetened Whipped Cream

Coffee

Serve a red wine

VII. Crabmeat Cocktail
(*Frozen Crabmeat, Relish, and Russian Dressing*)

Hot Garlic or Chive Bread

Breaded and Fried Chicken Breasts
or Wiener Schnitzel
Mushrooms in Cream
Mixed Salad of Canned Beets, Celery Root, and White Beans
with
French Dressing

Canned Babas heated in Rum
with
Whipped Cream

Coffee

Serve a dry Rhine or Moselle wine

LESSON II

CHICKEN SOUP STOCK, BEEF STOCK, VEAL STOCK, FISH STOCK,

With the disappearance of the coal stove, the pleasures of making stock in a stockpot on the back of the stove have almost disappeared. Present-day soups cannot sit on the back of a gas or electric stove and simmer for days on end, but a very good chicken stock can be produced, from market to table, inside of four hours.

Making a good basic chicken soup stock requires no special talent —it is as easy as boiling water. A little time is needed to assemble and prepare the vegetables and herbs that simmer with the fowl, but if time is short, a package of prepared soup greens and a little bag of herbs bought at the market can be used. The most difficult part of the whole thing is to find a butcher who not only has veal bones on hand, but will crack them for you. Place veal bones and well-cleaned fowl into a stockpot or kettle, add cold water, and bring slowly to a boil. The slower the water reaches the boiling point the better. The scum that rises to the surface as the water heats should be lifted off at intervals with a slotted spoon. When the water starts to boil, add the well cleaned and sliced or quartered vegetables, soup greens, herbs, seasonings, and spices. Cover the stockpot or kettle, reduce heat, and simmer slowly for 3 to 3½ hours. Some cooks start with a little less water and add ½ cup cold water every hour. After 3 to 3½ hours the stock will have reduced considerably. The French describe the slow simmering as letting the stock *smile*. It can be made to *smile* on the back of the coal range, but it is hard to classify on a gas or electric stove. The simmer must barely move the surface of the stock. It is *not* to boil slowly. Strain the stock through a fine strainer, cool, and refrigerate it. When it is cold the fat will form a surface sheet which should be carefully lifted off in large pieces. The stock should be entirely clear of fat and not left with little nodules which appear as hard lumps when the soup is served cold and as oily eyes when it is served hot. Strain the defatted stock again through a cloth wrung out in cold water and laid across a sieve. Place stock in a jar, seal, and refrigerate until needed. It is now ready to be used as a base for soups or sauces, or it can be reduced and *clarified* into a strong clear consommé or bouillon.

The moment the word *clarify* is used, complications set in and the first problems arise. The process of clarifying a soup has never been sufficiently explained for the young cook, and the clear soup she can obtain from a can looks infinitely more tempting and attractive than the cloudy soup stock she has just produced by boiling a fowl with vegetables in a stockpot.

Soup stock or broth is the unclarified liquid which is obtained when fowl, meat, game, and/or vegetables are cooked with water. Soup stock or broth may be used for all cream soups. It should always be carefully strained and defatted before it is sealed in jars. Properly refrigerated, it can be kept for ten days to two weeks. It can be stored in a freezer for two to three months.

Consommé or bouillon is the name applied to clarified and reduced soup stock or broth. The stock or broth is usually reduced for added strength and clarified into a translucent liquid which is used for clear soups, jellied soups, and some of the light and delicate cream soups and sauces.

Clarifying stock or broth means reheating the cold soup with cold ingredients that will draw all the sediment out of the stock and leave it clear, crystal clear if possible. The most important clarifiers are egg whites, raw meat, and egg shells. Egg whites may be beaten stiff or mixed with the raw meat. The clarifying agents should be stirred into the stock and brought to a boil, while stirring slowly. As soon as the stock reaches the boiling point, the heat should be reduced slightly and the stock should simmer, uncovered and untouched, for 30 minutes. The gathered sediment can then be lifted from the consommé with a spoon and the consommé should be strained through a cloth wrung out in cold water and laid across a sieve. Strain two or three times if necessary. Refrigerate the consommé in sealed jars until needed.

Excellent consommés and bouillons can be bought and should be used when time is short. We only urge that you learn how to make a basic soup stock before the simple art is forgotten.

ADVICE THAT APPLIES TO ALL SOUP STOCKS OF CHICKEN OR MEAT

If the chicken or meat that is cooked in the stock is of first consideration, as in Chicken Fricassee or Boiled Beef, do not start cooking it in cold water. By the time the water comes to a boil, all the flavor will have been drawn out of the meat. Bring the water to a rapid boil, add the meat, and bring the water back to a boil as quickly as possible. This seals all the juices in the meat and leaves it tender and juicy, but the stock will not be as strong.

When a strong stock is of primary importance and the meat will not be used as a main dish, place fowl or meat in cold water and bring it slowly to a boil. The meat will be dry and tough, but the stock will be strong and excellent.

When stock is reduced by rapid boiling in an uncovered kettle, the stock will become saltier as it reduces.

Recipes for basic stock are given in a quantity suitable for the average soup kettle. The stock should last the average household for about a week.

BASIC CHICKEN STOCK

1 5 to 5½ pound fowl, disjointed
1 pound veal knuckle bones, cracked
2 carrots, scraped and quartered
1 onion, stuck with 2 cloves
3 stalks celery with leaves
½ bay leaf
7 sprigs parsley
1 sprig thyme
3 to 4 peppercorns, bruised
1 teaspoon salt
3 quarts cold water

Place all ingredients in a large stockpot and bring to a boil as slowly as possible. Skim off the scum that rises to the surface and reduce heat. Cover and simmer for 3½ hours. Strain stock and cool. Lift fat from surface and refrigerate stock until needed.

Additional or Alternate Ingredients

2 leeks, white part only
1 turnip, peeled
1 parsnip, peeled
1 sprig chervil
1 tomato, quartered
1 additional onion

Alternate Method

Add vegetables, herbs, and seasonings only after the soup has been skimmed.

CHICKEN CONSOMMÉ

(*Clarifying Chicken Stock*)

3 quarts chicken stock
1 small onion stuck with 1 clove
½ carrot, scraped
1 celery stalk with leaves
½ bay leaf
1 sprig thyme
3 sprigs parsley
1 tablespoon tarragon vinegar
1 teaspoon lemon juice
½ pound ground beef
1 egg white and 1 broken egg shell
3 peppercorns

Simmer stock until it is reduced to half. Set it aside to cool. Mix onion, carrot, celery, herbs, and seasonings and add to soup. Stir beef with 1 tablespoon cold water and add to soup with the egg white, egg shell, and peppercorns. Bring soup to a boil, stirring constantly, until it reaches the boiling point. Reduce heat and simmer uncovered for 30 minutes. Season to taste and strain through a tammy (a straining cloth) or cheesecloth wrung out in cold water. Chill and use as recipes require.

Variation 1

Place the reduced, cold stock in a kettle with 3 stiffly beaten egg whites, 1 quartered tomato, 1½ tablespoons vinegar, and ¼ cup wine or sherry. Bring to a boil, stirring constantly. Take from heat, set aside for 15 minutes, strain, and use as above.

Variation 2

Place reduced cold stock in kettle with ½ pound ground raw chicken mixed with 2 unbeaten egg whites and the broken shells. Bring to a boil, stirring slowly. Simmer uncovered for 30 minutes without stirring. Strain and use as above.

Chilled Clear Consommés

Consommé Imperiale: Garnish chilled chicken consommé with 1 cold cooked artichoke bottom in each cup or plate. Pipe chicken liver purée into the artichoke bottom and add sherry to taste to the consommé.

Consommé with Oeuf Mollet: Serve iced chicken consommé with 1 cold Oeuf Mollet (a 6-minute egg cooled and carefully peeled) and sprinkle with freshly minced chervil, parsley, or chives.

Consommé with Port Wine or Sherry: Add good port wine or sherry to iced consommé, sprinkle with minced tarragon, and add an ice cube to each cup or plate.

Consommé Portugaise: To 3 parts chilled chicken consommé, add 1 part chilled tomato juice, season with cayenne, and garnish with peeled and seeded tomato slices.

Consommé Russe: To 3 parts chilled chicken consommé, add 1 part chilled and whipped sour cream. Pass minced watercress, sour cream, riced hard-cooked egg, and diced bologna sausage with the soup.

Consommé Sir James: ⅓ clear consommé, ⅓ green turtle soup, ⅓ Madeira, 1 shot brandy. Served chilled.

Consommé Viviane: This is a very simple consommé. Chill the soup and pour it into cups that contain disks of cold cooked chicken meat (these are cut from sliced chicken with a small cookie cutter or the center of doughnut cutter). Add as many truffles cut into matchstick thickness as you can afford and add a good sherry to taste.

BASIC BROWN STOCK I

2 pounds shin or brisket of beef
3 pounds knuckle of veal, cracked
7 quarts cold water
1 tablespoon salt
2 medium onions, stuck with 2 cloves
2 celery stalks
1 turnip, peeled and quartered
2 carrots, scraped and quartered
7 peppercorns, bruised
1 bouquet garni (2 bay leaves, 1 sprig of thyme, 7 sprigs of parsley)

Sear the beef and bones in their own fat in a large heavy kettle until well browned on all sides. Cover with cold water, add salt, and set aside for 1 hour. Bring slowly to a boil, skim off the scum. Add onions, celery, turnip, carrots, peppercorns, and bouquet and bring back to a boil. Skim off scum again and simmer covered for 6 hours, skimming occasionally. Take from heat, strain through a cloth wrung out in cold water, and chill. Lift off the layer of fat and use as a base for sauces and soups.

CLARIFYING

1 small onion, quartered
½ leek
1 carrot, scraped and quartered
1 stalk celery with leaves
1 bouquet garni
4 peppercorns
1 egg white with 1 egg shell
1 teaspoon lemon juice
1 tablespoon vinegar
½ pound ground lean beef mixed with 1 tablespoon cold water
12 cups stock

Mix all ingredients, except stock, well and place them in a clean kettle. Add the stock and set over low heat. Gradually bring the mixture to a boil, whisking all the time. Lower heat and simmer gently, uncovered, for about 25 minutes. Strain through a sieve covered with triple layers of cheesecloth wrung out in cold water. Store in refrigerator in a covered container up to 2 weeks. Use for clear soups and sauces.

BASIC BROWN STOCK II

3 pounds brisket of beef
2 veal knuckles, cracked
3 quarts water
1 small yellow onion, sliced
2 carrots, scraped and quartered
2 celery stalks
1 bouquet garni
6 peppercorns
Salt to taste
4 large mushrooms or 2 dried mushrooms
1 leek
1 2-pound chicken (optional)

Place beef and veal bones in cold water in a large kettle. Bring to a boil, skim off the scum, add vegetables, herbs, and seasonings. Cover and simmer for 2 hours. Add chicken and simmer 45 minutes longer. Strain stock and chill. Lift off fat, cover, and store in refrigerator.

TO CLEAR* AND IMPROVE THE STOCK

Place 6 cups clear stock in a large kettle and add:

3 tablespoons dry red wine
1 tablespoon dry sherry
2 teaspoons tarragon vinegar
2 tablespoons tomato paste
3 egg whites, beaten stiff

Set over medium heat, bring slowly to a boil, stirring constantly. Take from heat and set stock aside for 15 minutes undisturbed. Pour stock through a strainer lined with moistened cheesecloth. Rinse out and dry kettle, return stock to kettle, and reheat.

PETITE MARMITE

Serve the cleared stock with slices of beef and chicken and freshly cooked sliced carrots and turnips. Toast broken slices of French bread, sprinkle with grated Parmesan cheese, and brown lightly under the broiler until cheese is browned. Serve toasted bread pieces with the marmite. They are floated on the soup and eaten with it.

* Note that this *clears* the stock; for *clarifying* see page 40.

BASIC VEAL STOCK

4 pounds veal and knuckle bones, cracked
4 quarts cold water
2 medium onions, quartered
2 carrots, scraped and quartered
1 turnip, peeled and quartered
2 stalks celery
1 bouquet garni
1 clove garlic
1 tablespoon salt
6 peppercorns, bruised

Combine meat bones and water in a large kettle and set aside for 1 hour. Place over low heat and bring slowly to a boil, skim off scum, add vegetables, herbs, and seasonings and bring back to a boil. Skim again, cover, and simmer 5 hours, skimming occasionally. Take from heat, pour through a strainer lined with triple cheesecloth wrung out in cold water. Chill, remove layer of fat, and store in refrigerator in a covered container up to 2 weeks. Use for soups and sauces or clarify as for beef stock, page 40, before using.

BASIC FISH STOCK

3 pounds whitefish, halibut, flounder, or cod
Fish bones, heads, and trimmings
3 quarts cold water
1 onion, quartered and stuck with 2 cloves
1 carrot, scraped and quartered
1 teaspoon salt
7 peppercorns, bruised
1 bouquet garni

Place all ingredients in a large kettle, bring to a boil, reduce heat and simmer 1¼ hours. Strain through a hair sieve and store in a covered container in refrigerator up to 1 week. Clarify according to directions on page 40, omitting the ground beef. It is rarely necessary to clarify fish stock.

THE CLEAR SOUPS

Hot Bouillon and Consommé

Clear soups date back to the court of Louis XIV, and ever since the discovery that an egg white would clear all floating matter out of stock, we have devoted ourselves to finding things to put back into it.

We spike it with sherry, Madeira, or port wine (sometimes even with bourbon) and we combine clear chicken or beef stock with clam consommé and whipped cream. We combine it with gelatin for our jellied soups, and we give it, clear and strong, to our skiers and invalids.

The two clear soups that are better bought than made, unless you are steaming clams for supper, are green turtle soup and clam juice. Stock a few cans and bottles of these and your clear soup creations can go on indefinitely.

The garnishes for clear soups are endless. Turn to the choux paste chapter, page 227, for the little salty profiteroles the French love so well. Find noodles on page 160 or on the market shelf. Add cooked vegetables, pasta, marrow, dumplings, herbs, and sliced pancakes. The best known traditional clear soups are listed below, but you can use your imagination and many of your leftovers. Almost anything can go into a clear soup, including a whole squab or a quarter of a chicken.

Consommé Africaine: Spice with curry powder to taste, garnish with diced artichoke bottoms.

Consommé Andalouse: Heated Madrilene.

Consommé Ancienne: Chicken consommé garnished with toast spread with white sauce mixed with grated Parmesan cheese and browned.

Consommé Argenteuil: Clear beef consommé with cooked asparagus tips.

Consommé Bohemienne: Chicken consommé, choux paste "Peas," and riced goose liver purée.

Consommé Bouquetiere with Cooked Vegetables: Peas, carrots, green beans, asparagus, and turnips.

Consommé Cancalaise: Fish consommé garnished with poached oysters and pieces of cooked fish.

Consommé Carmen: Color bouillon with tomato juice, add seeded and diced tomatoes, cooked rice and chervil.

Consommé Carnegie: Add raviolis and chervil.

Consommé Colbert: Sliced root vegetables and 1 poached egg in each portion.

Consommé Christiana: Add choux paste puffs filled with salted purée of chestnuts.

Consommé Don Carlos: Add cooked rice, chervil, and steamed tomatoes.

Consommé Dumont: Add strips of cooked tongue and mushrooms.

Consommé Lady Morgan: Fish stock with poached shrimp, mushrooms, and oysters.

Consommé Mercédès: Add sherry.

Consommé Olga: Spike with port wine or Madeira, add diced celery.

Consommé Russe: Reddened with beet juice, garnished with a julienne of cooked vegetables.

Consommé St. Germain: Garnish with dumplings, page 206, green peas, and chervil.

Consommé Thérèse: Chicken consommé spiced with cloves; add chicken dumplings and chervil and serve chilled.

Consommé Trianon: Bouillon with 1 poached chicken breast for each portion, diced cooked tomatoes and cucumbers and chervil.

Consommé Victor Emanuel: Bouillon with tomatoes and cooked pasta served with grated Parmesan cheese.

JELLIED SOUPS

Jellied soups are clear soups with softened gelatin stirred into them while they are hot. Minced ingredients may be added to the cold soup, or cold jellied soup may be poured over cold cooked ingredients. The jellied soup should be ice cold, slightly thickened, and not under any circumstances stiff and quaking. It should be eaten with a spoon, not cut.

BASIC JELLIED SOUP

Use approximately 1 to 1½ envelopes gelatin for 6 cups clear soup in cool weather and 1½ to 2 envelopes gelatin in hot weather.

1½ envelopes gelatin
¼ cup cold bouillon, consommé, sherry, port wine, or any clear liquid
5¾ cups boiling clear bouillon or consommé

Stir gelatin into cold bouillon and set aside to soften for 15 minutes. Bring bouillon to a boil, take from heat, stir in gelatin until dissolved, cool, and chill. (Half the bouillon may be brought to a boil, the gelatin dissolved in it, and the other half added—this speeds chilling.)

Variations

Use for base:

1. Clear beef consommé, or bouillon.
2. Chicken consommé or bouillon.
3. Clear beet-flavored and colored consommé or borsch.
4. Clear green turtle soup.
5. Clear chicken and celery bouillon.
6. Clear tomato bouillon, madrilene.
7. ¾ Chicken consommé and ¼ beet juice.

If you desire, use sherry or port wine to soften the gelatin, but always use one or the other with the green turtle soup.

Additions to the Jellied Soups

1. To madrilene, add diced peeled and seeded tomatoes and chopped parsley.
2. As above, with a mixture of cold cooked vegetables.
3. Add a julienne of cold cooked beets and/or shredded cabbage to jellied beet bouillon or borsch.
4. Add caviar to jellied bouillon and garnish with hard-cooked riced egg.
5. Add minced parsley, mint, chives, dill, or any mixture of fresh herbs to any of the jellied soups after the gelatin has dissolved.
6. Pour jellied and sherried clam bouillon over a bed of minced clams, onions, and parsley.
7. Pour jellied chicken soup over a small crisp celery, cucumber, and onion dice.

Garnish jellied soups with:

1. Rosettes of salted whipped cream.
2. Center rosettes with a little black or red caviar.
3. Whipped sour cream sprinkled with minced dill or chopped chives.
4. Paper-thin lemon slices.
5. Lime wedges.
6. Very small cold melon balls.
7. Grated lemon or orange rind.

LESSON III

BASIC WHITE SAUCE—

Sauce Blanche

White sauce, in its darker moments, has been compared unfavorably with library paste. In its lighter moments it is our constantly recurring basic white sauce; reduced to its best it is France's sauce velouté. It is the base for at least half our sauces, cream soups, soufflés, puddings, casseroles, creamed and gratinéed dishes, croquettes, and hot canapés. There are literally hundreds of famous recipes, French and American, hot and cold, that can be added to the repertoire of the cook who has learned the simple process of making a smooth white sauce.

With that knowledge, almost anything is possible, from the creamiest chicken soup to those glossy white chickens or lobsters, decorated with truffles, that usually appear only on the most elaborate cold buffet tables. The latter are coated with sauce chaud-froid, which is nothing more nor less than basic white sauce with a little gelatin added. That is only the beginning: Restaurant Marguéry in Paris has glazed a million soles under a coating of sauce velouté (so named for its velvety smoothness) made with fish stock and dry white wine, instead of chicken stock. The process is always the same, and the changes are minor.

White sauce is thickened with butter and flour which are cooked together before the liquid is added. This essential thickening agent has a name of its own in every occidental cooking language except English. For us it is either butter-and-flour-cooked-together, or we fall back on the French word *roux*.

Some recipes can be cooked in almost any saucepan or kettle, but for a smooth white sauce the proper utensils and tools are absolutely essential:

a small, heavy saucepan with a rounded bottom
a wooden kitchen spoon
a French wire whisk

For making White Sauce II according to the double-boiler method, substitute for the saucepan a double boiler whose upper section has a rounded bottom.

WHITE ROUX

(*Roux Blanc*)

This is given as a separate recipe for those who wish to make a larger quantity of the roux in advance. It can be stored in a covered jar in the refrigerator for a week or more.

½ cup butter
¾ cup flour

Melt butter slowly in a heavy saucepan over low heat. Do not let it brown. Stir in flour with a wooden spoon until smooth. Continue to cook very slowly, stirring constantly until the roux becomes foamy and cream-colored. Do not let it brown. Cooking the roux very slowly is essential to obtain a smooth sauce. Cool and refrigerate roux in a covered container.

When needed, place at least 1 tablespoon roux per cup of liquid in heavy saucepan and stir in the liquid over low heat until the sauce is thickened and smooth. Reduce heat to simmer and cook the sauce, uncovered, stirring occasionally for at least 15 minutes. If there is time, reduce the sauce further. It will become smoother, thicker and creamier the longer it simmers. Simmer for 15 minutes to 1 hour, stirring occasionally, until the desired thickness is reached.

BASIC WHITE SAUCE I

(*Sauce Blanche*)

4 tablespoons butter
4 tablespoons flour
2 cups milk
¼ teaspoon salt

Melt butter slowly in heavy saucepan over low heat. Do not let it brown. Stir in flour with a wooden spoon and cook, stirring constantly, for at least 3 minutes until foamy and smooth. The roux will be cream-colored but must not brown. Stir milk in gradually with a wire whisk and cook gently, whisking constantly, until the sauce is thickened and smooth—about 7 minutes. Reduce heat to a simmer and cook sauce, stirring frequently, 12 to 14 minutes longer. Recipe makes approximately 2¼ cups of sauce. The sauce may now be used as recipes require. If there is time the sauce can be reduced and improved by simmering uncovered, stirring frequently for 15 minutes to 30 minutes longer. Recipe makes 1¾ to 2 cups reduced sauce.

When there is no time at all, add boiling milk to the roux, increase heat slightly, and boil the sauce gently, whisking constantly and vigorously for 5 minutes. Recipe makes 2¼ cups sauce.

If the sauce is not going to be used immediately, butter the surface with a few paper-thin slices of butter, cover tightly and place over hot water until needed.

WHITE SAUCE II

(*Double-Boiler Method*)

4 tablespoons butter
4 tablespoons flour
2 cups milk
¼ teaspoon salt

Melt butter in top of a double boiler over gently boiling water. Stir in flour, cover, and allow roux to cook for 7 minutes. Add milk, stir with a wire whisk until smooth, cover again, and let sauce cook 20 minutes longer. Stir vigorously with whisk until all lumps disappear and sauce is thickened and smooth. Cover, reduce heat, and leave sauce over simmering water until needed. Recipe makes approximately 2¼ cups sauce. This method is ideal for creamed dishes and soups. The meat, vegetables, or other soup ingredients can be added to the white sauce and kept hot until needed. Warm cream can be added to this hot mixture immediately before serving.

The thickness of white sauce and its descendant sauces depends upon the proportions of roux to liquid and the amount of time the sauce reduces. The following chart gives quantities, yields, and the purposes for which the various thicknesses are usually used.

A note on temperature of liquids and how to add them to white and brown sauces:

Anyone using two or more cookbooks is likely to read opposite directions on the temperature of the liquids that are added to the white and brown sauces and whether they are to be added *on* or *off* the heat.

Some authorities claim that lumps in the sauce result from using cold or unheated liquids. Others claim that adding the liquid while the roux is cooking over low heat is a mistake, that it must be stirred in until it is smooth *off* the heat, and that the saucepan should then be returned to the heat and the sauce stirred until it thickens.

The best rule in the matter lies in the *hand* of the cook: Do what is simplest.

If adding a cold or room-temperature liquid such as a freshly opened can of bouillon or a cup of dry white wine, use it as it comes. Add it over low heat so that the stirring will smooth the liquid into the roux at the same time that the roux expands and the thickening process starts.

If you are making a sauce from stock that is simmering on the back of the stove, ladle the stock into the sauce just as it comes.

In other words, use either hot or cold liquids and add them while the saucepan is over low heat. However, if you were taught to add liquids off the heat and it *feels* better to you, it doesn't matter—either method can be used.

What does matter and what does prevent lumps and what does break up lumps when they do occur is a really vigorous beating with a French wire whisk and the use of a saucepan with a rounded bottom that does not allow any of the sauce to escape the whisk.

If the roux is cooked slowly, the liquid stirred in gradually, the sauce whisked vigorously and then allowed to simmer for as long as possible, the liquid can be cold or boiling and it can be added on or off the heat. The sauce should only be strained if an ingredient, such as bay leaf, peppercorns, or cloves, was cooked in the sauce and it should be removed before the sauce is served. A sauce need not be strained to remove lumps: They can be broken and smoothed with the wire whisk, not with a gentle stirring but with a real beating.

WHITE SAUCES

DESIGNATIONS	BUTTER	FLOUR	LIQUID—MILK OR WHITE STOCK	OTHER INGREDIENTS	APPROXIMATE YIELD	USES
Very Thin White Sauce	2 tbs.	2 tbs.	2 cups	¼ teaspoon salt or to taste	2¼ cups; after reducing 30 minutes, 1½ cups	Thin soups, creamed vegetables
Thin White Sauce	3 tbs.	3 tbs.	2 cups	Salt to taste	2⅓ cups; after reducing 30 minutes, 1⅔ cups	Thick sauces, creamed soups, creamed vegetable soups
Medium White Sauce	4 tbs.	4 tbs.	2 cups	Salt to taste	2½ cups; after reducing 30 minutes, 1⅔ cups	Thick sauces, creamed soups, vegetable soups
Medium-Thick White Sauce I	5 tbs.	5 tbs.	2 cups	Salt to taste	2⅔ cups; after reducing 30 minutes, 1¾ cups	Creamed fish and meats, casseroles
Medium-Thick White Sauce II	5 tbs.	6 tbs.	2 cups	Salt to taste	2⅔ cups; after reducing 30 minutes, 1¾ cups	Gratinéed dishes
Thick White Sauce	6 tbs.	7 tbs.	2 cups	Salt to taste	2¾ cups; after reducing 30 minutes, 2 cups	Soufflés
Very Thick White Sauce	½ cup, 8 tbs.	10 tbs.	2 cups	Salt to taste	3 cups; after reducing 30 minutes, 1 cup	Croquettes

Basic white sauce should have a smooth, fine texture, which depends upon two factors, both of which are mentioned in the recipes. (1) The roux should be cooked *slowly* so that the starch in the flour can expand; (2) the liquid should be added *very slowly* and *stirred constantly* until it is thickened and smooth.

The utensils that are specified are important to prevent lumpiness in the sauce. A French wire whisk is rounded, and when it is used to stir a sauce in a saucepan with a rounded bottom, it reaches all of the sauce. If a square-bottomed saucepan is used, there is always a ridge of the sauce that is not reached. It cooks undisturbed and creates lumps when it is finally stirred into the sauce.

BÉCHAMEL SAUCE

Named for the Marquis de Béchamel, maître d'hôtel of Louis XIV.

2 tablespoons butter
1 tablespoon finely chopped onion
4 tablespoons flour
2 cups boiling milk
1 sprig parsley
¼ teaspoon salt
2 white peppercorns
3 tablespoons heavy cream

Melt butter in a heavy saucepan over low heat, add onion, and stir until onion is soft and transparent but not browned. Stir in flour and continue to stir until it just starts to turn a creamy gold color, about 3 minutes. Add milk gradually, stirring with a wire whisk, until the sauce is smooth and thickened, 5 to 7 minutes. Add parsley, salt, and peppercorns and cook slowly, stirring frequently for 30 minutes. Stir in cream, strain, and use béchamel as a base for other sauces or use with fish, poultry, and creamed vegetable dishes.

CREAM SAUCE

(*Sauce à la Crème*)

2¼ cups béchamel sauce
½ cup heavy cream
½ teaspoon lemon juice if sauce is to be served with fish

Simmer béchamel sauce, uncovered, over low heat, stirring frequently, until reduced to 1½ cups, about 30 minutes. Stir in cream, bring back to a boil, and serve. Add lemon juice just as sauce is taken from heat. Use for "creamed" foods, fish, eggs, and poultry.

MORNAY SAUCE

2¼ cups béchamel sauce
2 egg yolks
4 tablespoons heavy cream
1 tablespoon freshly grated Parmesan or Swiss cheese
whipped cream (optional)

Heat béchamel sauce in a heavy saucepan over low heat, or in the top of a double boiler over simmering water. Beat yolks into cream and stir slowly into the béchamel. Cook, stirring constantly, for 1 minute. Do not allow sauce to reach the boiling point. Add the cheese and continue stirring until cheese is melted and yolks have thickened and enriched the sauce. The sauce must always remain under the boiling point after the yolks have been added. Mornay sauce should be served as it is or as a masking sauce for fish, vegetables, or any dish that is to be gratinéed in the oven. Two or three tablespoons of the grated cheese may be sprinkled over the sauce before it is gratinéed in the oven. Two or three tablespoons of whipped cream may be folded into the top layer of the sauce before it is gratinéed. The cream makes it brown very smoothly.

VELOUTÉ SAUCE

The French word *velouté* means velvety. In order to achieve the necessary velvety smoothness, velouté must be cooked longer than white sauce. Since the sauce reduces in cooking, it should be made in larger quantities than white sauce or béchamel. There is no *quick* velouté sauce. If time does not allow for slow cooking, make basic white sauce with white stock, chicken stock, or fish stock and use as the recipe requires.

3 tablespoons butter
6 tablespoons flour
3½ cups white stock
2 white peppercorns
Salt to taste, depending on saltiness of stock
½ cup chopped mushrooms, mushroom stems, or peelings

Melt butter slowly in heavy saucepan over low heat. Do not let it brown. Stir in flour with a wooden spoon until foamy and smooth, about 3 minutes. The roux should just start to turn creamy gold, but not brown. Stir stock in gradually with a wire whisk and cook gently, stirring constantly until the sauce is thickened and smooth, about 7 minutes. Add seasonings and mushrooms and cook slowly, stirring frequently for 1 hour. The result is about 4 cups of sauce which should be reduced to about 2½ cups. Strain through a fine sieve and use at once or cool, stirring frequently. Store in a covered container in refrigerator up to 1 week. Use as a base for thickening other sauces.

CHICKEN VELOUTÉ SAUCE

Substitute 3½ cups chicken stock for the white stock.

FISH VELOUTÉ SAUCE

Substitute 3½ cups fish stock or 3 cups fish stock and ½ cup dry white wine for the white stock. Use to thicken fish sauces or as a fish sauce.

SUPRÊME SAUCE

Suprême sauce, like velouté sauce, calls for long cooking over low heat to reduce it to an even smoother and creamier consistency.

¼ cup sliced mushrooms, or stems and peelings
3 cups chicken stock
1 cup cream
½ recipe velouté sauce

Cook mushrooms in stock until it is reduced to 2 cups. Add velouté sauce and continue to cook over very low heat, stirring frequently, until sauce is reduced to 1½ cups.

Stir in the cream and, still stirring, cook only long enough to heat it. Serve at once. If it is to be held for a little while, butter the top with a few paper-thin slivers of butter, cover, and set aside. Serve with fish, eggs, and "creamed" foods.

Variations of the Basic White Sauces

The following white sauce recipes can be seasoned to taste, depending on the saltiness of the stock or other ingredients used.

Albert Sauce: Stir into 1 recipe chicken velouté sauce, ¼ cup finely grated or well-drained bottled horseradish, ¼ cup minced parsley, 2 minced shallots, and 1 teaspoon dry mustard. Simmer 5 minutes longer. Serve with boiled chicken, beef, or fish.

Allemande Sauce: Take 1 recipe suprême sauce from heat, beat into 2 egg yolks, and fold in ¼ cup heavy cream, whipped. Serve at once, or stir in ¼ cup unwhipped heavy cream. Serve with boiled chicken.

Sauce Ambassadrice: Stir into 1 recipe suprême sauce, ⅔ cup minced, cooked chicken. Simmer long enough to heat through. Just before serving, fold in ½ cup heavy cream, whipped. Serve with eggs, vegetables, chicken, or pancakes.

Admiral's Sauce: Stir into 1 recipe fish velouté sauce 1 to 2 teaspoons anchovy paste, 2 tablespoons each of minced shallot and small capers, and the grated rind of 1 lemon. Serve at once with fish.

Almond Sauce: Simmer in 1 recipe chicken velouté sauce, ½ cup blanched almonds, pounded to a paste. Serve with chicken.

Anchovy Sauce: Stir anchovy paste to taste into 1 recipe fish velouté sauce. Serve at once with fish.

Archduke Sauce: Just before serving, whip ½ cup champagne into 1 recipe suprême sauce. Serve with fish or chicken.

Aurora Sauce I: Stir into 1 recipe chicken velouté sauce, over medium heat, ½ cup each tomato purée and finely diced ham. Cook long enough to heat through. Serve with poultry and eggs.

Aurora Sauce II: Combine, heat, and serve, ½ recipe each, fish velouté sauce and tomato sauce, page 59. Serve with fish.

Béchamel Sauce: See page 52.

Bercy Sauce: Simmer in 1 recipe fish velouté sauce, 1 tablespoon minced shallots. Just before serving, stir in 2 tablespoons minced parsley and lemon juice to taste. Use for fish and baked fish dishes.

Sauce Berchoux: Prepare 1 recipe béchamel sauce using herb butter instead of plain butter, then finish off the heat as *allemande sauce*. Serve with chicken or use as *béchamel sauce*.

Sauce Blanche: See basic white sauce.

Brittany Sauce: Stir into 1 recipe fish velouté sauce, ¼ cup each, hot cooked sliced leek, diced onions, celery, and mushrooms. Reheat and serve with fish.

Caper Sauce: To 1 recipe basic white sauce, add 3 tablespoons small capers, or to taste. Serve with veal, boiled beef, or chicken.

Cardinal Sauce: Prepare fish velouté sauce with lobster butter instead of plain butter, add a minced truffle, and finish with yolks and cream. Serve with lobster or fish.

Celery Sauce: To 1 recipe basic white sauce, add ½ cup diced cooked celery and ¼ cup minced parsley. Use water in which celery cooked for part of the liquid in the sauce. Serve with chicken or eggs.

Chantilly Sauce: Just before serving, fold ⅔ cup heavy cream, whipped, into 1 recipe suprême sauce. Use as suprême sauce.

Chaud-Froid Sauce: Soften 1 envelope plain gelatin in ¼ cup cold chicken stock for 15 minutes. Take 1 recipe hot chicken velouté sauce from heat and stir in gelatin until dissolved. Cool, use to coat chicken or lobster, decorate with truffle cutouts. For detailed directions, see page 63.

Cheese Sauce: Stir into 1 recipe basic white sauce until melted, ½ to ¾ cup grated Cheddar or Swiss cheese. Do not use processed cheese. Serve with vegetables.

Cherbourg Sauce: Prepare 1 recipe fish velouté sauce with shrimp butter instead of plain butter. Add ½ cup diced cooked shrimp. Also called Dieppe sauce. Serve with fish or eggs.

Chivry Sauce: Prepare 1 recipe béchamel sauce, substituting herb butter for plain butter and 1 cup dry white wine for milk. Garnish sauce with chopped parsley. Serve with boiled chicken.

Clam Sauce: Prepare 1 recipe fish velouté sauce with clam juice instead of fish stock. Add ⅔ cup steamed littleneck clams or minced clams. Poached bay scallops may also be added. Serve with fish or pasta.

Cucumber Sauce: To 1 recipe chicken or fish velouté sauce, add ⅔ cup peeled, seeded, diced, and sautéed cucumber. Cook long enough to heat through. Serve with fish.

Curry Sauce: Prepare 1 recipe basic white sauce. Stir 1 tablespoon curry powder into ¼ cup of the hot sauce until smooth. Stir it back into the sauce and repeat until sauce is curried to taste. Add 2 teaspoons onion juice. Indian curry sauce is not thickened with flour. Use for curries of meat, poultry, fish, shellfish, or eggs.

Dieppe Sauce: See Cherbourg sauce.

Sauce Dugléré: Prepare 1 recipe fish velouté sauce, adding ½ cup white wine and ½ cup diced tomatoes. Scald, then simmer in the sauce, 2 minced shallots, ½ minced onion, and ¼ cup finely chopped parsley. Serve with fish.

Epicurian Sauce: Sharpen 1 recipe béchamel sauce with 1 tablespoon each walnut and mushroom ketchup and vinegar. Add more of either of the ketchups to taste. Add a pinch of cayenne pepper and serve. Use as béchamel sauce.

Etretat Sauce: Prepare 1 recipe fish velouté sauce and add ⅔ cup tomato purée and ⅓ cup chopped, sautéed mushrooms. Heat and just before serving, add ⅔ cup small poached oysters. Serve with fish.

Financier Sauce: Prepare 1 recipe chicken velouté sauce. Add ½ cup dry white wine, ½ cup each, hot cooked and minced chicken and mushrooms, 1 diced truffle, and minced herbs—parsley, chives, chervil and tarragon. Serve with veal, chicken, or eggs.

Finnish Sauce: Prepare 1 recipe béchamel sauce with 1 tablespoon paprika added. Simmer in the sauce ½ cup finely diced and scalded green peppers, ¼ cup diced pimento, and 1 tablespoon chopped parsley. Served with veal, chicken, or eggs.

Herb Sauce: Stir 2 tablespoons each, minced shallots, parsley, and chervil, 2 tablespoons cut chives, and ½ cup dry white wine into 1 recipe basic white sauce. The herbs can be changed according to availability. Basil, oregano, or tarragon can be substituted for chervil. If cut dill is used, reduce quantity to 1 teaspoon. Also called sauce fines herbs. Serve with eggs, fish, chicken, or veal.

Horseradish Sauce: Stir into basic white sauce, ½ cup freshly grated horseradish, or to taste. Add a pinch of sugar. If a fresh horseradish root is not available, use bottled horseradish, and squeeze it dry before incorporating in the sauce. Serve with fish or boiled beef.

Lobster Sauce: Prepare a basic white sauce with lobster butter instead of plain butter. Add yolks and cream as in basic white sauce recipe. Serve with lobster or fish.

Lyonnaise Sauce: To 1 recipe velouté sauce, add ½ cup dry white wine, ½ cup cooked onions, puréed, and 3 tablespoons chopped herbs, parsley, chives, and chervil. If preferred, ½ small clove garlic may be crushed into the sauce. Serve with fish, chicken, or vegetables.

Matelote Sauce: Combine 1 recipe fish velouté sauce with 1 cup oyster liquor, ½ cup each cooked, diced onions and mushrooms and a pinch of cayenne pepper. Serve with fish.

Mornay Sauce: See page 52.

Mushroom Sauce: Sauté ½ pound thinly sliced mushrooms with 2 tablespoons minced onion in 2 tablespoons butter until soft, about 5 minutes. Stir into 1 recipe chicken velouté sauce. Add ½ cup heavy cream. Serve with meat, poultry, vegetables, eggs, fish.

Mustard Sauce, also called Flemish Sauce: Stir Dijon or any preferred mustard or combination of mustards into 1 recipe basic white sauce. Add mustard according to taste. Beat in yolks and cream as on page 53. Serve with any meat, boiled beef, or fish.

Nantua Sauce: Prepare 1 recipe fish velouté sauce with shrimp butter instead of plain butter. Add 1 cup diced cooked shrimp to the sauce and thin with whipped sour cream. Serve with fish.

Newburg Sauce: Prepare 1 recipe basic white sauce, using cream instead of milk. Take sauce from heat, stir in 2 egg yolks and 2 to 3 tablespoons sherry to taste, and stir the sauce over very low heat until thickened and smooth. Do not let sauce return to a simmer after egg yolks have been added. Serve with lobster or seafood.

Normandy Sauce: Prepare 1 recipe fish velouté sauce, using oyster liquor and clam juice instead of fish stock. Whip the sauce into 2 beaten egg yolks and fold in ½ cup heavy cream, whipped. Serve with fish or oysters.

Onion Sauce: See Soubise sauce, page 58.

Oyster Sauce: Add to 1 recipe fish velouté sauce, 1 cup oyster liquor and 1 cup poached oysters. If oysters are small, leave them whole. Serve with fish or chicken.

Paprika Sauce: Flavor 1 recipe béchamel sauce with paprika to taste, stir paprika into a little of the hot sauce until smooth, then stir back into the sauce. Serve with chicken, veal, or eggs.

Parsley Sauce: Add minced parsley to taste to 1 recipe basic white sauce. Use as a white sauce.

Pea Sauce: Stir 1 cup puréed cooked green peas into 1 recipe basic white sauce. Excellent over boiled cauliflower.

Polish Sauce: Prepare 1 recipe béchamel or velouté sauce. Before serving, stir in ¼ cup freshly grated horseradish, ½ cup sour cream, whipped, and a little lemon juice to taste. Add finely diced fennel, about 3 tablespoons or to taste. Serve with fish, meat, or poultry.

Poulette Sauce: Enrich 1 recipe chicken velouté sauce with ½ cup sautéed minced mushrooms, ¼ cup chopped parsley, a few drops of lemon juice, and just before serving, stir in 1 tablespoon cold butter. Use with chicken, shrimp, pancakes, or vegetables.

Princess Sauce: Enrich 1 recipe béchamel sauce with 1 cup reduced chicken stock, a purée of sautéed mushrooms, and ½ cup heavy cream, whipped. Serve with chicken.

Shallot Sauce: Sautée 4 minced shallots in the butter before making the roux for 1 recipe béchamel sauce. Stir in ¼ cup minced parsley. Serve with fish, chicken, or eggs.

Smitane Sauce: See sour cream sauce, below.

Soubise Sauce: Stir into 1 recipe béchamel sauce 2 cups puréed cooked onions and 1 cup heavy cream. Serve with fish, veal, lamb, and sweetbreads.

Sour Cream Sauce: Whip into 1 recipe basic white sauce 1 cup sour cream. Sprinkle with cut chives. Serve with roast chicken or veal.

Spinach Sauce: Combine 1 recipe chicken velouté sauce with 1 cup cooked, puréed spinach. Serve with boiled chicken instead of fricassee sauce.

Suprême Sauce: See page 54.

Tomato Sauce: Combine ½ recipe basic white sauce with 1 cup thick purée of tomatoes and 1 teaspoon each minced onions and basil. Serve with meat, pasta, or eggs.

Velouté Sauce: See page 53.

Vénitienne Sauce: Prepare white wine sauce, below, with herb butter instead of plain butter and stir in 1 tablespoon each minced parsley, chervil, and tarragon. Serve with fish.

Vernet Sauce: Prepare 1 recipe béchamel sauce with herb butter instead of plain butter. Add finely chopped white of 1 hardcooked egg and ¼ cup diced and drained dill pickle. Serve with chicken or eggs.

Vin Blanc Sauce: Thicken 1 recipe fish velouté sauce made with fish stock and dry white wine with egg yolks and cream, as in basic recipe. Serve with fish.

White Wine Sauce: See vin blanc sauce, above.

FRICASSEES, WHITE STEWS, AND CASSEROLES BASED ON BASIC WHITE SAUCE

Basic White Sauce is the reason for being of all the Fricassees, Blanquettes, white stews, and casseroles. Boiled poultry or meat are apt to be dry unless they are served with or in a rich sauce. Examples of this are: boiled beef with horseradish sauce, and chicken or veal in paprika sauce. Another way of serving boiled meat and poultry is in its own stock; for example, chicken in noodle soup and Marmite. The stock from the boiled meat, thickened with roux, becomes the base of the sauce. In many cases other ingredients are added to the sauce. They can be anything from small onions or mushrooms to wilted spinach or tomatoes. It must be remembered that in dishes of this kind, the tenderness and juiciness of the meat is important. For this reason the meat must be added to boiling water to seal in the juices.

For the sauce floating about our flat dinner plates, we provide rice, biscuits, dumplings, noodles, pasta, or mashed potatoes to do a sort of elegant "dunking." The combination can be delectable and the only regret is that we no longer serve it properly in wide soup plates.

BASIC FRICASSEE USING CHICKEN

- 1 5 to 5½ pound stewing fowl, disjointed, or 2 frying chickens, quartered
- 1 carrot, scraped and quartered
- 1 onion
- 1 celery stalk
- 1 bouquet garni, consisting of 1 bay leaf, 2 sprigs parsley, and 1 sprig thyme
- 2 peppercorns
- Salt to taste (bear in mind that stock will be reduced)
- 3 tablespoons butter
- 4 tablespoons flour
- 1 cup cream
- 2 egg yolks (optional)
- 2 tablespoons chopped parsley

Place all vegetables, bouquet, peppercorns and salt in a large kettle with enough water to cover the chicken when it is added. Bring to a boil, add chicken and let it boil for 10 minutes after the water returns to a boil. Skim off scum, cover, and simmer from 20 minutes to 1 hour, depending on whether frying chicken or fowl is used. Take out the chicken, draw off the skin and any loosened bones, and set chicken aside. Reduce chicken stock in kettle to 6 cups by boiling rapidly, uncovered. Make a white roux of butter and flour in a large saucepan on top of a large double boiler, moisten it with reduced and strained stock, according to basic recipe on page 37. Whisk in cream and let it simmer until smooth. If egg yolks are being added, beat them into the cream and under the saucepan or double boiler reduce heat to a simmer. Beat a little hot sauce into the cream and yolk mixture, then beat it into the sauce. The sauce must not boil after the yolks are added. (This includes the water in the double boiler.) Season to taste. Add chicken pieces and serve sprinkled with parsley.

Variations

1. Substitute parboiled veal pieces, boil for 1½ hours. Add cooked baby onions, mushrooms and a little lemon juice to taste to the sauce. This is usually called a blanquette de veau.
2. To chicken fricassee, add 1 pound wilted fresh spinach.
3. Add 1 cooked cauliflower, broken into flowerets.

Basic Casseroles

Prepare meat, vegetables, and any other ingredient as above. Make a white sauce, pour it over the contents of the casserole, and bake in a low oven until heated through. Top with crumbs and/or cheese. Do not add eggs or egg yolks when planning this recipe for a casserole. Increase heat to 400°F. to brown top, or sprinkle with melted butter and place under broiler until brown.

Variations on Boiled Chicken in Basic White Sauce, Suprême, Béchamel, or Velouté Sauce

The chicken for these recipes is simmered in stock, page 37, until tender. The strained and defatted stock is used to moisten the sauce. When leftover cooked chicken is used, the sauce can be moistened with canned clear chicken consommé or chicken bouillon cubes dissolved in boiling water. Use small chickens, whole, halved, or quartered, or larger chickens, disjointed. Breast of chicken or suprêmes (the half breast with first wing joint left on) can also be used. Or the chicken can be cooked ahead, the meat taken from the bones and refrigerated in a little of the stock to keep it moist. The sauce and all other ingredients can be prepared ahead. Assemble everything and heat in the top section of a double boiler over boiling water or in a casserole in the oven. The skin should always be removed from the chicken before it is put into the sauce.

À la King: Chicken in cream sauce with slivered green peppers and pimentos. Served on toast triangles.

À l'Ancienne: Chicken in velouté sauce with button mushrooms and small white onions. Garnished generously with toasted bread croutons.

À l'Andalouse: Chicken in suprême sauce with diced pimentos. Surrounded by green peppers stuffed with rice and diced, sauteéd eggplant.

Cardinal: Chicken in suprême sauce tinted with tomato purée. Surrounded with tomatoes stuffed with rice and chicken giblets.

Doria: Chicken in velouté sauce with puréed cucumbers, surrounded by a border of steamed cucumbers sprinkled with chopped parsley.

Hongroise or Paprika: Chicken in velouté sauce with small onions and diced, seeded tomatoes. The sauce is flavored and colored with paprika. Serve in a border of cooked noodles.

Imperial: Chicken in soubise sauce.

Jeanette: Suprêmes of chicken, each arranged on a base of chicken liver pâté. Masked with chaud-froid sauce, garnished with truffle cutouts. Serve with vegetable salad and garnish with diced aspic, page 132.

Maintenon: Chicken in suprême sauce with a julienne (cut in matchsticks) of sliced tongue, and mushrooms and sprinkled with diced truffles.

Princesse I: Chicken in suprême sauce with diced artichoke bottoms. Serve with a border of rice or noodles.

Princesse II: Chicken in suprême sauce flavored with asparagus purée. Garnished with artichoke bottoms filled with asparagus tips.

Revue: Chicken in suprême sauce with broccoli spears, in a border of rice.

Spinach: Chicken in suprême sauce with spinach in a border of rice or noodles. Spinach is washed and cooked for a few minutes over low heat in just the water that clings to its leaves.

Sultan: Chicken in suprême sauce, covered with chopped pimento and pistacchio nuts, in a border of rice or saffron rice.

White Stew Variations

À l'Ancienne: Veal simmered in veal stock. Served in white sauce based on the strained veal stock with cooked onions, carrots, and mushrooms.

À la Menagère: Substitute lamb for veal, continue as for blanquette de veau.

À la Romaine: Substitute lamb for veal, flavor sauce lightly with lemon juice. Add diced artichoke bottoms or fill little tart shells, page 191, with artichoke purée and place around the stew.

Basic Gratinéed Dishes

Arrange hot poached fish fillets, cooked vegetables, poultry, pasta, or eggs in a shallow gratinée dish. Pour over hot medium white sauce, which should, if possible, be moistened with its own liquid—as fish stock for fish dishes and chicken stock for poultry dishes. Pour over enough sauce to coat the contents of the dish generously and brown surface in any one of several ways.

1. Sprinkle grated Parmesan cheese onto the sauce, sprinkle it with melted butter, and brown in a 400°F. oven or under a hot broiler. Keep oven door open and watch so that it does not burn.

2. Pour Mornay sauce over the prepared dish, sprinkle with grated

Swiss cheese, and then brown top lightly in a 400°F. oven.

3. A dish covered with hot cream sauce or hot hollandaise sauce mixed with cream sauce may be browned or "glazed" under a broiler for a moment before serving.

4. Cover a dish with white sauce combined with whipped cream and brown lightly under a broiler.

Chaud-Froid

The glossy white coating that transforms chicken breasts, whole chickens, turkey or lobster into the focal point of a cold buffet is called *hot-cold* or chaud-froid. It is a basic white sauce, whitened with cream and stiffened with gelatin. The application, however, is different from the other coated foods, where aspic is brushed on, layer by layer, and any little imperfections in the coating can be covered by the next layer. Chaud-froid is like a fondant icing: It goes on in a wide poured stream and that's it. For a thick coating the stream can be repeated, but the slightest little blemish shows. Pouring chaud-froid over chicken breasts, eggs, or lobster is easy. The food is set on a wire mesh, over a pan. A wide stream of chaud-froid is poured over its entire surface with complete abandon. Nine-tenths of the chaud-froid is then taken from the pan under the food and reused.

Coating a whole chicken or turkey is difficult but fun. The only secret is to make a great deal of chaud-froid and start with the largest surface, the breast. Tilt the bird on the mesh slightly backward and pour over enough chaud-froid in the widest possible stream (from a wide utensil) to cover the breast. Tilt the bird so that the flow covers it from back to front leaving out only the wings and legs. Do not worry about rough fringes at the under edges; every artist has artistic license, and these edges can be masked with parsley or the entire bird can sit in a nest of vegetable flowers or real flowers or cress. Gather the chaud-froid from the pan below the mesh, chill the bird and reheat the sauce to flowing consistency. Repeat the glazing as often as necessary to obtain an enamel-like cover. When the last coat goes on, press truffle cutouts into it. Some people add green tarragon leaves and pimento, which gives the chaud-froid a slightly less dignified look. Gather and reheat the last of the chaud-froid and pour it over the wings and legs, doing each one separately. A small bird can have its extremities dipped. A large bird has to be tilted on its side. Refrigerate it until it is to be garnished and served. Paper cuffs and an attelet, or spear, of vegetables complete the picture.

The chaud-froid chicken breast, called chicken Jeanette, is an excellent and "easy" dish. The whole bird should not be done for anything less than a celebration.

BASIC CHAUD-FROID SAUCE
JELLIED WHITE SAUCE

4 tablespoons butter	3 to 4 envelopes gelatin
6 tablespoons flour	1½ cups heavy cream
2 cups clear chicken stock	3 egg yolks (optional)
½ cup light, cold sherry	Salt, depending on saltiness of stock

(Use more gelatin in summer than in winter)

Make a roux of butter and flour in the top of a double boiler, stir in chicken stock as for basic white sauce, page 49. While sauce is cooking over boiling water, stir gelatin into sherry and soften for 15 minutes. Take sauce from heat and stir in the gelatin until dissolved. Reduce heat so that water is just below simmering and stir sauce well with a French wire whisk. Beat cream and yolks together and whisk them into the sauce until thick and smooth. Cool sauce to just before setting and use it to coat chicken breasts or birds as described on page 63. When sauce has to be reheated, set it over hot, *not boiling*, water.

Variations

1. Pink Chaud-Froid Sauce. Stir paprika into the basic white sauce to tint it to desired shade. Use about 1 tablespoon red paprika for every quart of sauce.

2. Brown Chaud-Froid Sauce. Prepare exactly as white chaud-froid, using basic brown sauce instead of basic white sauce.

CREAMED SOUPS

Most creamed soup recipes are a simple repetition of the white sauces with more liquid added. They can be classified as the "patient" recipes since they wait patiently, and without deteriorating, for the guest who arrives last. They can be prepared in advance and reheated in a double boiler, or prepared in a double boiler and pushed to the side of the stove until needed. They sound like wall flowers, but actually they are the hostess' greatest boon. Lunch can consist of a bowl of soup, crisp bread, cheese, and fruit. Dinner can start off calmly with a hot or cold creamed soup which was prepared (with very little effort) hours or days before.

Although we devoted all of Lesson 1 to learning how to make the basic soup stocks, the creamed soups can be based on canned bouillon, bouillon cubes, or granules or any of the various concentrates. The other ingredients should be either fresh cooked or frozen. Meat should be fresh cooked or leftover and fish should be fresh cooked, leftover, or frozen. The vegetables should be fresh or frozen. Some canned vegetables, such as corn and beets, make excellent creamed soups, but on the whole the flavor is better where fresh vegetables or fresh frozen vegetables are used.

The available canned clear soups are excellent, unless you have homemade soup stock in the refrigerator or freezer. It is a good plan to use jellied chicken consommé to moisten a cream soup that will be served chilled. The jelling agent in the base gives a very nice quality to the chilled cream soup.

CREAMED VEGETABLE SOUPS GROUP I

The following creamed vegetable soups are a combination of basic white sauce and a cooked and puréed, sieved, or blended vegetable. Part of the liquid used in making the white sauce can be the water in which the vegetable was cooked. If a leftover cooked vegetable is used without its own cooking liquid, use about ⅓ more stock, milk, or cream than in the basic cream of vegetable soup recipe.

The liquids can be altered to taste: More milk or stock can be substituted for the heavy cream, more vegetable water can replace the stock.

BASIC CREAM OF VEGETABLE SOUP, GROUP I

2 cups puréed or blended cooked vegetable, column 5 on chart
4 tablespoons butter
4 tablespoons flour
1 cup scalded milk
1 cup vegetable water or stock
1 cup heavy cream
½ teaspoon salt, depending upon amount of salt in stock or vegetable water
1 to 2 egg yolks, lightly beaten (optional)

Prepare vegetable, retaining 1 cup vegetable water; set both aside. In a heavy saucepan over low heat, or in the top of a double boiler, melt butter and stir in flour with a wooden spoon. Do not let it brown. Stir in milk and strained vegetable water gradually with a French wire whisk, until smooth and thickened. Reduce heat and simmer, stirring frequently for 15 minutes. Stir in puréed vegetable and cream and simmer, stirring occasionally until heated through. Simmer up to 30 minutes if a creamier, reduced soup is preferred. Correct seasoning.

For a still creamier soup, take from heat, beat a little of the hot soup into the egg yolks, then beat the mixture back into the soup. The soup can be reheated, but it must not simmer or boil after the yolks have been added.

The creamed vegetable soups in the chart on pages 68–73 are all prepared as basic cream of vegetable soup above and yield approximately 6 servings.

General Rules for Using Chart Recipes

Step 1. Prepare vegetable, column 5.

Step 2. While vegetable is boiling or after it is prepared, make a basic white sauce of the 3 ingredients in columns 1, 2, and 3, always adding the liquid slowly.

Step 3. Add the prepared vegetable, cream, or other called for ingredient. Season to taste, simmer at least 7 minutes, stirring. Serve at once, store and reheat, or chill before serving.

Step 4. Although the soups can be served as described in step 3, the thinner finished soups can be simmered over low heat, as basic white sauce is simmered, stirring frequently, from 7 to 35 minutes. The soup will be reduced by approximately ⅓ in quantity after simmering for 35 minutes and will be thicker, smoother, and creamier. The soup can also be cooked, uncovered, in the top of a double boiler, over boiling water, from 15 minutes to an hour.

Step 5. If the added enrichment of egg yolks or yolks and cream is preferred, take soup from heat. Beat yolks with 1 cup hot soup or with cream and beat the whole thing back into the finished soup and serve. For added thickening and smoothness, the soup can be returned to low heat and stirred for a few minutes.

Do not allow the soup to reach the simmering point after the yolks have been added or they will curdle immediately. Some heavy soup kettles retain heat so well that the soup goes on simmering after it is taken from the heat. Always add egg yolks after the simmering has stopped.

Any leftover vegetable or combination of vegetables can be puréed and substituted for those listed on the chart. There should be approximately 2 cups of puréed vegetables for 6 cups of soup, but even 1 cup of puréed vegetable will flavor a cream soup for 6 persons.

35 CREAMED VEGETABLE SOUPS

Season with salt and white pepper to taste

1	2	3	4	5	6	7
NAME	BUTTER	FLOUR	LIQUIDS	OTHER INGREDIENTS	GARNISH	SERVE
Cream of Artichoke Soup	3 Tbs.	4 Tbs.	2 cups strained stock, column 5 2 cups scalded milk 1 cup heavy cream	Boil 2 whole artichokes in 4 cups chicken stock for 40 minutes. Purée bottoms and tender part of leaves.	Diced artichoke bottoms reserved before puréeing, column 5	Hot or chilled
Cream of Asparagus Soup I	3 Tbs.	4 Tbs.	2 cups strained asparagus water, column 5 3 cups scalded milk	Boil 1 bunch asparagus to obtain 2 cups puréed asparagus	Asparagus tips, reserved before puréeing, column 5	Hot or chilled
Cream of Asparagus Soup II	4 Tbs.	4 Tbs.	2 cups scalded milk, add 2 cans room-temperature jellied chicken soup after white sauce has cooled	2 cups purée of cooked asparagus	2 hardcooked egg yolks and whites riced separately, chopped parsley	Chilled
Cream of Beet Soup I	5 Tbs.	5 Tbs.	1 cup beet juice, column 5 3 cups beef stock 1 cup medium cream	1 large can beets, drained and puréed, column 4	Sour cream topped with a little caviar	Chilled
Cream of Beet Soup II	6 Tbs.	6 Tbs.	3 cups scalded milk, 1 cup cream	2 cups purée of boiled beets	Whipped sour cream, cut or minced dill	Hot or chilled
Cream of Broccoli Soup Crème Tourangeau	4 Tbs.	4 Tbs.	4 cups chicken stock 1 cup heavy cream	1 bunch broccoli, trimmed and boiled in the stock for 40 minutes; strain stock, blend or sieve broccoli into a purée	Fried bread cubes for hot. Slivered lemon rind for chilled	Hot or chilled
Cream of Brussels Sprouts	2 Tbs.	2 Tbs.	2 cups strained Brussels sprouts water, column 5 2 cups stock 1 cup heavy cream	Boil 1 pound Brussels sprouts with 1 onion and 4 parsley sprigs, drain and purée	Bread croutons fried in curried butter	Hot

1 Name	2 Butter	3 Flour	4 Liquids	5 Other Ingredients	6 Garnish	7 Serve
Cream of Cabbage Soup *Soupe aux Choux*	3 Tbs.	3 Tbs.	3 cups scalded milk 3 cups strained cabbage water, col. 5	1 shredded cabbage and 1 onion boiled, strained, and puréed	Crisp crumbled bacon	Hot
Cream of Carrot Soup *Purée Crécy*	4 Tbs.	4 Tbs.	2 cups white stock 2 cups scalded milk 1 cup heavy cream	Boil 1½ pounds carrots with 3 stalks celery and 1 onion, drain, and purée	Chopped chervil or parsley	Hot or chilled
Cream of Cauliflower Soup	3 Tbs.	3 Tbs.	2 cups drained cauliflower water, column 5 2 cups scalded milk 1 cup heavy cream	Boil 1 2-pound cauliflower with 1 onion and 3 sprigs parsley. Drain and purée	Reserved cauliflower flowerets or toasted slivered almonds, cut or snipped dill	Hot or chilled
Cream of Celery Soup	4 Tbs.	4 Tbs.	2 cups drained celery water, column 5 2 cups scalded milk 1 cup heavy cream	Boil 1 bunch celery with 1 onion and 3 sprigs parsley, drain and purée. (optional: add ½ cup scalded almonds, pounded)	Toasted bread croutons or toasted slivered almonds or diced, drained tomatoes	Hot
Cream of Chestnut Soup	3 Tbs.	3 Tbs.	2 cups white stock 1 cup scalded milk 1 cup heavy cream	Boil 1 quart chestnuts 35 minutes. Peel* and boil until soft with 3 stalks celery and 1 slice onion. Drain and purée	Retained pieces of chestnut, column 5 chopped parsley	Hot
Cream of Corn Soup *Soup Sir Windham*	4 Tbs.	4 Tbs.	4 cups scalded milk In winter, add 1 shot brandy to finished soup	2 cups cooked fresh or frozen or canned corn kernels and ½ cooked onion, finely chopped or puréed together	Toasted croutons or crumbled, crisp bacon, paprika	Hot or chilled
Cream of Whole Kernel Corn Soup	2 Tbs.	2 Tbs.	4 cups scalded milk	1 large can corn heated with its liquid and 3 tablespoons minced onion	Popcorn or diced pimento	Hot
Cream of Cucumber Soup I	3 Tbs.	3 Tbs.	4 cups milk	Boil 4 peeled cucumbers and 2 small white onions until tender, about 14 minutes, drain and purée	Salted whipped cream or cut or snipped dill	Hot or chilled

*Peel off outer and thin inner shells.

NAME	BUTTER	FLOUR	LIQUIDS	OTHER INGREDIENTS	GARNISH	SERVE
Cream of Cucumber Soup II	3 Tbs.	3 Tbs.	1 cup cucumber water, column 5 2 cups medium cream	Boil 2 peeled and 1 unpeeled sliced cucumbers and 1 slice onion and 1 sprig dill for 14 minutes, drain, add 2 cans jellied chicken consommé (at room temperature) and blend or purée	Salted whipped cream sprinkled with cut chives	Chilled
Cream of Eggplant Soup	4 Tbs.	4 Tbs.	4 cups milk 1 cup medium cream	Boil 1 peeled and diced eggplant for 30 minutes, drain and purée	Tomato slices, chopped scalded green pepper, chopped pimento and parsley	Hot
Cream of Green Spring Onion Soup *Crème à L'oignon*	4 Tbs.	4 Tbs.	4 cups scalded milk 1 cup heavy cream	Boil 2 to 4 bunches (at least 24) green spring onions in water to cover about 30 minutes. Blend or purée with their own liquid	Chopped chervil sprinkled over oven toasted French bread slices	Hot
Cream of Leek and Potato Soup	4 Tbs.	4 Tbs.	3 cups scalded milk 1 cup heavy cream	Boil 1 bunch leek, white and tender part of green stalks, with 1 onion and 3 peeled potatoes in water to cover for 30 minutes, purée with their own liquid	Toasted bread croutons or cut chives	Hot or chilled
Cream of Lettuce Soup	3 Tbs.	3 Tbs.	4 cups scalded milk 1 cup thin cream	Boil 2 heads green lettuce, shredded with ½ onion, sliced thin, 1 bay leaf and 3 sprigs parsley. Drain, remove bay leaf, and blend or purée	Spring onion rings, chopped parsley or toasted, cheesed bread croutons	Hot or chilled
Cream of Lima Bean Soup	4 Tbs.	4 Tbs.	2 cups scalded milk 1 cup bouillon stock 1 cup heavy cream	2 cups cooked lima beans puréed with ½ cooked onion and ¼ small clove garlic	Bacon curls or thinly sliced cocktail frankfurters on hot soup. Chopped parsley on chilled soup	Hot or chilled

Name	Butter	Flour	Liquids	Other Ingredients	Garnish	Serve
Cream of Mushroom Soup	See Cream of Vegetable Soups, Group II, page 88, for all Cream of Mushroom soups and their variations					
Cream of Parsnip Soup	5 Tbs.	5 Tbs.	1 cup parsnip water, column 5 4 cups scalded milk	Boil 3 scraped and diced parsnips until tender, purée with ½ cup of parsnip water. Use 1 cup additional parsnip water for base, column 4	Salted whipped cream and minced parsley	Hot
Cream of Pea Soup	See page 76 for separate group of Cream of Green Pea soups and their variations.					
Cream of Potato Soup	2 Tbs.	3 Tbs.	4 cups scalded milk add 1 cup chilled heavy cream if soup is to be served chilled	Boil 4 peeled and sliced potatoes with 2 stalks scraped celery and 1 sliced onion for 30 minutes, drain and purée or blend with ½ cup potato water	Sprinkle heavily with cut chives	Hot or chilled
Cream of Mashed Potato Soup	3 Tbs.	3 Tbs.	4 cups scalded milk	2 cups hot mashed potatoes	Fried bread croutons and chopped parsley	Hot
Cream of Pumpkin or Squash Soup *Crème Bressane*	4 Tbs.	4 Tbs.	3 cups scalded milk 2 cups beef stock or bouillon	Boil 3 pounds peeled and diced pumpkin, ½ onion, sliced, 1 bay leaf and 3 sprigs parsley for 30 minutes or until pumpkin is soft. Drain and purée	Diced ham or fried bread croutons	Hot
Cream of Sauerkraut Soup *Kraut Suppe*	5 Tbs.	5 Tbs.	5 cups beef stock Add ½ cup dry white wine before serving	Boil 2 pounds cooked sauerkraut for 30 minutes, drain, add fresh water and simmer 2 hours longer with 1 bay leaf, 3 pepper corns and 3 sprigs parsley. Take out bay leaf and pepper, drain and mince	Sliced frankfurt sausages and toasted bread cubes	Hot
Cream of Sorrel Soup *Potage Germiny*	3 Tbs.	4 Tbs.	4 cups strained stock, column 5	Simmer 3 onion slices and 3 cups tightly packed sorrel	Salted whippd cream or garlic	Hot or chilled

Name	Butter	Flour	Liquids	Other Ingredients	Garnish	Serve
Cream of Sorrel Soup (continued)			1 cup heavy cream	leaves in 4 cups beef stock until tender. Drain and purée, use stock, column 4	croutons	
Cream of Spinach Soup Velouté à la Livonienne	5 Tbs.	5 Tbs.	Drained spinach water, column 5 1½ cups beef stock 2 cups milk 1 cup heavy cream	Simmer covered, over low heat, 1 pound washed spinach leaves, in only the water that clings to the leaves, until soft and wilted, about 7 minutes. Drain and purée spinach. Use spinach water, column 4	Small choux paste profiteroles filled with minced ham, page 234	Hot or chilled
Cream of Spinach Soup Potage Florentine	5 Tbs.	5 Tbs.	Spinach water, column 5 3 cups scalded milk 1 cup beef stock	2 packages frozen spinach cooked according to package directions and blended into a smooth purée. Use spinach water, column 4	6 warm or cold 6-minute eggs (oeufs mollet)	Hot or chilled
Cream of Squash Soup	5 Tbs.	5 Tbs.	3 cups scalded milk 2 cups beef stock	Boil 3 pounds squash, peeled and diced with ½ onion and 1 bay leaf until soft. Drain and purée	Toasted slivered almonds	Hot
Cream of String Bean Soup Velouté à la Mozart	4 Tbs.	4 Tbs.	3 cups scalded milk 2 cups bean water, column 5	Boil 1½ pounds diced string beans and 1 small onion in 2 cups water for 20 minutes. Strain and purée beans. Use bean water, column 4	Toasted slivered almonds or croutons	Hot
Cream of Tomato Soup	See page 80 for separate group of Cream of Tomato soups and their variations					
Cream of Turnip Soup	6 Tbs.	6 Tbs.	1 cup scalded milk 4 cups stock, column 5	Boil 2 cups diced turnip in 4 cups white stock. Strain and purée turnip. Use stock in column 4	Diced hardcooked eggs, chopped parsley	Hot

Name	Butter	Flour	Liquids	Other Ingredients	Garnish	Serve
Cream of Watercress Soup *Crème de Cresson*	3 Tbs.	4 Tbs.	4 cups strained stock column 5 1 cup medium cream	Simmer 3 onion slices and 3 cups tightly packed watercress leaves in 4 cups stock until tender, about 7 minutes. Drain and puree. Use stock, column 4	Salted whipped cream, reserved cress leaves	Hot or chilled
Cream of Wax Bean Soup *Crème Musart*	4 Tbs.	4 Tbs.	3 cups scalded milk 2 cups bean water, column 5	Boil 1½ pounds wax beans, chopped with ½ onion in 2 cups water for 25 minutes. Strain and purée beans. Use bean water, column 4	Chopped chervil, parsley and toasted bread croutons	Hot
Cream of Zucchini Soup	5 Tbs.	5 Tbs.	3 cups scalded milk 2 cups zucchini water, column 5	Boil 6 tender young zucchini sliced in 2 cups water with 3 beef bouillon cubes for 10 minutes. Drain and purée. Use zucchini water, column 4	Paper thin lemon slices	Hot

There are so many variations and descendants of cream of green pea soup that it follows here as a basic recipe with a variation chart.

BASIC CREAM OF GREEN PEA SOUP

2 pounds green peas, fresh or frozen
7 pea pods, if fresh peas are used
1 small white onion, quartered
1 large lettuce leaf, shredded
½ teaspoon salt, or to taste
1 pinch sugar
5 tablespoons butter
5 tablespoons flour
4 cups milk, scalded
1 cup heavy cream
1 pinch white pepper
2 egg yolks, well beaten (optional)

Boil peas, pods, onion, lettuce, salt, and sugar in 4 cups water until very soft, about 20 minutes. Drain and discard pods, retain ½ cup of the water. Purée the peas, onion, and lettuce shreds through a vegetable mill or blender or rub them through a sieve, with the retained water. Melt butter in a heavy saucepan, over low heat. Stir in flour until it is smooth and bubbling. Do not let it brown. Stir in milk with a French wire whisk until mixture is smooth and thickened, reduce heat, and cook gently for 14 minutes. Stir in puréed peas and heavy cream, add salt, if needed, and pepper. Bring to a boil, reduce heat, and simmer long enough to heat through, about 7 minutes.

For a creamier and richer soup, quickly beat ½ cup hot soup into the egg yolks, stir the mixture back into the soup, and stir soup for 3 minutes over very low heat. Do not let it come back to a boil after yolks have been added.

Serve plain or garnished with fried bread croutons, salted whipped cream, or any of the traditional garnishes suggested on the chart on page 68.

For special occasions go one simple step further and make the famous

BOULA GRATINÉE

½ recipe cream of green pea soup, omit heavy cream and egg yolks
1 large or 2 small cans clear green turtle soup, the type that contains turtle meat and sometimes sherry
½ cup sherry
1 cup heavy cream, whipped with:
  ¼ teaspoon salt
  ¼ cup grated Parmesan cheese

Heat the green pea and turtle soups with the sherry in the top of a double boiler over boiling water. Place 6 ovenware soup bowls on a cookie sheet or pan, near broiler. Stir soup well and pour it into soup bowls, filling them about ¾ full. Divide whipped cream over the 6 soup bowls. Work quickly with a spatula, sprinkle each bowl heavily with grated cheese, covering the entire surface, and push under a hot broiler. Depending on size of soup bowls, use top shelf of broiler or any shelf that will bring surface of soup about 1½ to 2 inches from broiler unit. Leave oven door open, watch carefully. The cream and cheese will swell and brown in a few seconds. Serve at once and pass a small decanter of sherry, which should be added to the soup to taste.

If individual soup bowls are not available, the soup can be poured into a shallow casserole. Cream and cheese can be added and browned under the broiler, but the surface of the soup has to be almost level with the top of the casserole.

CREAM OF GREEN PEA SOUPS USING BASIC RECIPE, PAGE 74

See also cream of chicken soups, page 83, for combinations of chicken and green pea soups

Name	Basic Cream of Green Pea Soup	Omissions	Additions	Time of Incorporation	Garnishes	Serve
Cream of Green Pea and Sorrel Soup Potage à l'Ambassadeur	½ recipe	Egg yolks	½ recipe cream of sorrel soup	Combine after soups are completed	Toasted bread croutons	Hot
Cream of Green Pea Soup with Rice Potage à l'Ambassadrice	1 recipe	Lettuce leaf and egg yolks	1 heart Boston lettuce, shredded, ½ cup sorrel leaves	Boil and purée lettuce and sorrel with peas	Add ½ cup boiled rice, just before serving	Hot
Cream of Green Pea Soup with Bacon Curls	1 recipe		A ham bone or ham rind (optional)	May be cooked with peas	Crisp bacon curls	Hot
Cream of Green Pea Soup with large cooked vegetables Potage Balvais	1 recipe	Egg yolks	Hot cooked vegetables, whole small white onions, thick carrot slices, large cauliflower and broccoli flowerets	At serving time	Mound vegetables in soup plates, pour soup around, sprinkle vegetables with chopped parsley	Hot
Cream of Green Pea and Lettuce Soup Potage Chantilly	½ recipe	Egg yolks	½ recipe cream of lettuce soup	Combine after soups are completed	Toasted bread croutons	Hot
Cream of Green Pea Soup with Toasted Bread Potage Clamart	1 recipe				Whole slices of oven-dried buttered French bread	Hot
Cream of Green Pea Soup with Ham Potage Fontanges	1 recipe		Blanched sorrel and chervil, shredded	Cooked in soup for last 15 minutes cooking time	Diced ham	Hot or chilled
Cream of Green Pea Soup with Chicken Crème Gounod	1 recipe		1½ cups cold cooked chicken cut in large dice	Heat chicken in soup		Hot

Name	Basic Cream of Green Pea Soup	Omissions	Additions	Time of Incorporation	Garnishes	Serve
Cream of Green Pea Soup with Sausage Slices *Grüne Erbsensuppe*	1 recipe	Egg yolks			6 skinless, hot frankfurters, cut across into thin slices	Hot
Cream of Green Pea and Tomato Soup *Potage Italienne*	½ recipe	Egg yolks	½ recipe or 1 can cream of tomato soup	Combine soups and cream at the last moment in such a way that each portion has a green, red, and white swirl	¾ cup cream, half whipped	Chilled or hot
Cream of Green Pea Soup with vegetables *Crème Jubilée*	1 recipe	Egg yolks	½ cup each steamed whole peas, diced carrots, celery, beans and diced cauliflower	Reheated in soup before serving	Minced parsley and chervil	Hot
Cream of Green Pea Soup with vegetables *Potage Longuedocienne*	1 recipe		Julienne of cooked vegetables	Reheat in soup before serving		Hot with homemade melba toast
Cream of Green Pea and Sorrel Soup *Potage Longueville*	½ recipe	Egg yolks	½ recipe cream of sorrel soup	Combine after soups are completed	Large cooked macaroni cut into thick rings	Hot
Cream of Green Pea Soup and Noodles *Velouté à La Maraîchere*	1 recipe	Egg yolks	1 cup diced onion, wide noodles cooked and drained	Add onion for last 15 minutes of cooking time, add hot noodles just before serving	Large pieces of torn white bread toasted slowly in oven	Hot
Cream of Green Pea Soup with vegetables *Potage à la Marigny*	1 recipe	Egg yolks	Whole cooked green peas, French-cut cooked green beans, shredded sorrel	Cooked in soup for last 15 minutes of cooking time	Chopped chervil	Hot

Name	Basic Cream of Green Pea Soup	Omissions	Additions	Time of Incorporation	Garnishes	Serve
Cream of Green Pea Soup with Shrimp *Crème de Pois et d'Écrevisse*	1 recipe	Egg yolks	½ cup sherry or to taste	Stir in after taking soup from heat	1 pound shelled and deveined shrimp, boiled 4 minutes and drained	Hot or chilled. Pass sherry decanter separately
Cream of Green Pea Soup with Shrimp *Potage de Pois à la Navarin*	1 recipe	Egg yolks	1 pound peeled and cooked shrimp	Just before serving	Whole cooked green peas, lots of finely chopped parsley	Hot
Cream of Green Pea Soup with Vegetables *Crème à la Polonaise*	1 recipe	Egg yolks	Julienne of cooked celery, leek, onions, and beets	Cook beets separately, add the entire julienne just before serving	Salted whipped cream	Hot
Cream of Green Pea and Potato Soup *Crème de Pois et Pommes*	½ recipe	Egg yolks	½ recipe cream of potato soup	Combine after soups are completed	½ inch croutons of white bread, fried in butter until golden and added just before serving	Hot
Cream of Green Pea Soup with Gratineéd Bread *Potage Rigoletto*	1 recipe	Egg yolks	Shredded spinach leaves	Cooked in the soup for the last 15 minutes cooking time	Toasted French bread slices spread with thick white sauce sprinkled with grated Parmesan cheese and browned under the broiler	Hot
Cream of Green Pea Soup with Salmon	1 recipe		2 small or 1 large poached salmon steak divided into chunks, or 1 can salmon, heated	Stir in just before soup is served; try to keep salmon in large pieces	2 tablespoons minced parsley or snipped dill	Hot

BASIC CREAM OF TOMATO SOUP

6 medium or 4 large ripe tomatoes, about 1½ pounds, peeled and quartered
1 cup tomato juice
2 tablespoons chopped celery leaves
2 tablespoons minced onion
1 teaspoon white or brown sugar
5 cups milk
1 bay leaf
1 clove
3 sprigs parsley
5 tablespoons butter
5 tablespoons flour
Salt and white pepper to taste
2 egg yolks (optional)
½ cup heavy cream (optional)

Cook tomatoes, juice, celery, onion, and sugar in a heavy soup kettle over low heat for 20 minutes, stirring occasionally. Scald milk with bay leaf, clove, and parsley, set aside to draw. Melt butter in a heavy saucepan over low heat. Stir in flour and cook, stirring about 2 minutes, until roux is creamy but not brown. Stir in the strained scalded milk gradually and continue to stir until the thin white sauce is smooth and thickened, about 5 minutes. Adjust heat to simmer and cook the sauce, stirring occasionally, for 15 minutes. Sieve or blend the tomatoes and their juice into a smooth purée. Stir it into the simmering white sauce, let it simmer 7 minutes longer, stirring frequently. Season and take from heat. For a richer soup, beat yolks with heavy cream, and beat into the soup. Serve at once or return to low heat and stir about 3 minutes; do not let the soup come to a boil after the yolks have been added.

CREAM OF TOMATO SOUPS USING BASIC RECIPE, PAGE 79

Name	Basic Cream of Tomato Soup	Omissions	Additions	Time of Incorporation	Garnishes	Serve
Cream of Tomato Soup with Whipped Cream	1 recipe				1 large rosette of salted whipped cream, piped on a slice of tomato and sprinkled with chopped parsley	Chilled
Cream of Tomato and Onion Soup I *Crème à l'Andalouse*	½ recipe	Egg yolks	½ recipe cream of onion soup, 1½ cups hot cooked rice	Combine rice and soups after both are completed	Shredded scalded green peppers, diced tomatoes	Hot
Cream of Tomato and Onion Soup II *Purée à la Gasçonne*	½ recipe	Egg yolks	½ recipe cream of onion soup	Combine when both are completed	Julienne of ham and chopped sautéed mushrooms	Hot
Cream of Tomato and Rice Soup *Velouté Carmen*	1 recipe		Hot boiled and drained rice	Add before serving	Julienne of ham and thin pancake	Hot
Cream of Tomato and Noodle Soup *Crème Chabrillan*	1 recipe		Hot boiled thin noodles or vermicelli	Add before serving	Chopped parsley	Hot
Cream of Tomato Soup Chicago	1 recipe		Add fresh or dried tarragon leaves	Cook with soup for flavor	Pearl onions and toasted croutons	Hot or chilled
Cream of Tomato Soup, Chilled *Potage Côte d'Azur*	1 recipe		3 tomatoes, peeled, seeded, and diced	Chill in soup for 15 minutes before serving	Salted whipped cream, toasted bread croutons	Hot or chilled
Cream of Tomato and Potato Soup *Purée à la Malakoff*	½ recipe	Egg yolks	½ recipe cream of potato soup	Combine soups when both are completed	Blanched shredded spinach leaves	Hot

Name	Basic Cream of Tomato Soup	Omissions	Additions	Time of Incorporation	Garnishes	Serve
Cream of Tomato Soup, Italian *Velouté à la Milanaise*	1 recipe	Egg yolks	Diced sautéed mushrooms and hot cooked macaroni broken into short lengths	Add mushrooms and macaroni to completed soup, reheat	Diced ham and sliced white truffles	Hot with grated Parmesan cheese served separately
Cream of Tomato and Vegetable Soup *Crème Murillo*	1 recipe		A julienne of steamed, hot vegetables	Combine with soup just before serving	Fish dumplings	Hot
Cream of Tomato and Fish Soup *Velouté à la Nimoise*	1 recipe	Egg yolks and 3 cups scalded milk	Substitute 3 cups fish stock for 3 cups scalded milk	Stir fish stock with scalded milk into roux	Fried bread croutons	Hot
Cream of Tomato and Shrimp Soup *Potage à la Russe*	$\frac{1}{2}$ recipe	Egg yolks	$\frac{1}{2}$ recipe cream of shrimp soup	Combine soups when both are completed	Diced cooked green beans	Hot or chilled
Cream of Tomato and Lobster Soup *Crème Washington*	$\frac{1}{2}$ recipe		$\frac{1}{2}$ recipe cream of lobster soup	Combine soups when both are completed	Diced cooked lobster meat, chopped tarragon	Hot or chilled
Cream of Tomato and Crab Soup	1 recipe	Egg yolks	$1\frac{1}{2}$ cups picked crab meat	Chill in soup for last hour before serving	Sherry and minced parsley	Chilled

BASIC CREAM OF CHICKEN SOUP

6 tablespoons butter
6 tablespoons flour
4 cups chicken stock*
Salt and pepper to taste if chicken stock is unsalted
1 cup heavy cream

Melt butter in heavy saucepan over low heat. Stir in flour with a wooden spoon and cook until bubbling but not brown, about 3 minutes. Gradually add chicken stock, stirring with a French wire whisk until soup is thickened and smooth, about 5 minutes. Reduce heat and let soup barely simmer for 14 minutes. Add cream, cook only long enough to heat. Serves 6. Cook soup in top of double boiler according to recipe for basic white sauce cooked in double boiler if soup is not going to be served immediately.

CREAM OF CHICKEN SOUP I

(*Potage à la Reine*)

Prepare 1 recipe basic cream of chicken soup. Garnish it generously with hot cooked chicken cut into strips, toasted bread croutons, and finely chopped parsley.

CREAM OF CHICKEN SOUP II

(*Velouté Agnès Sorel*)

Prepare 1 recipe basic cream of chicken soup. In the top of a double boiler, over boiling water, add large pieces of cooked chicken, all skin and bones removed, and cook until chicken is heated through. Garnish the soup with a julienne of cold tongue and thin mushroom slices sautéed for 5 minutes in butter.

* Homemade chicken stock, stock made from wingtips, neck, and giblets, canned clear chicken consommé, jellied chicken consommé, chicken bouillon cubes or granules, or a combination of any of the above may be used.

CREAM OF CHICKEN SOUPS USING BASIC RECIPE, PAGE 82

All soups on chart serve 6

Name	Basic Cream of Chicken Soup	Additions	Time of Incorporation	Garnishes	Serve
Cream of Chicken Soup with Green Peas *Potage à l'Ambassadeur*	1 recipe	1 cup heavy cream, 1½ cups small, cooked green peas		¼ cup chopped scalded sorrel	Hot
Velouté à la Colombine	1 recipe	1 cup heavy cream, anisseed flavor		Julienne of cooked squab	Hot
Crème Duchesse	1 recipe	1 cup light cream, hot cooked asparagus spears		Diced truffles or bread croutons	Hot
Potage à la Durham	1 recipe	2 cups cream of lobster soup		Spinach and dumplings	Hot
Potage Elisa	1 recipe	¼ cup scalded minced chervil, ½ cup scalded minced sorrel	Before simmering 14 minutes	Salted whipped cream optional	Hot or chilled
Potage Ésaü	3 cups	2 cups of cream of celery soup, ½ cup each cooked diced celery and mushrooms	Before simmering 14 minutes	Profiteroles filled with chicken liver or goose liver pâté	Hot
Potage Fanchette	½ recipe	3 cups cream of asparagus soup	Before simmering 14 minutes	Wilted lettuce leaves, rolled around chicken purée and heated in soup	Hot
Crème Favorite	½ recipe	3 cups cream of asparagus soup	Before simmering 14 minutes	Diced cooked chicken and cooked asparagus tips	Hot or chilled
Velouté à la Germinal	1 recipe	2 tablespoons each chopped chervil and tarragon (if dry herbs are used, substitute 2 teaspoons each)	Before simmering 14 minutes	Cooked asparagus tips	Hot or chilled

Name	Basic Cream of Chicken Soup	Additions	Time of Incorporation	Garnishes	Serve
Velouté à la Grenade	½ recipe	½ recipe cream of tomato soup	Before simmering 14 minutes	Diced chicken and tomatoes, chopped parsley	Hot or chilled
Velouté Judic	1 recipe	1 cup shredded lettuce leaves	Before simmering 14 minutes	Diced chicken	Hot
Velouté Jussienne	1 recipe	1 additional cup heavy cream	With chicken stock	Sliced or halved cooked chicken breasts	Hot
Potage Lavalliere	½ recipe	½ recipe cream of celery soup	Before simmering 14 minutes	Cut chives or chopped parsley	Hot
Potage Livonien	1 recipe	1 cup puréed tomatoes or 1 can cream of tomato soup	Before simmering 14 minutes	Peeled and seeded tomatoes, diced	Hot or chilled
Crème Lucullus	1 recipe	2 egg yolks beaten into the cream	Add as for basic recipe and heat, stirring, but do not allow to boil	Chicken liver carolines, see page 232	Hot
Potage McDonald	1 recipe	Stir curry powder, to taste, into ½ cup of the hot soup, then stir back into the soup, ½ cup purée of cooked onions	Before simmering 14 minutes	Diced sautéed cucumber, for hot, diced raw cucumber for chilled	Hot or chilled
Crème Mary Stuart	½ recipe	½ recipe cream of green pea soup	Combine before simmering 14 minutes	Toasted bread croutons	Hot
Velouté Marie Louise	1 recipe	2 cups cooked diced vegetables, any except beets	With cream	Chopped parsley	Hot
Velouté à la Medicis	1 recipe	1 cup puréed lobster or 1 cup or can lobster bisque	Before simmering 14 minutes	Heated pearl onions, heated diced lobster meat	Hot
Crème Marquise	½ recipe	½ recipe cream of lettuce soup	Before simmering 14 minutes	Cooked green peas	Hot

Name	Basic Cream of Chicken Soup	Additions	Time of Incorporation	Garnishes	Serve
Velouté Martha	½ recipe	½ recipe cream of onion soup	Before simmering 14 minutes	Steamed vegetables and chopped herbs, parsley, chives, and chervil	Hot
Potage à la Mogador	1 recipe			Riced goose liver pâté, diced chicken, and diced truffles	Hot or chilled
Potage Monte Cristo	1 recipe	1 cup diced artichoke bottoms	Before simmering 14 minutes	Chicken pieces, or diced chicken	Hot
Crème à la Montglas	1 recipe	1 cup chopped, sautéed mushrooms	Before simmering 14 minutes	Diced truffles	Hot
Crème à la Montmorency	1 recipe	1 additional cup chicken stock, 2 cups drained, cooked noodles	Add stock with other stock, add noodles after simmering 14 minutes	Hot cooked chicken wings, grated Parmesan cheese	Hot
Crème à la Montorgüeil	1 recipe	1 cup cooked vegetables, cutouts or diced	After simmering 14 minutes	Minced sorrel and chervil	Hot or chilled
Velouté à la Nelusko	1 recipe	If possible, use hazelnut butter instead of plain butter for basic cream of chicken soup		Chicken pieces, chopped, toasted hazelnuts, filberts	Hot
Potage à la Princesse	1 recipe	1 cup heavy cream, 2 egg yolks, well beaten with the cream	After simmering 14 minutes	4 tablespoons diced ham	Hot
Velouté à la Princesse	1 recipe	1½ cups hot cooked rice	After simmering 14 minutes	Cooked asparagus tips, diced chicken, chopped chervil	Hot or chilled
Crème Victoria	1 recipe	2 cups medium cream, ½ cup diced chicken, ½ cup diced ham, ½ cup diced sautéed mushrooms	Before simmering 14 minutes	2 hardcooked egg yolks, riced, 2 hardcooked egg whites, chopped, ½ cup chopped parsley	Hot

Name	Basic Cream of Chicken Soup	Additions	Time of Incorporation	Garnishes	Serve
Crème Raphael	½ recipe	½ recipe cream of celery soup	Before simmering 14 minutes	Diced cooked celery	Hot
Potage à la Reine	1 recipe			Toasted bread croutons, julienne of cooked chicken, heated pearl onions	Hot
Potage à la Reine Hortense	½ recipe	½ recipe cream of lettuce soup, blended or puréed scraps of cooked artichoke	Before simmering 14 minutes	Diced, cooked artichoke bottoms	Hot
Potage à la Reine Margot	1 recipe	1 cup almond milk (milk with pounded blanched almonds)	Before simmering 14 minutes	Pistachio nuts and chicken pieces	Hot
Potage à la Reine Wilhelmine	½ recipe	½ recipe cream of rice soup	Before simmering 14 minutes	Diced cooked carrots and cooked asparagus tips	Hot
Velouté à la Rossini	1 recipe			Profiteroles filled with goose liver pâté and minced truffles, page 232	Hot
Velouté à la Russe	1 recipe	½ cup additional cream, 1 cup puréed cooked lobster meat	Before simmering 14 minutes	Diced cooked lobster meat	Hot or chilled
Crème Senegalaise	1 recipe	Curry powder, to taste, stirred into ½ cup soup and then stirred back into soup	Before simmering 14 minutes	Salted whipped cream and toasted coconut	Hot or chilled
Velouté à la Toulousaine	½ recipe	½ recipe cream of mushroom soup	Before simmering 14 minutes	Diced cooked chicken and sautéed chicken livers	Hot
Crème Wellington	1 recipe	½ cup diced, cooked celery, 1 cup cooked rice	Before simmering 14 minutes	Chopped parsley	Hot

CHILLED CREAM OF CHICKEN SOUPS

CRÈME à la DOYEN

Garnish 1 recipe basic cream of chicken soup with ½ cup purée of cooked green peas mixed with 1 cup salted whipped cream. If possible, pipe the green cream onto the soup through a pastry tube and sprinkle with 2 tablespoons chopped parsley or mint.

CRÈME COMTESSE

Garnish 1 recipe basic cream of chicken soup with 1 cup cold cooked peas and ½ cup of rounds cut from lettuce leaves with the smallest available cookie cutter.

CRÈME DUCHESSE

Garnish 1 recipe basic cream of chicken soup with 1 cup cold cooked asparagus tips and 1 teaspoon grated orange rind.

DUNHAM SOUP

Garnish 1 recipe basic cream of chicken soup with ½ cup cold cooked diced lobster meat, 4 tablespoons finely chopped raw spinach, and 1 riced hard cooked egg.

POTAGE MEDICI

Garnish 1 recipe basic cream of chicken soup with 1 cup diced cold cooked lobster meat, ½ cup tiny cocktail onions, and ½ cup chopped cold chicken.

RED AND WHITE SOUP

Garnish 1 recipe chilled basic cream of chicken soup with 2 well-drained chopped pimentos. Sprinkle each serving with 1 teaspoon chopped parsley.

VELOUTÉ CLAIRE FONTAINE

Garnish ½ recipe basic cream of chicken soup mixed with ½ recipe cream of watercress soup with ½ cup chopped watercress and place a thin slice of orange on each serving.

CREAMED VEGETABLE SOUPS GROUP II

These creamed vegetable soups are a combination of basic white sauce and a sautéed vegetable. The butter used for the roux in the white sauce is first used to sauté the vegetable, the flour is then stirred into the butter-and-sautéed-vegetable mixture, and stock, milk, or cream is added, as for basic white sauce.

BASIC CREAM OF MUSHROOM SOUP

¾ pound mushrooms, chopped
¼ cup minced onion
4 tablespoons butter
4 tablespoons flour
1 cup chicken stock
3 cups scalded milk
1 cup thin cream
Salt and pepper to taste
¼ cup sherry (optional)

Sauté mushrooms and onion in butter, over low heat, for 7 minutes. Do not let them brown. Sprinkle with flour and stir until it is absorbed and smooth. Stir in the stock and cook 7 minutes longer. If a smooth mushroom soup is preferred, blend or purée at this point. To the chopped or blended mushroom base add scalded milk and cook over low heat, stirring frequently, for 20 minutes. Add cream and sherry and cook until heated. Serve with a garnish of salted whipped cream, sprinkled with minced parsley.

Variations and Additions

1. One bay leaf, 3 sprigs parsley, and 1 clove can be boiled in the stock for 15 minutes. Strain stock before using.
2. A pinch of nutmeg or a pinch of dry mustard may be added to the soup with the scalded milk.
3. Two egg yolks may be beaten into the cream before it is added to the soup. Cook, stirring, for 3 minutes, but do not allow the soup to come to a boil.

BASIC CREAM OF LEEK AND POTATO SOUP

(*Hot Potage Parmentier or Chilled Vichyssoise*)

1 large bunch leeks, about 1 pound, washed and trimmed
6 tablespoons butter
3 medium onions, sliced
2 tablespoons flour
3 cups chicken stock
3 large potatoes, peeled and diced
1 cup heavy cream
Salt and pepper, depending on saltiness of stock

Slice leeks, including the pale green sections. Melt butter in a kettle over medium heat, add leeks and onions and simmer about 15 minutes, stirring frequently; do not let butter or vegetables brown. Sprinkle with flour and stir until it is smooth and absorbed. Add the stock and potatoes and simmer covered, stirring occasionally, until vegetables and potatoes are very soft, about 20 minutes. Season to taste and purée or blend the vegetables. Add cream and reheat.

If soup is going to be served hot, garnish and serve at once or keep hot in the top of a double boiler over boiling water.

If soup is going to be served chilled, increase the cream to two cups. Chill the soup and the cream and combine them just before serving in chilled cups or plates.

Garnish hot leek and potato soup with toasted bread croutons or diced crisp bacon.

Garnish vichyssoise (chilled leek and potato soup) with cut chives.

Variations

1. Cream of onion and potato soup. Substitute 1 pound yellow onions for the leek.

2. Potage alenois (watercress soup). Omit 2 of the onions and substitute 1 bunch watercress, coarse stems removed. Serve hot or chilled garnished with a few sprigs fresh watercress.

3. Substitute one 1½ pound cauliflower, diced, for one of the onions and one of the potatoes. Serve hot or chilled with a garnish of small reserved cauliflower flowerets and finely diced ham.

4. Substitute 1 pound shredded spinach leaves for 2 of the potatoes. Garnish with salted whipped cream.

5. Combine ½ recipe cream of leek and potato soup with ½ recipe cream of mushroom soup.

6. Combine ½ recipe cream of leek and potato soup with ½ recipe cream of tomato soup. Garnish with peeled, seeded, and diced tomatoes and chopped parsley.

BASIC CREAM OF ONION SOUP

6 medium onions, sliced
4 tablespoons butter
2 tablespoons flour
4 large potatoes, peeled and diced
2 cups chicken stock
2 cups scalded milk
1 cup heavy cream
Salt and pepper, depending on saltiness of stock

Sauté onions in butter in a heavy kettle, stirring until they begin to turn golden, about 7 minutes; sprinkle with flour and stir until smooth. Add potatoes and stock and simmer, covered, for 35 minutes, stirring frequently. Purée or blend the soup, return it to heat, and add milk and cream and seasoning. Bring to a boil and take from heat.

Variations

1. Serve soup in heatproof cups, sprinkle top heavily with grated

Parmesan cheese, and push under the broiler until top is evenly browned. Leave oven door open and watch carefully.

2. Substitute 6 medium leeks, white part only, sliced, for 2 of the onions.

3. Brown onions in butter, sprinkle with flour, stir until absorbed, gradually add 4 cups scalded milk, and simmer, stirring frequently, for 20 minutes. Add cream and bring to boil. Cover each serving with thin slices of toasted French bread. Sprinkle with grated Swiss cheese and a grinding of black pepper.

4. Substitute strong beef stock for chicken stock, finish with a dash of Worcestershire sauce, sprinkle top of soup with grated American cheese.

5. Prepare basic cream of onion soup. Take from heat, beat in 2 egg yolks, and cover top of soup completely with toasted bread croutons.

6. Garnish basic cream of onion soup generously with crisp French-fried onion rings. Place on soup just before serving.

BASIC CREAM OF CUCUMBER SOUP

4 medium cucumbers
1 medium onion, sliced thin
4 tablespoons butter
2 tablespoons flour
4 cups scalded milk
Salt and pepper to taste
1 cup heavy cream

Cut cucumbers in half lengthwise, scrape out and discard the seeds and slice thin. If the soup is going to be blended instead of puréed through a sieve, it is not necessary to remove the seeds. Cook cucumber and onion slices in butter until soft and transparent, about 7 minutes. Stir frequently and do not let them brown. Sprinkle with flour and stir until absorbed and smooth. Gradually stir in the milk, season, and simmer covered, stirring occasionally, for 15 minutes. Purée or blend the soup, add cream, reheat, and serve hot, or chill and serve in chilled cups or soup plates.

Variations

1. Garnish with salted whipped cream and sprinkle cream with cut chives and paprika.

2. Prepare cream of green pepper soup by substituting 2 cups scalded and chopped green peppers for 2 of the cucumbers. Garnish with salted whipped cream and slivered pimento.

3. Substitute 6 zucchini for 3 of the cucumbers. Do not peel or seed. Garnish with minced parsley and lemon rind, grated into large slivers.

SOUFFLÉS BASED ON WHITE SAUCE

Most soufflés consist of a flavored white sauce which puffs up because stiffly beaten egg whites have been folded into it. Combine basic white sauce with the minced or puréed flavoring ingredient for which the soufflé is usually named. Stir in egg yolks, fold in stiffly beaten egg whites, and bake until puffed and brown according to one of the basic recipes. Soufflés are like all the other basic recipes. Make one soufflé successfully and you automatically know how to make about 250 more.

BASIC CHEESE SOUFFLÉ

1 pound Swiss cheese, coarsely grated or finely diced
1½ cups basic white sauce, medium thick
5 egg yolks, beaten
6 egg whites, beaten stiff after yolks are added to cheese sauce
Salt to taste, depending on saltiness of cheese

Preheat oven to 375°F. Make or reheat white sauce in a heavy pan over low heat. Stir in cheese until melted. Do not let it boil. Cool for 10 minutes, beat in yolks, little by little. Fold in egg whites and pour mixture into an unbuttered 1½ quart soufflé dish or straight-sided baking dish. Set dish into a pan of hot water, only a little larger than the dish. Bake for 35 to 42 minutes. If oven temperature has a tendency to sink, bake at 400°F. Do not open oven door for the first 30 minutes. Serve *at once.*

Additions and Variations

1. One tablespoon minced onion or 2 tablespoons finely cut chives

may be stirred into the white sauce with the egg yolks.

2. One-half teaspoon dry mustard or 1 teaspoon prepared Dijon mustard may be stirred into the white sauce with the egg yolks.

3. One cup grated natural Cheddar cheese may be substituted for the Swiss cheese.

4. Three-quarters of a cup grated natural American or Swiss cheese and ¼ cup grated Parmesan may be substituted for the Swiss cheese.

5. Arrange a layer of well-drained sliced tomatoes in the bottom of a 2-quart soufflé pan. Add ¼ cup minced chives to the basic cheese soufflé recipe and pour the soufflé mixture over the tomatoes. Bake as basic cheese soufflé.

6. Arrange tomato layer in a 2-quart casserole, as in variation 5. Cut 8 slices bacon into ½-inch squares with a sharp knife or scissors and sauté over low heat until transparent and lightly browned, but not crisp. Drain well and spread bacon over tomatoes. Pour 1 recipe basic cheese soufflé over the bacon and bake as basic cheese soufflé.

7. Arrange a thick layer of cooked shrimp in the bottom of a 2-quart soufflé pan. Add 2 tablespoons minced onion and 1 tablespoon cut dill or chives to the basic cheese soufflé mixture and pour it over the shrimp. Bake as basic cheese soufflé.

8. Add to basic cheese soufflé 1 cup peeled, seeded, and diced tomatoes, well drained, and 2 tablespoons each minced green pepper and onion. Add 1 additional egg white. Bake in a 2-quart soufflé dish, as basic cheese soufflé.

9. Add to basic cheese soufflé, 1 cup sautéed and well-drained chopped mushrooms and ¼ cup minced onion. Bake in a 2-quart casserole, as basic cheese soufflé.

10. Add to basic cheese soufflé 1 teaspoon Worcestershire sauce, ½ teaspoon dry mustard and ¼ garlic clove, crushed.

11. Cut lid from 6 very large tomatoes, scoop out pulp, and use for sauce. Drain tomatoes well. Prepare ½ recipe basic cheese soufflé and spoon it into the tomatoes. Set tomatoes in a baking dish with ½ cup water, and bake in a 350°F. oven until puffed, about 20 minutes.

12. Pour half the soufflé mixture into a 2-quart dish and arrange 6 cold poached or peeled 6-minute eggs on the soufflé mixture. Pour over remaining mixture and bake, as basic cheese soufflé.

13. Prepare 2 soufflé mixtures, ½ recipe of each, cheese and spinach or cheese and mushroom or tomato. Spoon mixtures into soufflé dish in 4 layers and bake as basic cheese soufflé.

14. One-half recipe cheese soufflé can be filled into a soufflé dish over ½ recipe ham or salmon soufflé mixture. Bake as cheese soufflé.

BASIC VEGETABLE, MEAT, OR FISH SOUFFLÉ

(For a 1½-Quart Soufflé or Straight-Sided Baking Dish or 4 to 6 Individual Baking Cups)

3 tablespoons butter
3½ tablespoons flour
1 cup liquid
½ teaspoon salt
Pepper to taste

1 cup finely diced, minced, blended, or ground cooked vegetable, meat, or fish
4 egg yolks, using large eggs
5 egg whites, beaten stiff with:
1 pinch salt

(For a 2-Quart Soufflé or Straight-Sided Baking Dish or 6 to 8 Individual Baking Cups)

4 tablespoons butter
4½ tablespoons flour
1½ cups liquid
½ teaspoon salt
Pepper to taste

1½ cups finely diced, minced, blended or ground cooked vegetable, meat, or fish
6 egg yolks
7 egg whites, beaten stiff with:
1 pinch salt

Prepare thick white sauce according to basic white sauce recipe on page 49. Take saucepan from heat as soon as liquid has been added and whip with a French wire whisk until it is very thick and smooth. Add seasonings, return to heat, whipping constantly, and boil gently for 1 minute. Cool soufflé base for 5 minutes, then whip in the yolks, one by one, until smooth. Stir in the prepared vegetable, meat or fish. Beat egg whites with pinch of salt until very stiff but not dry. Stir 1 heaping tablespoon stiff egg white into the soufflé mixture, then fold the rest in gently and lightly. Pour mixture into the prepared dish, set dish into a pan of water which is only a little larger than the soufflé dish and bake on the center shelf of a preheated 375°F. oven. Do not open oven door for at least 30 minutes. Bake 40 to 42 minutes for a soft soufflé, up to 1 hour for a dry soufflé.

If mixture fills or almost overflows baking dish, before baking, tie a firm wax paper collar around the baking dish to extend two inches above its edge all the way around. Tie it well around edge of dish and secure overlapping top with a paper clip. Butter the inside of the paper. Strip off paper collar when soufflé is ready to serve.

The following vegetable, meat, and fish soufflés are prepared in the same way. Slight changes and variations are noted next to the ingredients.

Variations

(*Vegetable Soufflés based on 1½-Quart Recipe*)

Use water in which vegetables cooked, or milk, unless otherwise specified.

Asparagus: 1 cup asparagus purée, 12 cooked asparagus tips, diced, ¼ cup minced onion.

Broccoli: 1½ cups cooked chopped broccoli, 1 tablespoon each minced onion and parsley.

Celery: Chop inside stalks and yellow leaves of 1 small bunch celery. Cook until tender. Use 1 cup cream of celery soup and ¼ cup grated Parmesan cheese.

Chestnut: 1½ cups salted purée of chestnuts, ¼ cup chopped and lightly sautéed onion, 1 cup milk.

Corn I: 1 or 1½ cups fresh corn kernels, cut from ear and well drained, or canned or frozen corn, chopped and well drained. Pack down tightly in cup measure. Use 1 cup cream.

Corn II: Add ¼ cup minced green pepper.

Corn III: Add 2 tablespoons minced green pepper and 1 tablespoon each minced onion and pimento.

Corn IV: Combine ½ or ¾ cup well-drained corn kernels with ½ or ¾ cup grated cheese. Use 1 cup milk.

Endive: 1 cup cooked and puréed endive, 2 tablespoons minced onion and parsley, 1 cup milk.

Green Pea: 1 or 1½ cups purée of cooked green peas, 1 tablespoon minced onion, 1 cup milk.

Mushroom Soufflé I: Use basic recipe with 1 cup cream. Sauté ¾ pound chopped mushrooms and ⅓ cup chopped onions in 3 tablespoons butter, drain and incorporate in soufflé base.

Mushroom Soufflé II: Add ½ cup cut dried mushrooms for a stronger flavor.

Mushroom Soufflé III: Use 1 cup cream of mushroom soup instead of cream.

Onion Soufflé: Sauté 3 cups chopped onion in 3 tablespoons butter, add 1 cup water, and simmer 10 minutes. Drain. Use liquid to moisten roux.

Potato Soufflé I: 2 cups hot mashed potatoes, ¾ cup cream, 2 tablespoons minced onion.

Potato Soufflé II: 1½ cups hot mashed potatoes, ½ cup grated cheese.

Potato Soufflé III: Bake 6 large potatoes, mash pulp. Fill soufflé mixture back into potato shells and bake 30 minutes in a 325°F. oven. Minced onion and parsley may be added to the potato soufflé base.

Spinach Soufflé: 1½ cups puréed or chopped spinach, tightly packed, 2 tablespoons minced onion (½ cup chopped ham, optional). Serve with mushroom sauce.

Succotash Soufflé: See corn soufflé III, page 95.

Sweet Potato Soufflé: 2 cups cooked mashed sweet potatoes, 1 cup milk, 1 tablespoon brandy, 1 tablespoon grated orange rind, 1 cup milk.

Tomato Soufflé I: 2½ cups drained canned tomatoes, ½ onion, minced, ½ cup milk, ½ cup juice from tomatoes, ½ cup breadcrumbs, and 2 tablespoons minced parsley. One can cream of tomato soup may be substituted for the other liquids.

FISH SOUFFLÉS

Sauté 2 tablespoons chopped onion in the butter before adding the flour. Add 1½ cups white fish or 2 1-pound packages poached for 5 minutes, then drained and mashed. Add minced dill or parsley to taste and bake as basic soufflé based on 1½-quart casserole.

Variations

1 cup shredded crabmeat, 1½ cups diced lobster or half lobster and half shrimp, and 1½ cups flaked salmon can all be used in the basic soufflé recipe. As fish is bland, herbs, onions, a little sherry or white wine, finely diced pickle or green pepper, minced olives, or mushrooms may be added. Fish stock, milk, or tomato juice can be used as the liquid.

MEAT SOUFFLÉS

Minced cooked meat, leftovers of cooked chicken, turkey, or game, minced ham, liver, or tongue can all be used in the basic soufflé recipe. Additions of mustard, diced pickle, chopped mint or chives, and cooked vegetables can be made. Unless the meat is of very soft texture, do not use more than 1½ cups. Tomato juice, meat stock, milk, or chicken stock can be used as the liquid.

Sweet Soufflés Based on Basic White Sauce

Follow recipe for basic vegetable, meat, or fish soufflé, page 94. Use flour, butter, and eggs as specified, substitute milk for liquid, omit salt and pepper and add other ingredients as listed below:

Almond Soufflé: ¼ cup sugar, 1 cup ground almonds, ½ teaspoon each almond and vanilla extract, 2 tablespoons rum.

Chocolate I: Add 3 squares semisweet chocolate, melted, to the basic soufflé base. Stir in ⅓ cup sugar or to taste, 1 teaspoon vanilla extract, 2 tablespoons rum, ½ cup ground almonds. Use milk for the liquid.

Chocolate II: Prepare as above, using 3 squares sweet chocolate and substituting 1 cup cold cocoa for the milk. Flavor with Curaçao instead of rum and use pecans instead of almonds.

Coffee I: 2 tablespoons instant coffee, 2 tablespoons rum, ⅓ cup sugar, 1 cup milk. Add 1 egg yolk and 2 egg whites.

Coffee II: 3 tablespoons instant coffee, ⅓ cup sugar, 1 cup finely chopped pecans or almonds, 1 cup cream, add 1 egg white.

Hazelnut Soufflé: ½ pound package hazelnut meats, ground, 1 cup milk, 1 tablespoon rum, ⅓ cup sugar.

Rum Soufflé: 18 crushed vanilla cookies soaked in ⅓ cup rum, ½ cup chopped pecans, ¼ cup sugar, 1 cup milk.

LESSON IV

BASIC BROWN SAUCE

Most of the brown sauces are made exactly like the basic white sauce except that they are based on brown roux and brown stock instead of white roux and white stock.

Some of the brown sauces can also be made right in the roasting pan or casserole in which the meat or stew which they are to accompany is cooking. When made in the roasting pan the sauces are usually called gravies. The finest brown sauces are still made in a separate saucepan, and many of them are a combination or variation of brown sauce, tomato sauce, Madeira sauce, and Espagnole.

Utensils for brown sauce are a little different from those for white sauce. Since the brown roux has to be cooked slowly until it is a rich brown, it is apt to scorch and become bitter if the saucepan is too thin. We asked for a *heavy* saucepan for basic white sauce. We insist that a heavy saucepan or small heavy frying pan is essential for a successful brown sauce. Use a wooden spoon to stir the sauce.

BROWN ROUX

(*Roux Brun*)

½ cup beef or pork fat or butter
½ cup flour

Melt fat in a very heavy saucepan or pan and cook until it turns golden. Stir in the flour and continue to cook, stirring constantly until the roux is a rich, deep brown. Remove from heat and use or store as white roux, page 48.

BASIC PLAIN BROWN SAUCE

¼ cup fat, beef, pork, or butter
¼ cup flour
4 cups rich brown stock or beef bouillon
2 tablespoons puréed, cooked tomatoes or tomato juice

Melt fat in a heavy saucepan over medium heat until it turns golden. Stir in the flour and continue to cook slowly, stirring constantly with a wooden spoon until the roux is a rich, deep brown. Add stock, cup by cup, stirring until all the stock is incorporated and the sauce is smooth and thickened. Reduce heat and cook the sauce slowly, stirring occasionally until reduced to half, about 1 hour. Stir in tomato purée or juice and cook 5 minutes longer.

Store the brown sauce in a covered jar in refrigerator up to 1 week. The top of the jar can be sealed with melted fat.

BASIC RICH BROWN SAUCE

¼ cup fat, beef, pork, or butter
½ carrot, scraped and diced
1 onion, chopped
½ cup flour
4 cups rich brown stock
3 parsley sprigs
1 bay leaf
Salt, depending on saltiness of stock
¼ cup puréed, cooked tomatoes or

3 black peppercorns
½ clove garlic, optional
½ clove garlic, crushed
1 stalk celery
tomato juice
2 cups rich brown stock (optional)

Melt fat, as for basic plain brown sauce, add carrot and onion and cook, stirring, until they are golden. Sprinkle in the flour and cook, stirring until it is evenly and richly browned. Add stock and all other ingredients, except tomatoes and additional stock, and cook, over low heat, stirring occasionally, until reduced to half, about 1 hour. Strain. Stir in tomato purée and cook 5 minutes longer. Use sauce at once or store as basic plain brown sauce. For a richer sauce, add additional stock and cook again until reduced to half, about 1 hour. Use basic rich brown sauce as it is with meat, poultry, or game, or as a base for other sauces.

ESPAGNOLE SAUCE

(*Also called Demi-Glace*)

2 tablespoons diced mushrooms or mushroom peelings
½ cup dry sherry
2 cups basic rich brown sauce
2 teaspoons beef concentrate, or beef extract

Cook mushrooms in sherry until reduced to 5 tablespoons. Add the basic rich brown sauce and beef concentrate and cook, stirring occasionally, for 20 minutes. Strain and serve with meat or game, or use as a base for other brown sauces.

MADEIRA SAUCE

Heat 1 recipe Espagnole sauce, add ½ cup Madeira wine, bring to a boil and serve with beef, veal, or ham.

Variations on Basic Brown Sauce

African Sauce: Prepare 1 recipe basic brown sauce with puréed cooked onions, Madeira wine, and a pinch of cayenne pepper. Garnish the sauce with 1 peeled truffle, diced. Serve with meat, poultry, or game.

Aromatic Sauce: Simmer 1 recipe basic brown sauce made with beef bouillon with 2 sprigs each, thyme, basil, and marjoram. Add a few blades of chives and 1 bay leaf. Strain the finished sauce and stir in 1 tablespoon each minced tarragon and chervil. Serve with veal, poultry, or filet mignon.

Bordelaise Sauce: Simmer until reduced to 1 cup, 2 cups red or white wine with 1 bay leaf, 2 sprigs each, thyme, parsley, and tarragon and ½ onion sliced thin. Take out the herbs and blend or purée the reduced wine and onion. Add the purée to 1 recipe basic brown sauce and simmer until heated through. Garnish with slices of poached marrow. Serve with steak.

Bressoise Sauce: Into 1 recipe basic Espagnole sauce, sieve 2 raw chicken livers. Add 2 minced shallots. Simmer 5 minutes and add 3 tablespoons orange juice. Much better than you'd think. Serve with poultry.

Broglie Sauce: Add ¼ cup diced, cooked ham, ¼ cup sautéed chopped mushrooms, and Madeira wine to taste to 1 recipe basic brown sauce. Serve with eggs, poultry, or meat.

Caper Sauce (Brown): Add dry white wine and small capers to taste to 1 recipe Espagnole sauce. Serve with veal or boiled beef.

Catalane Sauce: Prepare 1 recipe Espagnole sauce, add 1 tablespoon brown mustard, ½ clove garlic, crushed, and 3 tablespoons each minced parsley and onion, ½ cup Madeira, and a pinch of cayenne pepper. Simmer sauce 15 minutes longer. Serve with beef.

Chasseur Sauce: Prepare 1 recipe Espagnole sauce using game stock instead of brown stock. Properly, the blood of hare or venison should be added. Serve with game, red meat, or poultry.

Chateaubriand Sauce: A basic Madeira sauce into which dry white wine and parsley butter (Maître d'Hôtel) are beaten at the last minute. To 1 recipe Madeira sauce add 2 tablespoons parsley butter and wine to taste. Serve with filet or steaks.

Chaud-Froid Sauce (Brown): Use basic brown sauce instead of basic white sauce. Follow recipe on page 56. Use to mask cold poultry or meat dishes.

English Sauce: Stir into 1 recipe basic brown sauce lemon juice to taste and ¼ cup chopped parsley. Just before serving, stir in 1 tablespoon cold butter. Serve with any boiled meat.

Espagnole Sauce: See page 101.

Felix Sauce: 1 recipe basic brown sauce made with lobster butter instead of plain butter. Add a little lemon juice to taste. Serve with shellfish.

Garibaldi Sauce: Flavor 1 recipe basic brown sauce with 1 teaspoon each curry powder, mustard, and anchovy paste. Add 2 tablespoons small capers. Taste the sauce and add curry powder or mustard to taste. Serve with liver, rice, meat, or poultry.

Geneva Sauce: Prepare 1 recipe Espagnole sauce, add ½ cup diced sautéed mushrooms, ¼ cup chopped parsley, and ½ cup red wine. Simmer the sauce until slightly reduced, about 20 minutes. Serve with fish, eggs, or poultry.

Madeira Sauce: See page 101.

Miroton Sauce: Add to 1 recipe basic brown sauce, ½ cup purée of cooked tomato, ½ cup purée of cooked onions. Diced ham capers and diced pickles may be added to the sauce. With the additions, it is called sauce hachée. Serve with poultry, eggs, or boiled beef.

Onion Sauce (Brown): 1 recipe Espagnole sauce garnished with baked onion rings. Serve with fish, lamb, or veal.

Orly Sauce: Stir into 1 recipe basic brown sauce 1 cup thick tomato purée and ½ cup purée of sautéed mushrooms. Serve with fish, meat, or sweetbreads.

Paprika Sauce (Brown): Ladle half cup of 1 recipe basic brown sauce into a cup and stir into it 1 tablespoon paprika until smooth. Return the mixture to the sauce and repeat until the brown sauce is flavored with paprika to taste. Serve with veal, beef, or poultry.

Perigueux or Perigord Sauce: Prepare 1 recipe Madeira sauce, page 101, with as many diced truffles as you can afford. Serve with roast meats and poultry.

Piquante Sauce: Add to 1 recipe basic brown sauce, 2 tablespoons meat glaze, ¼ cup white wine, 3 chopped shallots, 1 teaspoon minced tarragon, and 1 chopped peppery pickle or ½ cup hot pickle relish. Serve with tongue and boiled meats.

Poor Man's Sauce: To 1 recipe basic brown sauce add 4 chopped shallots, 3 tablespoons chopped parsley, 1 tablespoon cut chives, roughly ground black pepper to taste, and from 1 to 1½ cups breadcrumbs. As the breadcrumbs thicken the sauce, more brown stock or water should be added. Serve with pork, game, sausages, or poultry.

Robert Sauce: Flavor 1 recipe onion sauce (brown) with ½ cup dry white wine, brown mustard to taste, and 1 pinch of sugar. Serve with roast pork.

Tomato Sauce (Brown): Simmer in 1 recipe Espagnole sauce 1 cup steamed and sieved tomatoes. Serve with roasts, pastas, or vegetables.

Victoria Sauce: In 1 recipe Espagnole sauce, dissolve ½ cup red currant jelly and add ½ cup port wine, or to taste. Serve with game or game birds.

Viennese Sauce: Stir into 1 recipe basic brown sauce, ½ to 1 cup sour cream to taste and the grated rind of 1 orange and ½ lemon. Serve with duck, game, or poultry.

Yorkshire Sauce: To 1 recipe Victoria sauce, add the slivered rind of 1 orange. Serve with roast duck or game birds.

BROWN CREAMED SOUPS

The brown creamed soups are based on basic brown sauce, as the white cream soups are based on basic white sauce. The brown roux is moistened with brown stock and the other ingredients are usually sautéed, braised, or browned before they go into the soup.

Prepare a basic brown sauce, page 100, using more liquid as the recipes specify.

MUSHROOM AND ONION SOUP

½ onion, chopped
6 tablespoons butter
2 cups thinly sliced mushrooms
6 tablespoons flour
3 cups rich brown stock or bouillon
1 teaspoon beef extract or gravy browning agent
1 cup heavy cream
¼ cup sherry
2 tablespoons minced parsley
Salt and pepper to taste

In a large heavy pan, sauté onion in butter until transparent, about 3 minutes. Add mushrooms and continue cooking until they are glossy and butter is brown, about 4 more minutes. Sprinkle flour over the mushrooms little by little and stir until it is absorbed in the butter and browned. Gradually stir in the stock, a cup at a time, until a smooth brown sauce is obtained. Reduce heat and simmer, stirring occasionally, for 20 minutes. Stir in beef extract, cream, sherry, and parsley and season to taste. Add stock or cream if a thinner soup is preferred.

Serve at once, cool and store in refrigerator, or hold in top of double boiler until ready to serve.

BROWN OYSTER STEW

Simmer 1 pint oysters, chopped, in their own liquor and enough water to make 2½ cups, for about 20 minutes. Brown 3 tablespoons butter in a wide pan, stir in 4 tablespoons flour, and gradually stir in the liquid drained from the oysters (set oysters aside). Stir until brown sauce is smooth and thickened, add the oysters, ½ cup diced celery, and 1 cup cream and simmer over low heat, stirring occasionally, for 30 minutes. Thin soup with additional cream to taste, and season with salt and pepper to taste, just before serving.

OX TAIL SOUP

(*Queue de Boeuf*)

Dredge 1 ox tail cut in 2-inch lengths with 6 tablespoons seasoned flour and brown well on all sides in 6 tablespoons fat or butter for about 12 minutes. Add 10 cups rich brown stock, stir until smooth, and simmer covered for 2 hours, stirring occasionally. Add ½ cup each diced carrot, celery, and onion and simmer 1 hour longer, stirring occasionally. Add 1 teaspoon each grated lemon rind, brandy, and ¼ cup sherry. Season to taste and sprinkle with chopped parsley.

VARIATIONS ON OX TAIL SOUP

Substitute 1 cup red wine for 1 cup stock and omit brandy and sherry. Brown onions in butter with meat before stirring in flour. Brown all vegetables with the meat.

CREOLE SOUP

Brown in 4 tablespoons butter ¼ cup each chopped onion, green pepper, mushrooms, and pimento, about 5 to 7 minutes. Sprinkle in 4 tablespoons flour and stir until absorbed and browned. Add 1 large can tomatoes, 2 cups strong beef stock, 2 tablespoons chopped parsley, and seasoning to taste. Stir well and simmer 20 minutes. Dice 4 slices cold bacon and fry in a small pan until golden. Drain on brown paper. Serve the soup hot, sprinkled with crisp bacon dice.

VARIATION ON CREOLE SOUP

Add 1 package frozen okra, cut into ½-inch lengths and thawed, or add 1 can okra during last 10 minutes of cooking time.

GULYAS SOUP

Gulyas soup is a beef stew, page 107, highly flavored with paprika. Cut meat, potatoes, and vegetables smaller than for stew, but make a greater quantity of sauce adding cream and stock until soup consistency is reached. Serve it in the early hours of the morning just before your late guests leave, or serve it at home after the ball is over.

BASIC BROWN STEW

Most brown meat, poultry, and game stews are cooked in water, stock, wine, or tomato juice or in a combination of liquids. When the meat has cooked until it is tender, the liquid is thickened by stirring a mixture of flour and water into it. The stew is then brought to a boil and cooked for a few minutes until thickened.

Another way of preparing the stew is to base it on a rich brown sauce made with the stew ingredients.

Any meat, poultry, or game may be substituted for the beef.

3 pounds chuck, rump, or preferred stewing beef, cut into 1½-inch cubes, trimmed of fat and gristle
¾ cup seasoned flour for dredging
6 to 8 tablespoons melted beef fat
1 onion, sliced
8 cups boiling liquid, stock, or water, or half red wine or half tomato juice with stock or water
Salt and pepper to taste
Herbs to taste: bay leaf, thyme, and parsley
4 tablespoons butter
6 tablespoons flour
3 tablespoons chopped parsley

In a deep heavy casserole or pan, lightly brown dredged meat on all sides in melted beef fat. Add the onion and continue to cook until meat is a rich, deep brown. Add the boiling liquid, seasonings, and herbs, cover, and simmer on top of the stove for 2 to 3 hours.

About 1 hour before meat is done, brown butter in a heavy pan, stir in the flour and cook, stirring constantly, until smooth. Strain 2 cups liquid from stew and stir them into the brown roux in the pan. Add 1 more cup, stirring slowly until thickened. Reduce heat and simmer uncovered, stirring occasionally, until meat is done. Strain liquid from casserole, cover casserole, and set aside. Measure 1½ to 2 cups liquid, according to taste and stir them into the simmering sauce in the pan. Use a French wire whisk if sauce is not smooth. Season to taste and pour over meat in casserole. Simmer long enough to reheat. Sprinkle with chopped parsley and serve.

Variations

Add small white onions and small peeled potatoes or large cubes of potatoes to the stew about 30 minutes before straining off the liquid. Add green peas, beans, cauliflower flowerets, mushrooms, peeled and quartered tomatoes, or quartered carrots about 10 minutes later.

Cook all the above vegetables in the stew for the last hour.

Pour ½ cup heated sour cream over stew just before serving. Stir it into the stew at the table.

Cook stew in ¼ cup tomato juice, and add 2 tablespoons tomato purée or paste to sauce.

Brunswick Stew: Substitute one 4½- to 5-pound disjointed fowl for beef, simmer in chicken stock, add tomatoes, lima beans, cooked corn, and mushrooms, and sprinkle with ¼ cup chopped parsley.

LESSON V

THE EGG SAUCES—

Mayonnaise Sauce and Hollandaise Sauce

There are only two basic egg sauce recipes to be learned, one cold and one warm. Both were originally French and both were prolific. Between them they have mothered more than seventy worthy descendants such as béarnaise and remoulade, and knowing how to make two means knowing how to make them all.

The creation of mayonnaise is attributed to Cardinal Richelieu—not to his chef but actually to him. In the course of three hundred and fifty years, sauce Mayonnaise has come to be spread on several million American sandwiches every day, and it binds another million salads. The name probably derives from Moyeu, the Old French word for egg yolk. There is no French city or district called Mayon.

Hollandaise was what the French called a Netherlands fish which was served with melted butter. Somewhere along the way a Frenchman beat some egg yolks into the warm melted butter and the sauce remained while the fish was forgotten.

Hollandaise is served at table as a separate sauce or it is poured over certain dishes before serving. It is also spread over some poached dishes and browned in the oven just before serving.

Mayonnaise is served as a separate sauce or it is folded into certain ingredients as an integral part of them. The gastronomy of certain districts leans heavily upon them. In France a filet mignon calls for a sauce béarnaise while in America, cauliflower and broccoli are at their best under a hollandaise.

Both recipes should be learned, although both sauces are available in jars or packages. There is also an easier blender method for making both of them, for which recipes also follow.

HOLLANDAISE SAUCE

The experienced saucemaker can whip up a beautiful hollandaise sauce in a small, round-bottomed saucepan over a wide pan of simmering water, simply by raising and lowering the saucepan in the steam above the water. The process depends so completely on the feel of the sauce while it is being whipped that it cannot be explained in a written recipe. The proper way to make hollandaise sauce is in the top of a double boiler, but the success of the sauce depends more on what is going on in the lower section of the double boiler than in the top.

The first rule is that the sauce does not cook over simmering water, it cooks in the steam above simmering water. The bottom of the upper section of the double boiler must not come in contact with the simmering water in the lower section. This sounds unimportant, but it is so vital to the success of the sauce that it is worth bringing out a ruler to establish just how much space there is between the two sections.

The second rule is that the water in the lower section, even though it does not touch the upper section, must not boil. It should simmer just enough to produce steam to envelope the upper section while the sauce is being whipped. There has to be enough warm steam to melt the butter, but not enough to melt it quickly. If the butter appears to be melting too quickly, raise the upper section for a moment to allow some steam to escape. If it is not melting fast enough, increase heat under the double boiler very slightly.

Read basic directions above before starting.

BASIC HOLLANDAISE SAUCE I

3 or 4 large egg yolks
1 tablespoon water
¼ teaspoon salt
1 cup soft butter cut in 14 pieces

1 teaspoon lemon juice
Cayenne
1 tablespoon hot water (optional)

Whisk egg yolks, water, and salt in the top section of double boiler until light. Add 1 piece butter, place over lower section of double boiler over low heat, keeping the water in the lower section hot, but just under simmering. Whisk the sauce until the butter is absorbed. Continue to whisk in the pieces of butter, one after the other, alternating with a few drops of lemon juice. Whisk until all the butter has been incorporated. Take from heat, add a few grains cayenne and stir with a wooden spoon until glossy. Stir in hot water for a lighter sauce.

If sauce separates, because it is too hot or has cooked too quickly, gradually stir in 2 tablespoons boiling water. Serve at once.

BASIC HOLLANDAISE SAUCE II

(*made in electric blender*)

¾ cup butter
4 egg yolks
2 tablespoons lemon juice
¼ teaspoon salt
1 pinch white pepper

Melt butter, do not brown. Place all other ingredients in container of blender, cover, and turn to high. Uncover and add hot melted butter in a very thin stream until all butter is incorporated and sauce is thick and smooth. Correct seasoning and serve with fish, vegetables, eggs, or poultry.

Holding or Storing Hollandaise Sauce

Keeping hollandaise warm, when it has to be prepared in advance, is just as much of an art as making it. When it has been whipped to the moment of absolute perfection, do not leave it in the saucepan. If it cannot be served at once, transfer it to a room temperature china or glass bowl and set it in a second bowl or pan of lukewarm water. The water can be renewed to keep it constantly lukewarm if the sauce has to be kept for any length of time. Do not store hollandaise-based egg sauces in metal containers and do not leave them in the double boiler in which they were made. Kept over warm water they will separate; set into lukewarm water, they will keep well. If the sauce becomes too thick, stir in a little heavy cream.

BASIC BÉARNAISE SAUCE I

¼ cup tarragon vinegar
¼ cup dry white wine
1 small shallot, chopped
4 peppercorns
4 sprigs tarragon, chopped
4 sprigs chervil, chopped
4 egg yolks
1 tablespoon water
⅛ teaspoon salt
1 cup soft butter cut into 14 pieces
A few grains cayenne pepper
3 sprigs chopped tarragon—leaves only
3 sprigs chopped chervil—leaves only

Simmer vinegar, wine, shallots, peppercorns, and herbs until reduced to 4 tablespoons. Beat yolks with water and salt in top of double boiler until light and creamy, add strained reduced mixture and 1 piece of butter, and set over lower section of double boiler, over hot but not simmering water. Whip sauce until smooth. Gradually whip in remaining pieces of butter until each addition is well blended. Correct seasoning, stir in herbs, and serve with filet of beef, steaks, other meats, or fish.

BASIC BÉARNAISE SAUCE II

(*made in electric blender*)

3 tablespoons tarragon vinegar
3 tablespoons white wine, or 6 tablespoons vinegar
2 chopped shallots or 2 tablespoons chopped onion
4 sprigs tarragon
4 sprigs chervil
½ teaspoon salt
¼ teaspoon pepper
4 egg yolks
¾ cup butter
2 teaspoons minced tarragon
2 teaspoons minced chervil

Boil vinegar, wine, shallots, and herbs until reduced to 3 tablespoons. Strain and add salt and pepper. Heat butter to just simmering, or when it starts to bubble. Place yolks and reduced vinegar in container of blender, cover, and turn on. Uncover and add hot melted butter in a thin stream. Add herbs and blend only until sauce is thick and butter is incorporated. Serve with steaks and other meats and fish.

Variations

SAUCE ANCIENNE

½ cup peeled, seeded, and chopped cucumber
2 tablespoons minced onion
2 tablespoons butter
½ cup or 1 can chopped mushrooms
1 recipe basic hollandaise sauce #1
2 truffles, peeled and diced

Sauté cucumber and onion in butter until onion is transparent, about 4 minutes. Add mushrooms and sauté 3 minutes longer. Make hollandaise sauce, add the well-drained vegetables, and serve with fish, meat, eggs, or poultry.

SAUCE BÂTARDE

1 recipe sauce béarnaise, prepared with 6 tablespoons fish stock and 2 tablespoons vinegar in place of ¼ cup vinegar and ¼ cup wine. Serve with boiled or poached fish from which fish stock was obtained.

SAUCE BAVAROISE

(*Sauce Écrevisses*)

Prepare 1 recipe hollandaise sauce #1 using shrimp butter, page 118, instead of plain butter. Add 1 drop orange vegetable color if desired. Serve with fish. Diced shrimps may be added to the sauce.

For sauce nonpareille, prepare as above, substituting lobster butter, page 118, and lobster meat for crayfish or shrimps.

SAUCE BEAUHARNAISE

1 recipe sauce béarnaise
2 tablespoons puréed tarragon leaves
Salt and pepper

Crush enough tarragon leaves in a mortar to make 2 tablespoons tarragon purée. Press through a fine sieve and whip into béarnaise sauce. Correct seasoning and serve with meat or roast duck.

SAUCE CAPERS

Add 3 tablespoons finely minced or small, well-drained capers to 1 recipe hollandaise sauce #1 or 2. Serve with meat, fish, poultry, or cauliflower.

SAUCE CHORON

(*also called Sauce Française*)

1 recipe sauce béarnaise
¼ cup tomato purée
Salt and pepper

Beat tomato purée into sauce béarnaise and season to taste. Serve with fish, chicken, or meat.

SAUCE DAUMONT

Prepare hollandaise sauce #1 using oyster liquor instead of vinegar in its preparation. Add ¼ cup sautéed and well-drained mushrooms and 1 or 2 peeled and chopped truffles. Add whole poached oysters to the sauce just before serving.

SAUCE HENRI IV

1 recipe sauce béarnaise, prepared with 6 tablespoons strong veal stock and 2 tablespoons vinegar in place of ¼ cup vinegar and ¼ cup wine. Serve with veal roast, chops, or cutlets.

SAUCE LOMBARDE

Add ½ cup lightly sautéed or canned sautéed mushrooms to 1 recipe hollandaise sauce #1 or 2. Add 2 tablespoons finely chopped parsley and serve with poultry, meat, or fish.

SAUCE MAGENTA

1 recipe sauce choron
2 tablespoons chopped parsley
½ tablespoon chopped chervil
½ tablespoon chopped chives
1 teaspoon chopped tarragon

Stir chopped herbs into sauce and serve with meat or fish.

SAUCE MALTAISE

Combine 1 recipe hollandaise sauce #1 or 2 with 3 tablespoons strained orange juice and grated rind of 1 orange. Serve with asparagus.

SAUCE MARGUERY

Prepare hollandaise as for sauce daumont, add ¼ cup oyster purée and omit remaining ingredients. Both sauces are served with fish.

SAUCE MARSEILLAISE

1 recipe hollandaise sauce #1 or 2
2 tablespoons tomato purée

Serve with fish, meat, or vegetables. Chopped parsley, oregano, or chives may be sprinkled over the sauce.

SAUCE MEDICI

1 recipe sauce choron prepared with ¼ cup red wine instead of ¼ cup white wine. Serve with meat or fish.

SAUCE MOUSSELINE

1. Combine 1 cup hollandaise sauce with ¼ cup cream, whipped. Serve with asparagus, broccoli, or artichokes.
2. Combine 2 cups hollandaise sauce with ½ cup cream, whipped, and 1 stiffly beaten egg white. Serve with fish or vegetables.

MUSTARD SAUCE

(*Sauce Moutarde*)

Add 2 tablespoons prepared mustard, or to taste, to 1 recipe hollandaise sauce #1 or 2. Serve with meat or fish.

SAUCE NOISETTES

Combine 1 recipe hollandaise sauce #1 or 2 with ¼ cup grated, toasted hazelnuts (or filberts), season well, and serve with chicken, fish, or asparagus.

SAUCE AUX OEUFS

To 1 recipe hollandaise sauce #1 or 2 add 1 riced hardcooked egg. Serve with vegetables or fish.

SAUCE OIGNONS

Sauté ½ cup small onion rings in butter until transparent. Drain well and serve with the onion rings on top of 1 recipe hollandaise sauce #1 or 2. Serve with fish.

SAUCE PALOIS

Add 3 tablespoons finely minced mint leaves to 1 recipe hollandaise sauce #1 or 2. Serve with fish, meat, or poultry.

SAUCE TYROLIENNE

3 tablespoons tomato purée
Salt and pepper to taste
3 egg yolks
¾ cup butter
3 tablespoons minced herbs: parsley, chives, tarragon, chervil, or any combination

Beat tomato purée, salt, pepper, and egg yolks in top of double boiler, as for sauce béarnaise. Whip in butter gradually, correct seasoning, and thin by beating in 1 to 2 tablespoons of hot water if desired. Add herbs and serve with meat or fish.

FLAVORED BUTTERS

To substitute for plain butter in making hollandaise sauce to accompany fish dishes.

LOBSTER BUTTER

½ pound soft butter
Shell of 1 lobster
Coral and fat of 1 lobster
½ cup water
¼ cup ground lobster meat
Salt to taste

Pound and crush lobster shell with butter, coral, and fat. Add water and cook in top of double boiler for 20 minutes. Strain, cool, and chill. Lift off the butter, stir in ground lobster meat, season, and chill until needed. Mix into hollandaise sauce instead of plain butter.

SHRIMP BUTTER

6 cooked shrimp
½ cup soft butter

Crush, pound, or grind shrimp to a smooth paste. Combine with butter and chill until needed.

MAYONNAISE SAUCE AND ITS DESCENDANT SAUCES

BASIC MAYONNAISE SAUCE I

2 egg yolks
½ teaspoon salt
¼ teaspoon dry mustard
1 pinch white pepper
2 teaspoons tarragon vinegar
1 teaspoon lemon juice
1 cup oil

Beat yolks, salt, mustard, pepper, and 1 teaspoon vinegar with electric or rotary beater until smooth. Gradually add 4 tablespoons oil, drop by drop, while beating constantly. Add remaining vinegar and beat in half of remaining oil slowly, in a thin stream. Add lemon juice and remaining oil slowly, still in a thin stream. Stop beater 3 or 4 times while mayonnaise is thickening to scrape sides of bowl with a spatula and to make sure that all oil is being absorbed before more is added.

BASIC MAYONNAISE SAUCE II

(*made in electric blender*)

1 large egg
2 tablespoons lemon juice
½ thin curl lemon rind cut with potato parer and slivered
½ teaspoon salt
½ teaspoon mustard
1 pinch white pepper
½ cup olive oil
½ cup salad oil, or 1 cup salad oil in all

Place egg, lemon juice and rind, salt, mustard, and pepper in blender container. Cover and blend 5 seconds, open lid, and add oil in a thin stream until mayonnaise is thick and smooth. Stir with spatula, blend a few seconds longer, and chill before serving.

Variations

1. Substitute lemon juice and vinegar for tarragon vinegar and add 1 curl lemon rind.
2. Add 2 sprigs parsley, stems removed, after oil is incorporated. Blend only until parsley is minced.
3. Add ½ small clove garlic, crushed, and omit lemon rind.
4. Substitute tarragon vinegar for lemon juice, omit lemon rind, and add 3 tablespoons crumbled soft blue cheese or Roquefort cheese after oil is incorporated.
5. Add 2 tablespoons prepared mustard after oil is incorporated.

To store mayonnaise: Beaten or blended mayonnaise made with salad oil can be stored without separating. Place in a tightly covered jar or container and refrigerate. Do not freeze mayonnaise.

Beaten or blended mayonnaise made with olive oil will separate when stored in refrigerator and it will separate if it stands too long before being served. To avoid the latter, beat in 1 teaspoon hot bouillon after the mayonnaise is completed. To avoid the former, store in a tightly sealed container in a cool place, up to 1 week.

To restore separated mayonnaise: Mayonnaise made in a blender does not separate. Stirred or beaten mayonnaise will separate if oil is added too quickly or if ingredients are not all at room temperature. Should the sauce separate, stop beating at once. Beat an egg yolk in a separate bowl and gradually beat the separated mayonnaise into it. A second egg yolk may be required.

Commercial mayonnaise: Beat commercial mayonnaise with a fork or whisk. It will become lighter and smoother. If, after long storage, oil rises to the top, drain off the oil and beat until smooth.

SAUCE AMERICAINE

1 cup mayonnaise
1 tablespoon prepared mustard
⅓ cup lobster coral
Salt and pepper to taste

Combine all ingredients. Serve sauce with cold lobster or add lobster meat to sauce and serve with cold poached eggs or cold eggs mollet.

Additions:

1. Add 1 tablespoon brandy.
2. Add 3 tablespoons finely diced lobster meat.

SAUCE ANDALOUSE

1 cup mayonnaise
¼ cup tomato purée
1 diced pimento
Salt and pepper to taste

Combine all ingredients and serve with meat, fish, or eggs.

Variations

1. Sauce Antiboise: Omit pimento and substitute 1 tablespoon chopped tarragon and 1 teaspoon anchovy paste.
2. Sauce Trianon: Add 2 tablespoons minced onion, 2 tablespoons chopped dill pickle, and 1 teaspoon chopped tarragon.
3. Sauce Tyrolienne: Combine tomato purée and mayonnaise, season well, and omit pimento. Add 1 teaspoon oregano if desired.

SAUCE ANGLAISE

1 cup mayonnaise
2 teaspoons dry English mustard
Salt to taste

Stir mustard into 2 tablespoons of the mayonnaise until smooth. Return to the remaining mayonnaise and stir well. Mustard may be increased to taste—the sauce should be sharp but not bitter. Serve with cold meats.

Variations

1. Curry Mayonnaise: Substitute curry powder to taste for the dry English mustard.
2. Mustard Mayonnaise: Substitute brown mustard for dry mustard.

SAUCE CHANTILLY

1 cup mayonnaise
½ cup heavy cream, whipped
¼ cup freshly grated horseradish, or to taste (optional)
Salt and white pepper to taste

If bottled horseradish is used, drain well before adding to sauce. Serve with fish or meat.

Variations

1. Horseradish Cream Sauce: Increase horseradish to ½ cup and freeze the sauce until it is set.

2. Sauce Suédoise: Add 1 tablespoon prepared mustard and chill before serving with meat or fish.

COCKTAIL SAUCE

1 cup mayonnaise
⅓ cup chili sauce
1 tablespoon pickle relish, drained
Salt and pepper to taste

Combine and serve with shrimp, crabmeat, avocado, melon balls, or lobster cocktail.

Additions or variations:

1. 1 tablespoon horseradish
2. 2 teaspoons lemon juice
3. 1 teaspoon Worcestershire sauce
4. 1 dash Tabasco sauce
5. 1 tablespoon chopped chives
6. 1 tablespoon chopped onion
7. 2 tablespoons chopped stuffed olives

SAUCE EPICURIENNE

1 cup mayonnaise
¼ cup minced cucumber
1 teaspoon anchovy paste, or to taste
3 tablespoons chopped chutney
Pepper to taste
½ cup whipped cream

Peel, seed, chop, and drain cucumber well. Stir anchovy paste, chutney, pepper, and cucumbers into the sauce. Fold in the whipped cream and serve with meat or fish.

SAUCE FIGARO

½ cup mayonnaise
2 tablespoons tomato purée
2 drops orange vegetable color
Salt and pepper to taste

½ cup mayonnaise
3 tablespoons spinach purée
1 drop green vegetable color
Salt and pepper to taste

Prepare the red and green sauces separately. For the green sauce crush and pound raw spinach leaves into a smooth purée. Place sauces side by side in a sauce bowl and just before serving swirl a spoon through both sauces to make a red and green pin wheel in the sauce bowl. Serve with fish, meat, vegetables, or salad.

SAUCE GENOISE

1 cup mayonnaise
2 tablespoons finely minced herbs
2 tablespoons chopped pistacchio nuts
2 tablespoons minced pine nuts
1 drop green vegetable color
Salt and pepper to taste

Combine all ingredients and serve with fish or meat.

GLOUCESTER SAUCE

1 cup mayonnaise
¼ cup sour cream
2 teaspoons Worcestershire sauce
1 teaspoon dry mustard
Salt and cayenne pepper

To make a very sharp sauce, increase the ingredients to taste. Serve with fish or meat.

MAYONNAISE CHAUD-FROID

(*also called Mayonnaise Collée*)

1 envelope gelatin
¼ cup water
1 cup mayonnaise
Salt and pepper to taste

In a small bowl, soften gelatin in water for 15 minutes. Set bowl in boiling water and stir until gelatin is liquified, adding a little water if necessary. Fold into mayonnaise and use to coat eggs or chicken.

SAUCE MEXICAINE

1 cup mayonnaise
3 tablespoons diced pimiento
3 tablespoons diced green pepper
1 teaspoon anchovy paste, or to taste

Combine and serve with fish, meat, or hardcooked sliced eggs.

SAUCE MOUSSELINE

½ cup mayonnaise
½ cup whipped cream

Fold cream into mayonnaise and serve with cold cooked vegetables or cold fish.

SAUCE RAVIGOTE

1 cup mayonnaise
2 tablespoons minced dill pickle
2 teaspoons chopped parsley
2 teaspoons chopped capers
2 teaspoons chopped shallot
1 teaspoon chopped tarragon
1 teaspoon chopped chervil
½ teaspoon anchovy paste (optional)

Combine all ingredients and serve with chilled lobster or crabmeat. Also good with eggs in aspic.

SAUCE REMOULADE

1 cup mayonnaise
2 tablespoons chopped dill pickle
1 tablespoon minced parsley
2 teaspoons anchovy paste
1 teaspoon dry mustard
1 teaspoon minced chervil
½ teaspoon garlic salt (optional)
Salt, pepper, and cayenne to taste

Combine all ingredients and serve with cold meats, fish, or cooked vegetables.

Additions and Substitutions

1. Substitute 1 tablespoon Dijon or other prepared mustard for dry mustard.
2. Add 1 tablespoon minced green pepper.
3. Add 3 chopped stuffed olives and omit dill pickle.
4. Add 1 teaspoon Worcestershire sauce.
5. Substitute chopped gherkin for dill pickle.

SAUCE RUSSE

Prepare 1 recipe remoulade sauce, above, add 3 tablespoons grated horseradish, or to taste. Serve with shellfish, fish, or meat.

SPANISH SAUCE

1 cup mayonnaise
¼ cup finely minced ham
½ garlic clove, crushed
2 teaspoons prepared mustard, or to taste
1 teaspoon paprika

Stir all ingredients into the mayonnaise, chill, and serve with cold cauliflower, asparagus, chicken, or eggs.

SAUCE TARTAR

1 cup mayonnaise
1 tablespoon minced onion
1 tablespoon minced capers
1 tablespoon minced chives
1 tablespoon minced gherkin
Salt and pepper to taste

Combine and serve with meat or fish, breaded fried foods, especially good with shrimps, scallops, or mushroom fritters.

SAUCE VERDI

1 cup mayonnaise
½ cup sour cream
¼ cup finely chopped dill pickle
2 tablespoons chopped chives
2 spinach leaves, minced and pounded
Salt and pepper to taste

Combine all ingredients and serve with fish, meat, or chicken.

SAUCE VERDURETTE

1 cup mayonnaise
8 spinach leaves, stems removed
3 sprigs parsley, stems removed
3 sprigs chervil, stems removed
2 tablespoons white breadcrumbs
1 teaspoon Dijon mustard
Salt and pepper

Pound the spinach and herbs with the breadcrumbs into a smooth paste, add all other ingredients, and fold into mayonnaise. Serve in place of sauce verte.

SAUCE VERTE

(*Green Sauce*)

1 cup mayonnaise
4 sprigs parsley
12 stems chives
2 sprigs tarragon

6 spinach leaves
2 sprigs chervil
6 sprays watercress
Salt and pepper

Remove coarse stems from herbs, scald with boiling water, dry well and pound into a paste in a mortar. Press paste out well and add the juice to mayonnaise. If preferred, paste may be added to mayonnaise with the juice.

Serve with cold eggs, meat, fish, poultry, potato salad, cauliflower, in fact with almost anything. It is good with hot meat, fish, or eggs.

SAUCE VERT-PRÉ

Prepare ravigote sauce, page 124, omitting anchovy paste and pickle, and substituting 2 minced spinach leaves and ⅓ cup whipped cream. Serve with cold fish. Especially with cold salmon.

BASIC OIL AND BUTTER SAUCES

BASIC FRENCH DRESSING

1 CUP

¼ cup vinegar, preferably tarragon
1½ teaspoons salt
Freshly ground black pepper, to taste
⅔ to ¾ cup oil, salad or olive oil, or half and half

Stir vinegar into seasoning, stir in oil. Chill, but not long enough to solidify oil. Shake before serving.

Variations

1. Add ½ teaspoon dry mustard, 1 teaspoon paprika, 1 teaspoon sugar, optional.
2. Add minced herbs to taste, chervil, basil, tarragon, parsley.
3. Add minced onion to taste.
4. Blend any combination in electric blender for an emulsified, heavier dressing.
5. Substitute lemon juice for vinegar.
6. Add 1 clove garlic to dressing, remove before serving.
7. Blend basic dressing with ½ small clove garlic, 1 teaspoon oregano, and 1 dash Magi seasoning.

BASIC WARM BUTTER SAUCE

Melt fresh butter in a small heavy pan until it foams.

Variations

1. Onion or Shallot Butter Sauce: Pour foaming butter over finely chopped onions or shallots and parsley. To 1 cup butter use ⅓ cup each onion or shallot and parsley.
2. Brown Butter Sauce: After butter is foaming, continue to cook until browned to taste.
3. Brown Butter and Crumb Sauce: Add ½ to ⅔ cup dry breadcrumbs to each cup of butter as it browns and stir until crumbs and butter are browned to taste.
4. Black Butter Sauce: Brown butter very slowly up to the moment when it turns almost black.

CLARIFIED BUTTER

Heat butter slowly in a heavy saucepan or in top of a double boiler over boiling water. When butter is melted, the clear "oily" butter separates from the "creamy" whey. Pour off the clear or clarified butter and discard the whey.

BASIC COLD BUTTERS

Cream butter, add flavoring and/or seasoning, and cool or chill. Shape after butter is cool and before it is stiff. If butter is to be used as a spread, as for bread, use at once.

1. Anchovy Butter: To ½ cup butter, creamed, add 1 to 3 teaspoons anchovy paste to taste.
2. Curry Butter: To ½ cup butter, creamed, add 1 to 2 teaspoons curry powder.
3. Garlic Butter: To ½ cup butter, creamed, add 2 to 3 garlic cloves, crushed, and salt and pepper to taste.
4. Herb Butter: To ½ cup butter, creamed, add 6 tablespoons minced herbs, chives, parsley, tarragon and/or chervil, ½ teaspoon dry mustard, and salt and pepper to taste.
5. Maitre d'Hôtel Butter: To ¾ cup butter, creamed, add 3 tablespoons each minced parsley, chives, lemon juice, and salt and pepper to taste.
6. Meunier Butter: Add 2 teaspoons lemon juice and 2 tablespoons minced parsley to brown butter.
7. Mustard Butter: To ½ cup butter, creamed, add 2 to 3 tablespoons brown mustard, Dijon or Düsseldorf, if possible.

LESSON VI

ASPICS, MOUSSES, FROZEN CREAMS, AND PUDDINGS

When building a cooking repertoire, especially for the summer, gelatin is the thing to know about. At one time making an aspic was a labor of Hercules, involving calves feet, veal bones, and thick flannel cloths. Now it has all been boiled down into a packet of little envelopes in a box. Preparing aspic out of gelatin is easy; learning to mold and shape, glaze, varnish, and garnish with it is a different, but still easy, matter. Learn its possibilities, learn how to handle it smoothly (lumplessly), and you have not only learned all jellied soups, creams, molded salads, and desserts, you will also know how to gild the salmon.

Predominately, aspic is a molding agent for cold concoctions of meat, fish, vegetables, or fruit. By itself it is a garnish. Allowed to set in a shallow pan it can be diced or cubed or cut into ornamental shapes with small cookie cutters and used as decorations.

Its usual base is clear chicken stock, bouillon, or fish stock to which sherry or wine has been added. In short, aspic is a gelatinized stock, seasoned to enhance and compliment the flavor of whatever foods it is used to mold together or glaze. Always served cold, it ranges from a simple tomato aspic to elaborate cases in which foods are lavishly displayed like jewelry in a showcase, making it appetizing.

Aspic is also a summer haven for leftovers. It is a way of making a simple ingredient into a party dish. Best of all, it can be made in advance and left in the refrigerator until needed.

The basic rules are simple. One envelope plain gelatin is enough to "set" one pint, 2 cups, of liquid. Soften the gelatin by stirring it into ¼ to ½ cup cold liquid and set it aside for 15 minutes. Stir it well so that no particles of dry gelatin powder remain. The gelatin does not really soften: It actually absorbs the liquid and forms a "lump." The remaining 1½ or 1¾ cups of liquid are then heated to a boil, taken from the heat, and the "lump" is stirred into it until it is dissolved.

The hot liquid is the base of the aspic and so it might as well have the proper character for what is needed. A bland aspic is worse than none. Although cold water is usually suggested as the softening agent for the gelatin powder, sherry is much nicer. Soften the gelatin in ½ cup cold sherry. Then dissolve it in 1½ cups boiling bouillon. Let it cool and use it as a glaze before it is set, or pour it into a mold and chill it until it sets. The aspic is ready to enhance, bind, or decorate a dish as soon as it is dissolved. In some cases it has to be used immediately, in others it has to cool. Use it for any of the following purposes:

1. *To line* a mold to which other ingredients will be added, such as molded salads.

2. *To pour over* a dish which is in a shallow container, such as poached eggs in ramekins, or cold trout on a fish platter.

3. *To glaze:* Brush layer of liquid gelatin over a cold fish or fowl and chill between applying the layers until a deep, glossy coat is obtained.

4. *To bed or garnish:* Pour liquid gelatin on a platter. Chill until set and arrange cold meats or fish on it, or pour liquid gelatin into a shallow dish and dice it after it is set. Use the dice as a bed for cold poached eggs or use the dice to garnish pâtés, fish, or cold platters.

5. *To coat with chaud-froid:* Pour liquid aspic into basic white or brown sauce, add cream, and cool until thick but not yet set. Use white chaud-froid to coat chickens, as for chicken Jeanette, and use brown chaud-froid to coat chicken Tallyrand.

Mold aspics in dishes or molds rinsed out in cold water and unmold them by dipping the mold into hot water for a moment. After they are unmolded and garnished they can be held in the refrigerator until ready to serve. They are among the "patient" dishes, provided they are kept cold.

TO SHAPE ASPICS

Besides pouring or brushing liquid aspic over various dishes or foods, it can be poured into a mold containing various ingredients. There are five ways of doing this.

1. Pour the liquid aspic into a rinsed mold after it is cold, but before it sets. Lower or submerge the desired cold food into it and chill until set. Unmold and serve. This has the disadvantage that the food sinks to the bottom, which does not matter in some cases, especially if there is so much fruit or other ingredient that it fairly fills the mold.

2. Coat mold with liquid aspic by applying many coats and chilling after each application. Then fill with pâté, mousse, or any desired food.

3 Pour half an inch of liquid aspic into the rinsed mold, chill until set, fill with a firm paste or pâté or any large piece or pieces of food, pour liquid aspic around and over it, and chill again. Add more food and more aspic until filled. This applies to molds of poached eggs or chicken breasts suspended in aspic.

4. Fill mold with liquid aspic and suspend food into it. This can be done by means of skewers from the side of the mold.

5. Pour liquid aspic into a rinsed *chilled* mold and chill. As aspic sets first around the cold mold, pour out the unset center, and fill cavity with food. This is the neatest but hardest method. The inside becomes too stiff to pour out only a very short time after the edges are perfect.

JELLIED SOUPS

Basic jellied soup and many variations will be found at the end of Lesson II on pages 44 and 45.

MOUSSE

Fashions in food seem to change almost as frequently as they do in clothes. Fortunately no hemline has ever gone up without coming down again, and no favorite dishes of the past have disappeared without making a simplified comeback. So with the mousse. It is back.

Mousse is a French word which means froth or foam. A vin mousseuse is a sparkling or foaming wine. A mousseline sauce is hollandaise lightened with whipped cream. A mousse is a light dessert of sweetened, flavored whipped cream, which is frozen without stirring. It is also a gelatin dessert combined with whipped cream and egg whites, or an unsweetened concoction containing fish, cheese, or meat which can be served hot or cold. A cold lobster mousse can start a meal off glamorously, a hot chicken or ham mousse can be the centerpiece of a dinner or buffet. A cucumber or avocado mousse can act as a salad or luncheon dish, and a frozen peach or apricot mousse is an incomparable dessert.

The mousse, in a sense, is a combination of a soufflé and an aspic in that it almost always combines the basic egg of the soufflé and the gelatin of the aspic. Like the soufflé and the aspic, it utilizes almost any leftovers. It can be made the day before it is used, or it can be made on the day it is to be served and left to poach or bake while the table is being set.

The soufflé is always hot, the aspic is always cold, and incorrectly served these achievements collapse or melt or run, but not the mousse, which is another patient dish that waits for the belated guest. It is also a year-round dish, since it can be hot or cold depending on the season.

THE BASIC MOUSSE RECIPES

This chapter goes out of its way to avoid the plural of mousse, which is mousses.

There are three basic mousse recipes and countless variations:

Type I is a combination of a basic ingredient or flavoring agent, whipped cream, and gelatin. It takes about 2 hours to set, but it can be held in the refrigerator up to 3 days. It can be sweet or salty.

Type II is a combination of a basic fruit or flavoring agent, whipped cream, and possibly stiffly beaten egg whites. It is frozen, unstirred, and served as a dessert. It is also called a parfait. It does *not* contain gelatin.

Type III is a combination of ground ingredients, egg whites, and cream. It is poached in a mold and unmolded before serving. It is served hot.

BASIC COFFEE MOUSSE—TYPE I

1 envelope gelatin
¼ cup cold coffee
1 tablespoon heavy rum
½ cup cream
½ cup confectioners sugar
2 tablespoons instant coffee or coffee essence
2 egg whites, beaten stiff
1 cup heavy cream, whipped

Sprinkle gelatin over the cold coffee and rum, stir well, and set it aside for 15 minutes. Heat cream, sugar, and coffee essence in the top of a double boiler over boiling water until hot, stir in the softened gelatin until it is dissolved, take from heat, and cool. After mixture is cold, fold in the stiffly beaten egg whites and whipped cream. Pour into an oiled 1-quart melon or similar mold and chill for 2 hours. Unmold and serve with a warm mocha-chocolate and almond sauce.

Variations

1. Maple Mousse: Use ½ cup shaved maple sugar, maple flavoring, and dissolve gelatin in ½ cup hot maple syrup. Omit egg whites and use 2 cups heavy cream, whipped, as above.

2. Chocolate Mousse I: Add 2 squares sweet chocolate (2 ounces) melted slowly over hot water and cooled, to the gelatin mixture, substitute cold cocoa milk for the cold coffee, and omit the instant coffee.

3. Chocolate Mousse II: Melt 7 ounces sweet chocolate in ¼ cup orange juice over hot, not boiling, water. Cool. Beat in 4 large egg yolks and 2 teaspoons Curaçao. Fold in the stiffly beaten egg whites. Pour the mixture into a dessert bowl or 6 individual dessert glasses and chill for 3 to 4 hours. Serve sprinkled with grated orange rind.

4. Chocolate Mousse III: Melt ½ pound semisweet chocolate over hot, not boiling, water. Stir in 5 well-beaten egg yolks, 1 cup sugar, 2 tablespoons rum, 1 tablespoon vanilla, and ½ cup heavy cream. Fold in the stiffly beaten egg whites and 1 cup heavy cream, whipped. Pour into a dessert bowl and chill for at least 3 to 4 hours. Sprinkle with chopped walnuts and grated orange rind and serve. This was a specialty in Budapest.

BASIC APRICOT MOUSSE—TYPE I

2 envelopes gelatin
¾ cup juice from apricots
1 #2½ can apricots, skinless
1 teaspoon vanilla
2 cups heavy cream, whipped
½ cup sugar

Sauce: 1 jar apricot jam melted over boiling water, spiked with ¼ cup apricot brandy, or to taste. Add ½ cup apricot nectar and ¼ cup slivered almonds.

Blend or stir pitted apricots into a smooth purée. Soften gelatin in ¼ cup juice from apricot can for 15 minutes. Heat ½ cup juice to boiling, take from heat, and stir in gelatin until dissolved. Add the blended fruit and cool. Flavor with vanilla, and fold in the whipped cream. Pour into a 1½-quart melon mold rinsed out in cold water and chill for at least 2 hours. Serve with hot apricot sauce.

Variations

1. Peach Mousse: Substitute blended peaches for the apricots, use juice from can for liquid, and flavor sauce with peach brandy.
2. Strawberry Mousse: Crush or blend 1 quart fresh strawberries and substitute for the apricots. Retain a few big berries to garnish the mousse.

BASIC COLD CRAB MOUSSE—TYPE I

2 envelopes gelatin
6 tablespoons cold fish stock
6 tablespoons lime juice
2 tablespoons lemon juice
4 cups crabmeat, picked over
Salt and pepper to taste
Pinch of English mustard
½ cucumber, seeded and chopped fine
1½ cups heavy cream, whipped
½ cup thick mayonnaise
2 tablespoons finely cut dill

Soften gelatin in cold fish stock for 15 minutes. Heat lime and lemon juice in top of double boiler, stir in gelatin until dissolved. Cool. Put crabmeat through meat grinder, season to taste, and add the English mustard. Stir in the cold gelatin and the finely chopped cucumber and beat until smooth. Whip the cream, fold in the mayonnaise and dill, and fold in the crab mixture. Pour into a well-oiled mold and refrigerate for 2 hours. Unmold and serve with curried mayonnaise.

COLD AVOCADO MOUSSE

Soften 2 envelopes gelatin in ½ cup heavy cream for 15 minutes. Stir until dissolved into ½ cup boiling lime juice. Cool. Add 3 cups crushed avocado, 1 tablespoon lemon juice, 1 tablespoon minced onion and chili powder, and salt and pepper to taste. Fold in ½ cup sour cream beaten with ½ cup mayonnaise. Pour into an oiled 1½ quart mold and chill for at least 2 hours. Serve with French dressing or lemon mayonnaise, page 119.

COLD CHICKEN MOUSSE

Soften 2 envelopes gelatin in ½ cup chicken stock for 15 minutes. Stir until dissolved into ½ cup boiling chicken stock, cool. Add 2½ cups ground cooked chicken, 1⅓ cups thick white sauce made with chicken stock, page 37, 2 tablespoons minced onion, and salt and pepper to taste. Fold in 2 cups heavy cream, whipped, pour into a rinsed or oiled 2-quart mold, and chill at least 2 hours. Serve with curried mayonnaise, page 121.

BASIC MOUSSE MIXTURE WITHOUT GELATIN—TYPE II

(*Pâte à Bombe*)

15 tablespoons sugar
10 tablespoons water
5 egg yolks
2 cups heavy cream, whipped
2 teaspoons vanilla or coffee extract

Boil sugar and water without stirring for exactly 5 minutes. Cool. Beat yolks in the top of a double boiler, over hot, not boiling, water. Gradually beat in the cooled sugar syrup and vanilla in a thin stream, and continue stirring constantly until thickened and smooth. Set top of double boiler over ice and beat until cold. The cooling off should be done as quickly as possible. Whip the cream, fold it into the cold yolk mixture, and pour it into an oiled bombe mold, or ice cream mold.

Variations

1. Coffee Mousse: Beat 2 tablespoons instant coffee or coffee extract into the yolk mixture after it is cold. Omit vanilla.
2. Chocolate Mousse: Beat ½ cup melted and cold sweet chocolate into the yolk mixture after it is cold. Omit the vanilla.
3. Liqueur of Rum Mousse: Flavor as Variation 1, with 1 to 2 tablespoons liqueur or rum. Omit vanilla.
4. Fruit Mousse: Stir into yolk mixture after it is cold, ½ cup purée of strawberries, peaches, apricots, or raspberries. Flavor with suitable liqueur. Omit vanilla.
5. Add crushed macaroons, praline powder, marrons glacé, or nesselrode fruits to yolk mixture after it is cold.

BASIC FROZEN VANILLA MOUSSE OR PARFAIT—TYPE II

Parfaits are frozen, without stirring, in a deep freeze or a freezer compartment or packed in ice and salt. A mousse or parfait frozen in an ice cube tray is not as satisfactory as one that is frozen in a freezer.

3 egg whites
¾ cup powdered sugar
3 cups heavy cream
2 teaspoons vanilla extract

Beat egg whites until half stiff. Gradually add 6 tablespoons of the sugar while beating until stiff. Whip cream in the same way, adding the remaining sugar after it is half stiff. Do not beat until it looks like thunderheads, just until it is stiff but still creamy and smooth. Add vanilla and fold stiff egg whites into cream. Pour into an oiled 2-quart bombe mold and freeze in deep freeze or seal tightly and bury in equal parts crushed ice and salt. Dip in hot water to unmold.

Variations

1. Serve with cherries jubilee.
2. Serve with brandied peaches or apricots.
3. Serve sprinkled with crushed praline powder.
4. Chocolate Mousse or Parfait: Melt 2 squares sweet chocolate (2 ounces) slowly over hot water, beat in 2 tablespoons heavy cream, and cool. Fold the beaten egg whites lightly into the mixture and fold in the whipped cream. Omit the vanilla.

BASIC RUM MOUSSE—TYPE II

6 egg yolks
¾ cup sugar
½ cup rum
2 cups heavy cream
Grated rind of ½ lemon

Stir the yolks, sugar, and ¼ cup rum in the top of a double boiler over boiling water. Stir constantly until the mixture coats the back of a spoon. Take from heat and beat until cold. Stir in the remaining rum and lemon rind. Whip the cream until stiff and fold into the rum mixture. Rinse a 1½-quart mold in cold water, pour the mousse into it, and freeze for at least 2 hours.

Variations

1. Rum Raisin Mousse: ½ cup raisins, puffed in the rum before it goes into the mousse, are added before the whipped cream is folded in.
2. Marron Rum Mousse: Add ¾ cup chopped marrons, drained of syrup, before the whipped cream is folded in.

MAPLE MOUSSE OR PARFAIT

Stir 4 egg yolks with a pinch of salt and 1 cup maple syrup in the top of a double boiler, over boiling water, until thick. Chill. Fold in the stiffly beaten egg whites and 2 cups heavy cream, whipped. Freeze mousse in freezer compartment or deep freeze for about 2 hours, in a 1½-quart mold, rinsed out in cold water. Dip mold into warm water and unmold on a platter.

BASIC EGG YOLK FROTH: SABAYON

6 large egg yolks
3 tablespoons sugar
12 tablespoons Marsala

Beat yolks and sugar in the upper section of a double boiler over simmering water until slightly thickened. Gradually add Marsala little by little, beating constantly until the mixture is thick and about doubled in bulk. Pour into stemmed glasses and serve at once or chill the filled glasses before serving.

Variations

1. Substitute sherry for Marsala.
2. Substitute half orange juice and half Curaçao for the Marsala and sprinkle top with grated orange rind.
3. Substitute 2 tablespoons brandy for 2 tablespoons Marsala.
4. Substitute 2 tablespoons apricot brandy for 2 tablespoons Marsala.

BASIC HOT FISH MOUSSE—TYPE III

1½ pounds salmon, halibut, or flounder
4 egg whites
1⅓ cups heavy cream
Salt and pepper to taste
2 tablespoons chopped dill
Vegetable oil for the mold

With a sharp knife cut meat from bones of salmon, remove skin, scrape the jelly-like layer next to the skin, and incorporate it with the raw fish. Set the skin and bones aside for the sauce and put the meat through the finest blade of the meat grinder 3 times and put it in the freezing compartment or freezer for about 15 minutes. Also place the heavy cream in the freezer to chill it thoroughly. Take fish from freezer and beat in the unbeaten egg whites very slowly, one after the other, with a French wire whisk. Return fish to the freezer. If there is no freezer available, beat over chopped ice. Add the 2 cups of unwhipped cream, whisk them in very slowly, and chill the mousse between the two additions. The action of the cold and the beating should result in a very stiff mousse. Add salt to taste and press the preparation into a well-oiled fish mold. (The mold can be decorated with truffle cutouts before the mousse is added.) Cover the mold closely with foil and place in 1 inch hot water in a pan in a 350°F. oven. Poach for 45 minutes, or until the mousse feels solid to the touch. The mold can remain in the oven longer if necessary, but should not stay long enough to form a crust. Take from heat and let stand for about 7 minutes so that it will shrink a little from the mold. Insert a sharp knife around the edges and invert on a platter. Sprinkle top with chopped dill or parsley and serve with hollandaise sauce.

Variations

1. Lobster Mousse: Pound lobster meat, then grind it as above, add tarragon instead of dill. Serve with lobster sauce.
2. Crab Mousse: Prepare as above, add grated lemon rind and serve with cucumber mousseline sauce.

BASIC HOT CHICKEN OR HAM MOUSSE—TYPE III

1½ pounds cooked chicken, ham, or other meat
1½ cups heavy cream
4 egg whites, unbeaten
Pinch of English mustard
¼ cup cold chicken or ham broth

Grind chicken or ham in the meat grinder three times. Chill it and beat in the egg whites very slowly, one after the other, chilling between each addition. Add a little of the broth if the meat is very dry. Stir in the unbeaten cream, very slowly, as for salmon mousse, chilling again. Pour the chilled mixture into an oiled mold and poach in the oven in a pan containing 1 inch of water. Poach for about 30 minutes or until set. Serve hot with watercress or mustard sauce.

FROZEN CREAMS

BASIC BISCUIT TORTONI

Dry 12 to 24 macaroons, depending on size, in a 200°F. oven for about 30 minutes until crisp. Crush with a rolling pin to obtain 2 cups macaroon crumbs.

Prepare 1 recipe frozen vanilla mousse, Type II. Omit the vanilla and substitute ¼ cup sherry. Add half the macaroon crumbs and pour into paper cups or ramekins. Sprinkle tops with remaining macaroon crumbs and freeze according to basic directions.

FROZEN SOUFFLÉS

The whole point of the frozen soufflé is that it should look exactly like a hot soufflé. The guest is supposed to be startled when he doesn't burn his mouth on the first bite. If the guest has eaten around, he won't be startled, but he will enjoy seeing his mousse half in and half out of the dish.

BASIC FROZEN SOUFFLÉ: Raspberry

Tie a thick band of wax or brown paper around the outside of a 7- or 8-inch soufflé mold, to extend 2 inches above the mold. Secure the top edge with freezer tape or a paper clip and butter or oil the inside lightly.

2 envelopes gelatin
⅓ cup raspberry juice or syrup
½ cup purée of raspberries
1 cup heavy cream, whipped

3 eggs, separated
½ cup sugar
1 tablespoon lemon juice
1 basket ripe raspberries (optional)
1 tablespoon cocoa powder

Stir the gelatin into the raspberry juice and set it aside to soften for at least 15 minutes. With a French wire whisk beat yolks and sugar in the top of a double boiler over hot boiling water until they are as thick as very heavy cream. Add lemon juice and softened gelatin and stir until gelatin is dissolved. Add raspberry purée (which must be very thick) and cool the mixture. Whip egg whites stiff, whip cream, and fold both into the cold raspberry mixture. Pour into the prepared mold, pulling the paper up higher if necessary. Chill in refrigerator for about 3 hours. Remove paper band by running a knife dipped in hot water around the paper as it is being pulled off. Sieve top of soufflé with cocoa powder and serve. If preferred, a deep hole can be scooped out of center and filled with fresh raspberries. Part of the scooped-out cream can be smoothed over the top of the hole and cocoa can be sieved over the top to hide completely this additional ruse to confound the innocent guest.

PUDDINGS: BAKED AND STEAMED

Pudding is a word that means different things to different people and different nations. In England, where pudding is at its best, it usually means something wrapped in a pudding cloth, firmly tied, and boiled, while the molded American pudding, to the British, is a "shape," quaking, or frozen into immobility.

For easy reference, we break up our puddings into various chapters and refer here only to three kinds.

1. Pudding mixtures poured into a mold or form, sealed, and steamed in a covered kettle of water on top of the stove or in the oven, such as plum pudding.
2. Salty pudding mixtures baked in an open or covered baking pan in the oven, such as corn or macaroni pudding. (These are often referred to as casseroles.)
3. Sweet pudding mixtures baked in an open or covered baking pan in the oven, such as rice or bread pudding.

For other puddings:

1. See cold, clear, gelatinized puddings under aspic, page 131.

2. See cold frozen cream puddings under mousse, page 133, or frozen soufflé, page 142.

3. See other puddings on pages 143 to 146.

BASIC STEAMED PUDDING—TYPE I

(*Victoria Pudding*)

1 cup butter
1 cup sugar
4 eggs
1½ cups flour
2½ cups breadcrumbs
½ cup raisins, chopped
½ cup currants, chopped
½ cup candied cherries, chopped

Cream butter and sugar together until light. Beat in the eggs, one by one. Stir in the flour and breadcrumbs and the chopped fruits. Pour mixture into a well-buttered pudding form, cover with waxed paper and adjust the lid firmly. Steam gently in a covered kettle of simmering water for 2 hours, replenishing the water with boiling water when necessary. The simmering water should always reach ⅔ up on the mold. Turn the pudding out on a hot platter and serve with rum-flavored whipped cream or soft ice cream sauce.

Variations

Substitute chopped figs or dates, melted chocolate, or any preferred ingredients such as nuts or orange rind for the currants and cherries.

ENGLISH CHRISTMAS PLUM PUDDING

½ pound beef suet
2½ cups breadcrumbs
1¼ cups sugar
1 pinch each salt and nutmeg
1½ cups raisins, chopped
1½ cups currants, chopped
¾ cup candied orange and lemon peel
¾ cup almonds scalded and chopped
8 eggs
½ cup brandy
additional brandy
brandy hard sauce

Mix finely chopped suet with crumbs in a large bowl. Add sugar, salt, nutmeg, raisins, currants, and the diced peels. Add almonds and beaten eggs. Mix in the brandy and set the covered pudding aside for one week. Stir once a day and add a little brandy to taste. Fill pudding mixture into a buttered bowl, tie over a scalded and floured cloth, firmly, and boil 12 hours, well covered at all times with boiling water. Leave pudding covered and hang it in a cool place until wanted. Before serving, boil or steam for 1 more hour.

Drench with warm brandy and flame. Serve with brandy hard sauce.

BASIC BAKED PUDDING—TYPE II

(*A Luncheon Main Course Dish*)

⅔ cup broken macaroni, cooked and drained
1 cup milk, scalded
1 cup cream, scalded
1 cup breadcrumbs
3 eggs, well beaten
¼ cup melted butter
1 green pepper, chopped fine
1 pimento, chopped fine
¼ onion, chopped fine
2 teaspoons minced parsley
½ cup grated Parmesan cheese
Salt and pepper to taste

Cook macaroni according to package directions and drain.

Pour hot milk and cream over crumbs. Reserve 1 cup of this mixture and set it aside. Add all remaining ingredients to the milk-and-crumb mixture and pour into a deep, buttered ovenware baking dish. Top with the remaining crumb mixture and bake in a 350°F. oven for about 1 hour, or until set and browned. Test as a custard, if a knife blade comes out clean, the pudding is done. Serve with tomato sauce.

BASIC BAKED PUDDING—TYPE III

(*Dessert Course*)

1 cup rice
2 cups milk
½ teaspoon salt
3 yolks
3 tablespoons sugar
1 cup heavy cream
½ cup raisins (optional)
¼ cup slivered almonds (optional)

Place rice in the top of a double boiler, over boiling water, with milk and salt and let it cook until the milk is absorbed, about 30 minutes. Beat yolks with sugar until creamy. Beat in cream. Cool rice and stir it into the yolk-and-cream mixture. Pour into 1 large shallow, or individual shallow, buttered baking dishes and bake in a 350°F. oven until heated through and browned, about 15 minutes. Serve cold with heavy cream.

Variations

Add puffed raisins, slivered almonds, or vanilla flavoring to taste.

LESSON VII

FRITTERS, CROQUETTES, PANCAKES, WAFFLES, OMELETS, STRUDEL AND NOODLE PASTE

French cooking, which is at times enormously elaborate, is also very frugal. The French often achieve imposing results with simple ingredients or leftovers. Knowing how to make fritters means that cold cooked meats and vegetables can be utilized for some of those lovely dishes that have made French cooking famous.

Like the mousse or soufflé, fritters cover the entire meal: miniature fritters with cocktails, a light fish fritôt, or cod fish balls, for lunch; meat fritters for the main course; corn or sweet potato fritters with the chicken; fruit and cream fritters for dessert. The repertoire of the homemaker who has learned the basic batter is again increased enormously.

The difference between fritters and regular deep-fat-fried foods lies in the preparation of the main ingredient. When the main ingredient retains its own shape, it is deep-fat-fried, as in fried chicken. When it is a composite of batter and ingredients that puff into a round shape, it is a fritter, as in corn fritters. When it blows up to magnificent proportions, it is a French beignet and can be found under choux paste, page 233. When the mixture is bound with thick white sauce and shaped and breaded, it is a croquette, page 150. The jelly doughnut was originally a yeast beignet, out of it grew our doughnut, which is a cousin of the fritter.

Meat, fish, and poultry fritters are usually served with a sauce. Vegetable fritters usually benefit by the sauce or gravy of the roast they accompany. Corn fritters are often served with maple syrup and fruit fritters are served with fruit or custard sauces or whipped cream.

Some ingredients require so little cooking that their immersion in hot fat suffices to cook the interior as well as the exterior of the fritter. These ingredients include fruits, shrimp, tender corn kernels, eggplant, and mushrooms.

BASIC FRITTER BATTER

1½ cups flour
¼ teaspoon salt
¼ cup salad oil
1½ cups lukewarm water
2 eggs, separated

Sift flour and salt into a warm bowl. Make a well in the center, pour in oil, water, and beaten egg yolks. Beat quickly into a smooth batter; do not over beat. Set aside for 3 to 4 hours to ripen. Fold in stiffly beaten egg whites just before using the batter.

For a thicker batter, use 2 cups flour, 2 tablespoons oil, and 2 whole eggs. All other quantities and methods remain the same.

Variations

1. Mix and sift 1 cup flour, 1 teaspoon baking powder and a pinch of salt. Gradually beat in ¾ cup milk and 1 well-beaten egg. Use for peach beignets or french fritters.

2. Mix and sift 1 cup flour, 1 teaspoon baking powder, 3 tablespoons sugar, and a pinch of salt. Gradually beat in ¾ cup milk, 1 tablespoon melted butter, and 1 well-beaten egg. Use for apple fritters or other fruit fritters.

BASIC FRENCH FRYING BATTER

2 cups flour
½ teaspoon salt
2 eggs, separated
5 tablespoons oil
1 tablespoon brandy
1 cup milk

Sift flour and salt into a bowl. Make a well in the center and put yolks, oil, and brandy into it. Stir the flour gradually into the yolks and oil, adding milk as you stir. Add more milk, if necessary, until batter is smooth and has consistency of heavy cream. Rest batter 3 to 8 hours. Just before using, fold in 2 stiffly beaten egg whites.

BASIC BATTER FOR EASTERN DEEP-FAT FRIED FOODS

(*Tempura*)

1 cup flour
2 tablespoons cornstarch
2 teaspoons baking powder
1 teaspoon salt
¼ cup tepid water
2 large eggs

Sift dry ingredients into a bowl. Stir in water and eggs, beaten together. Increase water, if necessary, to make a thick batter. Dip split shrimp, chicken, shellfish, fish, vegetables or pieces of meat into the batter and fry in deep fat at 350°F. until brown, about 5 minutes.

APPLE FRITTERS

3 apples, peeled and cored
2 tablespoons sugar
1 cup white wine
¼ cup raisins, chopped
¼ cup apple jelly
2 tablespoons brandy

Prepare 1 recipe basic fritter batter, variation 2, page 148. Slice apples ½ inch thick and poach with sugar and wine until just soft. Fill cavities with a mixture of raisins, jelly, and brandy. Dip in batter and deep-fat-fry at 375°F. until golden, about 5 minutes.

BEIGNETS SOUFFLÉ

(*French Fritters*)

In a deep-fat fryer, melt enough vegetable shortening to reach a depth of 3 inches for small beignets and a depth of 5 inches for large beignets. Heat shortening to 370°F. or if fryer has a temperature chart, heat to correct stage for *fritters.* If fryer is not equipped with a thermometer, heat shortening until a 1-inch cube of bread turns golden in 1 minute. Shape 1 recipe choux paste into 1½-inch balls with 2 spoons dipped in hot fat or with an ice cream scoop dipped in hot fat. Fry a few at a time in deep hot fat at 370°F. Let them cook until they are golden. They will turn themselves and each should show a crack down one side. Do not cook too many at once. Dust with powdered sugar in which a vanilla bean has been stored. Keep beignets hot in a 250°F. oven until all are completed. Serve with a sauce of whipped cream folded into soft vanilla ice cream.

See Lesson XI for basic choux paste recipes.

CROQUETTES

Croquettes, which sound like something your grandmother probably loved, are well worth reinstating in your cooking repertoire. Besides being another ideal haven for leftovers, they are among those patient dishes that sit and wait while others drink cocktails. They have the further advantage that they can be prepared in three ways.

1. Prepare the mixture, shape it into croquettes, bread them, and refrigerate until a few minutes before serving. Deep fat fry and drain them just before they come to the table.
2. Prepare and fry croquettes until they are pale golden. Take them out and set them aside. Refry just long enough to heat through and brown.
3. Prepare, fry, and drain them; keep them warm in a covered pan in a warm oven.

These methods are worth thinking about when you shape small cheese croquettes for your cocktail party or when you transform dreary mashed potatoes, which your family has seen before, into potato croquettes that can be rolled in ground almonds. The slivers of turkey that you hate to throw away can be the basis of a ladies' luncheon: turkey croquettes, mushroom sauce, a crisp salad . . . and then there is the day when the budget is low and a buffet party lies ahead. One inexpensive fowl can be cooked, ground and shaped into croquettes, spiked with sherry and herbs to feed a large party for practically a song. Finally there is visual appeal to consider. For a gala or holiday dinner, when you cannot bear to bring forth one more sweet potato under marshmallows or one more dish of kernel corn, make them into croquettes and heat them at the last minute.

When making croquettes out of mashed white or sweet potatoes, chestnut purée, or any similar mixture, beat in 1 tablespoon butter or 1 egg yolk. Use more of the mashed or puréed ingredient and less of the thick white sauce, such as 2½ cups thick purée to ½ cup white sauce. Roll croquettes in grated or chopped nuts, or add nuts to the mixture and egg and breadcrumb in the usual way.

The simplest method for preparation is to shape all the croquettes at once. Dip them all into egg and roll in crumbs, and so on, rather than dip each croquette into egg—crumbs—egg—crumbs. The egg and crumbs go further and the dipping is easier.

When raw corn or other ingredients are used the fat should not be quite as hot as when all ingredients are cooked.

Use imagination in flavoring, herbs, and sauces. Under certain conditions a croquette is even worth a diced truffle.

For other white sauce recipes, see Lesson III.

BASIC MEAT, POULTRY, FISH, OR GAME CROQUETTES BASED ON THICK WHITE SAUCE

USING CHICKEN

Make a thick basic white sauce, page 49, using 4 tablespoons butter and 5 tablespoons flour. Moisten the roux with ½ cup heavy cream and ½ cup chicken stock. Add 1½ cups diced cooked chicken meat and ½ cup chopped mushrooms, sautéed in 1 tablespoon butter. Add the juice of ½ lemon and salt, pepper, and a little sherry to taste.

Spread the mixture in a shallow pan and cool. When cold, shape into 12 small barrels or pyramids with floured hands. Dip the croquettes into 2 beaten eggs and seasoned breadcrumbs. Let them dry for a few minutes and then dip in egg and roll in breadcrumbs again. Let them dry again for 10 minutes. Fry in deep fat or shortening at 375°F. until golden, about 5 to 7 minutes.

Variations

1. Substitute 1½ cups diced or ground cooked meat, fish, shellfish, game, or any combination of meat or fish and ½ cup cooked vegetable for the chicken and mushrooms. The white sauce can be changed to brown sauce, fish sauce, or any thick, flavored sauce, pages 54 to 59.

2. Substitute ¼ cup chopped almonds for ¼ cup chicken or ½ cup cooked green peas or corn for part of the fish for fish croquettes.

BASIC VEGETABLE CROQUETTES BASED ON THICK WHITE SAUCE

USING CORN

Prepare thick basic white sauce of 4 tablespoons butter, 5 tablespoons flour, and ½ cup each vegetable water or stock and heavy cream. Cut into a bowl kernels from 6 medium ears of corn. Scrape the cobs with the back of the knife to obtain the remaining milk. Stir in the white sauce and season to taste with salt and pepper and 1 teaspoon sugar. (If 1½ cups canned corn are used, drain off all liquid and use ¼ cup for the basic white sauce.) Spread mixture in a shallow pan, cool, and chill. Shape cold mixture into 12 barrels, cones, or pyramids. Dip them in egg and roll in seasoned bread- or cracker-crumbs. Dry a few minutes and dip again in egg and crumbs. Dry for at least 10 minutes and fry in deep fat or shortening at 365°F. until golden. Drain on absorbent paper and serve at once.

BASIC PANCAKES

(*Crêpes*)

Thin pancakes should be baked in a pan that is kept solely for that purpose. An 8-inch rounded pancake pan makes the traditional 6-inch pancakes. The pan, like an omelet pan, should never be washed. It should be cleaned with a paper towel and hidden away until needed. Washing the pan makes pancakes stick. It is not necessary to butter the pan when the batter contains melted butter or oil, although a soft cloth dipped in melted butter may be run around the inside of the pan before starting each fresh pancake.

After mixing pancake batter, let it "rest" in a cool place for at least 2 hours. If the recipe calls for stiffly beaten egg whites, fold them into the batter after the rest period. Pour from 1½ to 3 tablespoons batter into the pan and swirl it around to cover the bottom surface of the pan evenly. If batter does not flow easily, add a little more milk. It may be necessary to add a little milk to the batter while making the pancakes, as the batter tends to thicken. Cook over medium heat for about 1 minute, turn pancake with spatula or lift and turn with fingers, and cook about 1 minute longer on second side. If stove-top burners are equipped with a dial, set heat at #4. Depending on heaviness of pan, increase or decrease cooking time. Cook first pancake until it is lightly browned and edges start to dry. Turn and cook it until second side is browned. Adjust the remaining pancakes to the same cooking time. Keep finished pancakes warm in a covered casserole in a warm oven or in a covered dish set over simmering water.

BASIC PANCAKE BATTER I
PÂTÉ À CRÊPES

(*Dessert Pancakes*)

1½ cups milk
2¼ cups flour
3 large eggs, separated
3 tablespoons sugar
¾ cup melted butter
Melted butter for pan

In a bowl, beat milk and sifted flour until smooth. Beat in egg yolks and sugar. Stir in butter and set batter aside, in a cool place, for 2 hours. Fold in stiffly beaten egg whites and make thin pancakes as directed above.

BASIC PANCAKE BATTER II

(*With Whole Eggs*)

1 cup flour
2 eggs
1 pinch salt
2 tablespoons sugar
1 cup cold milk
2 tablespoons melted butter
½ teaspoon vanilla (optional)
½ tablespoon brandy or rum

Sift flour into bowl, break eggs over it, and add salt, sugar, and milk, all at once. Beat or whisk into a smooth batter. Add butter and flavoring and rest batter in a cool place or in refrigerator for 3 hours. Batter will make about 12 6-inch pancakes.

Variations

1. Omit sugar and flavorings, add ½ teaspoon salt, and fill with savory fillings.
2. Omit sugar and flavoring. Roll up pancakes and cut them across into ¼-inch slices. Use in place of noodles in clear soups.
3. Prepare as above. Before rolling up pancakes, sprinkle with grated Parmesan cheese and a little melted butter. Roll up. Slice and use as above.
4. Omit butter and replace half the milk with heavy cream.

CRÊPES SUZETTE

Make a hard sauce of 6 tablespoons each soft butter and sugar and 1 tablespoon brandy. Spread the mixture over 12 small crêpes and fold them into quarters. Hold them until needed in a small covered dish. Melt ½ cup unsalted butter in a crêpe pan, or wide shallow pan, add 4 lumps sugar, previously rubbed on 1 orange and 1 lemon until saturated with flavor from the peel. Add 3 tablespoons sugar to the juice from the orange and lemon. Set over a burner. Bring sauce to a simmer, lay folded crêpes into it, and turn them gently until they are heated through. Pour 1 jigger each warmed brandy and cointreau over the crêpes and flame. Serve as soon as the flame dies down. Grated orange and lemon rind may be added to the sauce.

Pancake Fillings, Sweet

Spread fillings on medium or small pancakes, roll up, and sprinkle with powdered sugar, or as variations require.

1. Pancakes or Crêpes Georgette: Fill with drained pineapple dice or crushed pineapple, flavor with Maraschino.
2. Crêpes Gil Blas: Fill with hazelnut butter, butter creamed with sugar, and toasted ground hazelnuts, flame with brandy.
3. Crêpes Mancelle: Fill with sweetened purée of chestnuts flavored with Maraschino.
4. Hungarian Pancakes or Palatschinken: Fill with strawberry jam.
5. Hungarian Pancakes with Cheese Filling or Topfen Palatschinken: Stir cream cheese with egg yolks to spreading consistency, add sugar to taste and raisins puffed in brandy.
6. Danish Crêpes: Fill with chocolate-flavored pastry cream and serve sprinkled with grated sweet chocolate. Pass sweetened whipped cream separately.
7. Mocha Pancakes: Fill with coffee-flavored pastry cream and serve with hot mocha-flavored chocolate sauce, or softened coffee ice cream sauce.

Pancake Fillings, Savory

(*Omit Sugar in Basic Recipe*)

1. Fill pancakes with chicken hash and serve with mushroom sauce. Garnish with chopped parsley.
2. Fill pancakes with minced and creamed veal. Serve with a well-seasoned and herbed tomato sauce.
3. Fill pancakes with spinach, sprinkle with grated cheese, and brown under the broiler.
4. Fill pancakes with creamed mushrooms.
5. Fill pancakes with creamed turkey and serve with cranberry jelly.
6. Fill pancakes with creamed crabmeat and serve with shrimp, lobster, or cucumber sauce.
7. Fill pancakes with herbed tomato purée and serve with a light onion sauce (sauce soubise, page 58).

BASIC SWEDISH PANCAKES

Swedish pancakes require a special "Plett" pan which bakes seven evenly sized pancakes at one time.

2 eggs
2 cups milk
⅔ cup flour
½ teaspoon salt
2 teaspoons sugar
1 teaspoon melted butter
½ cup powdered sugar

Beat eggs with milk. Gradually beat in the sifted dry ingredients until smooth and add the butter last. Butter the "Plett" pan well, set over medium heat, and fill the seven cavities with 1 tablespoon each of the batter. Bake until the underside browns and bubbles show on the top. Turn and brown the other side. Spread pancakes on a heated plate, sieve with powdered sugar, and serve each guest with 1 pan of pancakes as they are browned. Pass wild strawberry jam or lingonberry preserve separately. (A very good swedish pancake mix is available at most markets if you are pressed for time.)

Griddle Cake Variations

Thin griddle pancakes: Sift 1¼ cups flour with 1 pinch salt and 1 tablespoon sugar. Beat in 1½ cups milk, 1 tablespoon melted butter, 1 egg, and ¼ teaspoon vanilla. Bake on buttered griddle. Makes about 18 very small griddle cakes. Increase the milk to 2 cups and use the same recipe to make 12 thin 6-inch pancakes in a lightly buttered pancake pan.

Griddle Cake Accompaniments

Fried and well-drained bacon, ham, or sausages. Whipped butter, maple syrup, shaved maple sugar. Strawberry jam, stewed blueberries, well-drained stewed corn kernels. Caviar and whipped sour cream.

BASIC WAFFLE BATTER*

3 eggs, separated
2½ cups cake flour
2 cups milk
3 ounces butter, melted
1½ tablespoons baking powder

* The same recipe may be used for pancakes.

Place yolks in bowl, sift in flour, and stir in milk and butter. Beat egg whites stiff, put them on the batter, sprinkle baking powder over them, and fold into the batter. Bake in heated waffle iron following manufacturer's directions.

Variations

Serve waffles with butter and maple syrup; crushed strawberries or raspberries and a small scoop of vanilla ice cream; creamed chicken or mushrooms; crisp bacon or broiled sausages. Add grated nuts or cheese to basic recipe for variety.

OMELETS

Buy a heavy omelet pan and keep it for the sole purpose of making omelets. An omelet pan must be rounded with sloping sides so that the egg can flow easily as the pan is shaken or tilted during the cooking, and so that the finished omelet can slide easily out of the pan. An omelet pan measuring about 9 inches across the top is ideal for a 3- to 4-egg omelet. Season the new pan, if it is cast iron or cast aluminum, by rubbing it with dry steel wool and then with oil. Don't let it get near water. Fill clean pan with oil and let it stand for 48 hours. (You can use the oil for something else.) Wipe the pan with a soft cloth, set it over low heat, and let it get hot slowly. It is now ready for its first omelet. Wipe the pan with a dry cloth each time it has been used. Never wash it. If it is a French copper omelet pan, treat it the same way but omit the steel wool.

BASIC FRENCH OMELET

(for two)

3 fresh eggs, extra large
2 teaspoons water
Salt and pepper to taste
1 tablespoon butter

Beat eggs with water and seasonings with a fork until well mixed but not foamy. Melt butter over medium heat in omelet pan, pour in eggs, and stir with a fork in the one hand while shaking the pan with the other hand. Do this until the eggs begin to firm. Stir more slowly toward the center of the pan, lifting the cooked eggs around the edge so that the uncooked eggs can flow down to the bottom. Let cook undisturbed for a few seconds. When omelet is lightly browned and the center is soft but not liquid, fold over half the omelet from the handle side to the outside edge of the pan. Hold a warm plate at the outside edge and invert the omelet onto it by lifting the handle until the omelet falls over onto the plate. This folds it again and gives it that conventional French omelet look. Serve plain or fill just before folding. The whole thing should take less than 3 minutes.

Make several small omelets with 3 eggs. Do not make larger omelets with more than 4 eggs.

Variations

1. Finely ground or minced ingredients, such as minced onion, herbs, or grated cheese, can be mixed with the eggs.
2. Grated cheese may also be sprinkled on the omelet just before it is folded and/or sprinkled over the top.
3. Other fillings are usually laid across the finished omelet (in the direction of the fold) just before folding.
4. Fillings are also laid alongside of the omelet, or they are divided, part inside and part outside.
5. A line of filling or garnish can be laid down the length of the omelet, or laid across it in straight or diagonal lines.

Fillings

Hot asparagus spears with the omelet, hot browned butter passed separately.

Cooked and drained asparagus spears, broccoli, cauliflower, spinach, or any preferred vegetable.

Creamed crabmeat, shrimp, or lobster

Crisp bacon dice with chopped parsley

Crisp bacon dice with grated cheese

Crushed garlic

Curried crabmeat, shrimp, or lobster

Diced cooked meats
Diced cooked potatoes
Diced ham, tongue, or bologna
Grated cheese
Hash brown potatoes and 1 tablespoon diced onion
Leftover meats, game, or poultry warmed in brown sauce
Minced herbs
Minced onion
Red or black caviar arranged on the omelet with a line of sour cream next to the omelet
Sautéed eggplant dice with minced pimento
Sautéed onions, tomatoes, mushrooms, or a combination of all three
Sautéed mushrooms with crisp bacon dice
Sautéed tomatoes with mixed green herbs
Strips of smoked salmon and capers next to the omelet

BASIC STRUDEL PASTE

2 cups flour
1 egg
lukewarm water
1 pinch salt
1 tablespoon sugar
1 tablespoon melted butter

Sift flour onto a pastry board, break egg into a cup measure, and beat well. Add enough lukewarm water to fill the cup. Pour into a small pitcher and beat in sugar and butter. Pour the mixture gradually into the well while working it into a smooth paste with the hands. Beat the paste by throwing and beating it against the board until the board and hands are clean and the paste is glossy and shows a slight inclination to bubble. Leave paste on lightly floured board and cover with a warmed bowl. Rest it for 1 hour.

Cover a large table with a plain cloth, dust it very lightly with flour, and roll out the paste on the center of it, in all directions, to make the largest possible round. Discard rolling pin, take off your rings and with the backs of your hands under the paste raise and stretch it toward yourself as far as it will go. If you cannot, get two or three other people to do this with you. Keep moving round and round the table until the paste is paper thin. Cut off thicker edge. Patch any holes with scraps from the edge and sprinkle entire surface, in order listed, with:

½ cup melted butter
1 cup toasted breadcrumbs (toasted in a low oven until golden)
¾ cup sugar mixed with ½ teaspoon cinnamon
6 green apples, peeled and thinly sliced
1 cup raisins
1 cup slivered almonds, scalded
1 cup toasted breadcrumbs
½ cup melted butter
¾ cup sugar mixed with ½ teaspoon cinnamon
Grated rind of 2 lemons

Fold in the edges of the paste and roll into a tight roll by lifting one side of the tablecloth and letting the strudel roll slowly over on itself. (I was fourteen before I realized that the cloth was not baked in the strudel.)

Lift strudel with hands and slip it onto your arms to get it into a heavily buttered roasting pan in a horseshoe shape. Sprinkle ½ cup melted butter over it and bake in a 400°F. oven until golden. It may take from 45 to 60 minutes, depending on quality of apples used. If the top seems to be too brown, reduce heat to 375°F. and cover with buttered paper or foil.

Try to remove the strudel from the pan in one piece. If this is too difficult, cut it in half and rejoin the 2 halves on the platter. Sprinkle generously with powdered sugar and serve warm, cold, or reheated.

BASIC NOODLE PASTE

2 cups flour
1 teaspoon salt
1 tablespoon vegetable shortening
¼ cup water
2 eggs, well beaten
½ cup flour

Sift flour and salt into a bowl. In a saucepan, heat vegetable shortening with water over low heat until dissolved. Take from heat. Beat eggs well and beat them into the warm water. Pour the mixture into the flour and stir until smooth with a wooden spoon. Turn out on a floured board and knead in flour, little by little, until ½ cup additional flour has been absorbed. Rest noodle paste under an inverted bowl for 1 hour. Divide dough in half, roll out to the largest and thinnest possible rounds, and dry for 1 hour. Fold dough over into a roll and cut into long thin strips. Shake strips apart and dredge them with a little flour. Use as needed. To cook, boil in a generous amount of salted water until tender, about 6 to 8 minutes.

Use cooked homemade or packaged noodles as an accompaniment for meat or poultry. Use in casseroles and soups; fry them in deep fat or bake them in puddings. Pour brown butter and crumb sauce over them, or add sugar and chopped walnuts and serve them as dessert.

LESSON VIII

BASIC RECIPES AND COOKING METHODS

Everything depends on the method of cooking and although you probably know all these methods, we repeat them here. While they are not, strictly speaking, basic recipes, they are the basic instructions which apply to the cooking of all foods according to our accepted practices.

TO COOK

To prepare food by any of the following methods. While this includes roasting, baking, and broiling, the word usually implies cooking on top of the stove.

TO BAKE

To cook in an enclosed oven in a covered or uncovered heat-proof container. Hot air circulates around the container.

1. When applied to bread baking: The containers are usually open pans, or loaves are placed on baking sheets. See Lesson XIII, Yeast Baking, for basic recipes and variations.

2. When applied to cakes, cookies, pastries, and pies: The containers are usually open pans, molds, or baking sheets. See Lessons X through XIII for basic recipes and variations.

3. When applied to casseroles, pot roasts, and puddings: The containers are either open or closed. Frequently they are closed and then opened for a specified time. See basic recipes following, page 164.

4. When applied to fish and sea food: The containers are usually open. See basic recipes following, page 166.

5. When applied to fruit and vegetables: The containers are either open or closed.

6. When applied to meat, poultry, and game: Baked in an open pan, the process is usually called roasting. See basic recipes and charts, page 180.

7. When applied to soufflés: The container is always open and frequently set into a shallow pan of water. See basic soufflé recipes and variations, page 92.

BASIC RECIPE FOR QUICKLY BAKED CASSEROLES USING COOKED INGREDIENTS: I

- ¾ cup chopped onion
- 3 tablespoons fat, oil, or butter
- 2 cups sliced mushrooms, peppers, or other sliced vegetables
- 2 to 3 cups cooked meat, poultry or fish, in pieces, chunks, or cubes
- 4 tomatoes, peeled and quartered, or canned tomatoes
- About ¼ pound cooked noodles, rice, or pasta, well drained
- 2 to 3 cups thin brown sauce or leftover gravy, or white sauce if poultry or fish is used

In a casserole, sauté onion in fat until golden. Add mushrooms or other vegetables and stir until they are lightly coated with fat. Take from heat and add layers of meat, tomatoes, and/or other ingredients. Top casserole with noodles and pour over gravy or sauce. Cover and bake in 350°F. oven until heated through, about 35 minutes. Casserole may be uncovered for later part of cooking time to brown top, or it can be dotted with butter and baked uncovered. Cheese can be sprinkled over the butter for a gratinéed top. Casseroles can be made up of almost any combinations of ingredients but they must be moistened or contain moist ingredients, such as tomatoes.

BASIC RECIPE FOR LONG-BAKED CASSEROLES USING UNCOOKED INGREDIENTS

3 pounds meat, chicken, or other main ingredient, cut into chunks or quartered
¼ cup butter
½ cup wine or sherry
12 small white onions, peeled
4 carrots sliced, or any other vegetable such as turnip or eggplant
¼ pound mushrooms, quartered
3 tablespoons flour
1 tablespoon tomato paste
2 cups stock or stock and wine
1 herb bouquet
3 tablespoons chopped parsley

In a heavy casserole, brown meat slowly on all sides in 3 tablespoons butter, add wine or sherry, and turn to absorb flavor. Take out meat, add remaining butter and vegetables, and cook, stirring, for 7 minutes. Take from heat, stir in flour, tomato paste, and stock. Stir over low heat for 5 minutes. Return meat to casserole, with herbs, cover tightly, and simmer on top of stove or in oven until meat is tender. Serve from casserole. Sprinkle with chopped parsley.

BASIC OVEN-BAKED POT ROAST

4 to 5 pounds pot roast of beef
2 tablespoons butter
2 large yellow onions, sliced
1 bay leaf
3 parsley sprigs
1 lemon slice, seeded
1 large can tomatoes
1 cup water or red wine
salt and pepper to taste
3 tablespoons flour
¼ cup cold water

Brown beef on all sides in butter in a heavy kettle. Add onions, bay leaf, parsley, lemon, tomatoes, water or wine, and salt and pepper to taste. Cover and bake in slow oven (250°F.) until meat is tender, about 4 hours, or about 50 minutes per pound of meat. Take out meat. Stir flour and water until smooth. Over low heat, stir into the liquid left in the kettle. Simmer until thickened. Correct seasoning and return meat to kettle. Simmer 3 to 4 minutes longer.

BASIC OVEN-BAKED PUDDING

This category covers vegetables, rice, pastas, bread, fish, meat, and sweet puddings. Raw or cooked ingredients are arranged or layered in an open baking dish, barely covered with white or brown sauce or other liquid and baked until pudding is cooked through and browned on top. The pudding is served from the baking pan.

Corn Pudding based on custard: Combine and stir in a buttered oven dish 3 cups tender corn cut from the cob, drained canned corn, or thawed and drained frozen corn, 2 tablespoons each minced onion, parsley, and green pepper, 1 teaspoon each salt and sugar, and ¼ teaspoon pepper. Add 1 cup milk and ½ cup cream beaten with 4 egg yolks. Fold in the 4 stiffly beaten egg whites and pour 2 tablespoons melted butter over top. Bake in a 325°F. oven for 35 minutes or until top is browned and pudding is set.

BASIC PUDDING BASED ON SAUCE—MACARONI PUDDING

Cook macaroni or any preferred pasta according to package directions and drain well. Stir with tomato, meat, or any preferred sauce. Pour into a well-buttered baking dish, dot top with butter, and sprinkle with grated Parmesan cheese. Bake uncovered in a 350°F. oven for about 35 minutes until top is golden. Use at least 1 cup sauce to every 2 cups of cooked pasta.

BASIC BAKED FISH

Fish may be marinated for a short time in herbed and seasoned wine, diluted vinegar, or thinned French dressing. Depending on size, marinate from 30 minutes to 1 hour longer for larger fish.

Arrange whole fish, cut portions, steaks, or split fish in a well-buttered baking pan or on a layer of heavily buttered brown paper. Bake in a 400°F. oven until tender and done. Small whole fish bake about 24 minutes per pound or 1½ minutes per ounce. Large fish, such as cod or haddock, or large fish pieces, bake about 9 to 10 minutes per pound; striped bass and similar fish bake about 12 to 15 minutes per pound. Add about 2 minutes if head is removed.

BARBECUE

To broil meat or poultry slowly on a spit over hot coals or on an outdoor grill. To broil over or under an open heat unit indoors. The foods are usually marinated in and basted with a highly seasoned barbecue sauce.

BASIC RECIPE FOR BARBECUE SAUCE

2 onions, minced
2 cloves garlic, crushed
3 tablespoons butter
2 teaspoons celery seed
2 teaspoons chili powder
2 teaspoons salt
½ teaspoon roughly ground black pepper
1 pinch cayenne, or to taste
½ cup soy sauce
½ cup Worcestershire sauce
½ cup vinegar
½ cup brown sugar or honey
3 cups tomato catsup
3 cups bouillon or water

Sauté onions and garlic slowly in butter in a heavy kettle over low heat for 5 minutes, stirring. Stir dry ingredients into a paste with the soy sauce and stir it into butter in pan. Add remaining ingredients and simmer gently, stirring occasionally, for 20 minutes. Use at once as a marinade for meat or chicken and baste the meat or chicken with the same sauce while it is broiling or spit roasting.

TO BOIL

To cook in liquid in a covered or uncovered container on top of the stove. It is a preliminary stage of cooking of some meats and the only form of cooking for many greens and vegetables. To fricassee usually applies to chicken, veal, or rabbit and means cooking in a small quantity of liquid, which is then used to moisten the white sauce in which the fricasseed meat is served.

For basic boiled beef or chicken, see soup stocks, page 37. For a strong soup stock, place meat or chicken in cold water and bring to a boil. For boiled beef or a juicy chicken and a weaker stock, place meat or chicken in boiling water.

See page 60 for basic fricassee of chicken and blanquette de veau.
See vegetable boiling chart on page 176.
See page 173, to steam.

TO BRAISE

To cook slowly in a tightly covered utensil in a small amount of liquid on top of the stove or in the oven. Braised meats are usually browned in a small quantity of fat before the liquid is added. Braising is often done on a bed of vegetables.

BASIC BRAISED BEEF

3 pounds beef, rump or top round
1 onion, sliced
1 clove garlic, crushed
6 peppercorns
3 tablespoons oil
Salt to taste

4 tablespoons fat or butter
2 carrots, sliced
1 herb bouquet of bay leaf, parsley, and thyme
2 celery stalks
1 cup red or white wine, cider, or tomato juice

Place meat with onion, garlic, peppercorns, oil, salt, and wine in an enameled or china bowl and turn it frequently for 7 hours. Remove meat, dry well, and brown on both sides in fat. Take out the meat and sauté the carrots or any other vegetable lightly in the fat remaining in the pan. Add herb bouquet, celery, and liquid and return the meat to the pan. Add the liquid in which the meat was marinated and enough water to ¼ cover the meat. Cover tightly and braise slowly in a 300° to 325°F. oven for 2½ to 3 hours, basting frequently. Use liquid in pan to moisten a brown sauce, page 100.

Braise other meat, chicken, game or game birds in the same way. Braise until tender.

TO BROIL OR GRILL

To cook over or under direct open heat in broiler oven, portable broiler, infrared broiler, or over charcoal.

BASIC BROILED CHICKEN

Set broiler at 350°F. or moderate. Rub split or quartered broilers with butter and season to taste. Place them skin-side down on greased rack under broiler so that top of broilers will be 3 inches from open flame or heating unit. Turn after 7 to 10 minutes, brush with butter or fat, and continue to turn and brush for 35 to 45 minutes in all until tender and brown. Broil skin-side up for shorter periods than skin-side down.

Variations

1. Brown broilers for 10 minutes on each side, transfer them to a pan, or a casserole. Lay a bacon strip or pat of butter on each piece. Add ½ inch chicken stock, cover, and bake, basting frequently for 30 to 35 minutes, in a 350°F. oven.

2. Place 4 chicken quarters in a bowl, pour over about ¼ cup French dressing, turn, set aside for 20 minutes, turning frequently. Broil as above at 500°F.

3. Brush chicken with maître d'hôtel butter or garlic, curry, mustard, or anchovy butter. Place a teaspoon of butter in cavity when broiling skin-side down. Be sparing with anchovy butter.

4. Sprinkle broilers very lightly with onion juice, lime juice, or curaçao before broiling.

TO PAN BROIL

To cook meats uncovered in a hot, heavy pan without additional fat, or by pouring off all fat as it accumulates.

BASIC PAN-BROILED MEAT

Place meat in hot dry pan and cook uncovered without liquid or fat. If meat is very lean, the pan should be lightly brushed with fat. Turn meat frequently to brown it evenly. If fat accumulates in pan, pour it off as the meat should not fry. Allow half as much time for pan broiling as for oven broiling.

FRYING
(*Panfry or Sauté*)

To cook lightly in an open pan in a small amount of fat over direct heat. Use little fat so that food browns as quickly as possible.

BASIC PANFRYING OR SAUTÉEING

Brown meat on both sides in small amount of fat or fat which comes from the meat itself. If meat is floured or breaded a little additional fat will be needed. Continue to cook lightly, leaving the pan uncovered and turning the meat occasionally until it is done. If fat smokes, turn down heat and add a little more fat. Panfrying is a process that should cook the meat while it is browning. If the meat browns too fast it will be uncooked inside.

TO FRY

To cook uncovered in a heavy pan over direct heat in a shallow layer of fat. The fat can be up to 1 inch deep. Use this method for breaded and coated foods.

BASIC FRIED CHICKEN

Have chicken cut for frying. Weigh chicken pieces and dredge in a mixture of ¼ cup flour, ½ teaspoon each salt and paprika, and ⅛ teaspoon pepper per pound of chicken. Dry dredged chicken pieces for at least 10 minutes. Heat fat in a heavy pan to come to a depth of ½ inch. Start frying the thickest pieces first. Do not crowd the pieces. Turn them to brown all sides evenly. Fry slowly, use 2 pans if necessary, until all pieces are golden, about 15 to 17 minutes. Add 2 to 3 tablespoons chicken stock to the pan, cover it tightly, and continue to cook, turning several times until done, depending on size, about another 10 to 15 minutes. Uncover pan and cook 5 minutes longer.

Use same method for breaded chops and cutlets, Weiner Schnitzel, and Chicken Kiev, reducing cooking time depending on thickness of meat.

TO DEEP-FAT FRY

To cook covered or uncovered in fat, deep enough to submerge the frying food completely. Fat should be at least 5 inches deep. A deep-fat fryer is equipped with a basket to facilitate lowering the food into the fat, and lifting it out when it is completed. Electric deep-fat friers are thermostatically controlled and usually equipped with a temperature chart.

BASIC DEEP-FRIED FOODS

Lower breaded or batter-dipped fish balls, fritters, beignets, chicken pieces, potatoes, or doughnuts into hot fat according to the following schedule. Turn pieces while frying, if necessary. Take out when done, drain and season, or sugar and serve.

Deep-fat Frying Schedule

Fry dredged, breaded, or batter-covered chicken pieces for 12 to 15 minutes at 365°F.

Fry breaded or batter-covered raw shrimp or fish pieces for 3 to 6 minutes at 365°F.

Fry breaded croquettes for about 4 minutes at 365°F.

Fry all fritters at 365°F.

Fry beignets at 365°F. See page 233.

Fry doughnuts and potato chips for 3 minutes at 365°F.

Fry French-fried potatoes for 7 to 8 minutes at 385°F.

TO POACH

To cook slowly in simmering liquid over low heat, or sometimes a low oven. The liquid should barely submerge the poaching food and it should not reach a boil.

BASIC POACHED FISH

Place fish, fish fillets or fish steaks in a single layer in a shallow pan. Barely cover with seasoned liquid. Cover pan and simmer until fish flakes easily—about 5 to 10 minutes.

BASIC POACHED EGGS

Break eggs, one at a time, into simmering water in a shallow pan. Simmer until eggs are set—about 4 minutes. Lift out with a slotted spoon. Trim and serve.

TO ROAST

See To Bake, page 163.

TO STEAM

To cook in a small amount of liquid in a tightly covered kettle so that the food is cooked in the steam. Food cooked on a rack in a covered kettle over simmering water is also steamed. The water does not touch the food. Special kettles with racks are made for steaming asparagus or fish.

Food mixtures placed in a mold are steamed in a covered kettle in boiling water which should reach ½ to ¾ way up the side of the mold. Food is also cooked in steam in a pressure cooker. Food cooked in the upper section of a double boiler over, but not touching, the boiling water is also cooked in steam.

TO STEW

To cook slowly in barely enough, or less, liquid than required to cover the food. The liquid which reduces in cooking then forms the sauce in which the stew is served. A stew should be cooked gently so that meat or fish and vegetables can absorb flavor from each other and from seasonings, herbs, and spices.

BASIC BEEF STEW

(*Boeuf Bourguignon*)

2 pounds stewing beef cut in cubes
2 cups red wine
2 jiggers brandy
2 onions, sliced
2 carrots, sliced
2 celery stalks
1 bay leaf
2 sprigs thyme
6 bruised peppercorns
Salt to taste
1 clove garlic, crushed
Flour for dredging
2 tablespoons fat for searing
3 tablespoons butter
½ pound mushrooms, quartered
24 small white onions, peeled
¼ cup flour for thickening sauce (optional)

Marinate meat for 3 to 4 hours in wine and brandy with onion, carrot, celery, herbs, seasonings, and garlic. Stir meat frequently. Drain meat well, dredge it with flour, and sear it on all sides in fat. Use a heavy kettle or Dutch oven. Drain liquid from vegetables, bring it to a boil, and add it to the seared meat. Fry vegetables in butter until glossy, add mushrooms, and stir until they are transparent, about 3 minutes. Add vegetables and onions to meat, cover and simmer 2 hours. If a thickened sauce is preferred, thicken with flour as in making gravy.

TO TOAST

To brown or dry out in dry heat. Usually applied to breads. Long toasting at a low temperature is also called oven drying and results in very crisp toast, such as melba toast or zweiback.

BASIC DIRECTIONS FOR MAKING TOAST

Use sliced or unsliced bread that is at least 1 to 2 days old. Slice ⅛, ¼, or ½ inch thick and toast in any of the following ways.

Toast ready-sliced bread or bread cut into ⅛- to ½-inch slices in electric toaster in the usual way. Trim off crusts or leave them on as preferred. The bread can also be trimmed before it is toasted. Spread hot toast with soft or melted butter and serve at once.

Variations

1. Sprinkle buttered top with 7 parts sugar combined with 1 part cinnamon, shaved maple sugar, finely minced herbs, or use any flavored butter such as curry or anchovy butter.

2. Arrange bread slices on broiler rack and toast under broiler flame or heat unit until golden. Turn to toast second side. For soft toast, cut bread thicker and toast more quickly in a preheated broiler. For crisper toast, cut bread thinner and turn several times on broiler rack while bread slices are toasting.

3. For melba toast or oven-dried breads, slice bread very thin, brush with melted butter and arrange on a baking sheet in a 250°F. oven. Bread slices will dry out slowly, then suddenly turn evenly brown. Depending on the thickness of the slices, this can take from 30 minutes to an hour; watch after 20 minutes. If oven does not brown evenly, turn baking sheet several times.

VEGETABLE COOKING CHART

Vegetable	Covered or Uncovered	Amount of Water	Approximate Cooking Time in Minutes
Artichokes, Globe	Uncovered	To cover	24–40
Artichokes, Jerusalem	Uncovered	To cover	30–35
**Asparagus*	Uncovered	To cover	10–20
Asparagus tips	Uncovered	To cover	5–12
Beans, green	Uncovered	To cover	18–25
Beans, wax	Uncovered	To cover	15–25
Beans, lima	Uncovered	To cover	20–30
Dried lima	Covered	Large amount	1–2 hours
Dried beans	Covered	Large amount	1–2 hours
Beets, young	Covered	Large amount	15–25
Beets, old	Covered	Large amount	40–60
Beet greens	Uncovered	Large amount	13–15
Broccoli	Uncovered	Large amount	18–19
Brussels sprouts	Uncovered	Large amount	10–15
Cabbage, quartered	Uncovered	Large amount	10–15
Cabbage, shredded	Uncovered	To cover	3–8
Cabbage, red, shredded	Uncovered	To cover	7–14
Carrots, young, sliced	Covered	Small amount	10–15
Carrots, old, sliced	Covered	To cover	15–20
Carrots, young, whole	Covered	Small amount	15–20
Carrots, old, whole	Covered	To cover	20–30
Cauliflower, large	Uncovered	Large amount	18–22
Cauliflower, small	Uncovered	Large amount	15–18
Cauliflower, divided	Uncovered	To cover	12–15
Celery, diced	Uncovered	To cover	15–18
Celery, root	Covered	To cover	20
Chard	Covered	Only as much as clings to leaves after washing	10–12
Chestnuts, peeled	Covered	To cover	20–28
Collards	Uncovered	Large amount	15–18
Corn on cob	Covered	To cover	5–8
Corn kernels	Covered	To cover	3–7

* If asparagus is steamed, cook covered in small amount of water and increase cooking time by about one half.

VEGETABLE COOKING CHART (*Continued*)

VEGETABLE	COVERED OR UNCOVERED	AMOUNT OF WATER	APPROXIMATE COOKING TIME IN MINUTES
Cucumber	Uncovered	To cover	5–10
Eggplant	Covered	Small amount	10–15
Kale	Uncovered	To cover	15–22
Kohlrabi	Uncovered	Large amount	25–30
Leek	Uncovered	Large amount	15–20
Lentils	Covered	Large amount	1–2 hours
Lettuce	Covered	Almost no water	5–7
Mushrooms	Covered	Almost no water	5–8
Okra	Uncovered	To cover	15–20
Onions, small	Uncovered	Large amount	12–18
Onions, large	Uncovered	Large amount	20–25
Onions, scallions	Uncovered	To cover	7–14
Parsnips	Uncovered	To cover	10–20
Peas	Uncovered	Small amount	7–15
Peppers	Uncovered	To cover	5–10
Potatoes, large	Covered	To cover	20–30
Potatoes, medium	Covered	To cover	18–25
Potatoes, quartered	Covered	To cover	15–18
Potatoes, sliced	Covered	To cover	4–6
Radishes	Uncovered	To cover	15–18
Rutabagas	Uncovered	Large amount	20–25
Salsify	Covered	To cover	25–40
Spinach	Covered	Only as much as clings to leaves after washing	4–7
Squash, Hubbard, cubed	Covered	Small amount	20–35
Squash, summer	Covered	Small amount	10–20
Squash, winter	Covered	Small amount	20–25
Sweet Potatoes	Covered	To cover	20–30
Tomatoes, whole	Covered	Very little	5–10
Turnips, whole	Uncovered	Large amount	20–25
Turnips, sliced	Uncovered	Large amount	15–18
Turnip greens	Uncovered	Large amount	18–20

TIME-TABLE FOR ROASTING

Cut	Approx. Weight (Pounds)	Oven Temperature Constant	Interior Temperature When Removed From Oven	Approx. Time (Min. per lb.)
Beef				
Standing rib	6 to 8	300°–325°F.	140°F.(rare)	23 to 25
measures 6 to 7			160°F.(medium)	27 to 30
inches from chine			170°F.(well)	32 to 35
bone to tip of rib	4 to 6	300°–325°F.	140°F.(rare)	26 to 32
			160°F.(medium)	34 to 38
			170°F.(well)	40 to 42
Rolled rib	5 to 7	300°–325°F.	140°F.(rare)	32
			160°F.(medium)	38
			170°F.(well)	48
Delmonico (rib eye)	4 to 6	350°F.	140°F.(rare)	18 to 20
			160°F.(medium)	20 to 22
			170°F.(well)	22 to 24
Tenderloin, whole	4 to 6	425°F.	140°F.(rare)	45 to 60 (total)
Tenderloin, half	2 to 3	425°F.	140°F.(rare)	45 to 50 (total)
Rolled rump (high quality)	4 to 6	300°–325°F.	150°–170°F.	25 to 30
Sirloin tip (high quality)	3½ to 4	300°–325°F.	150°–170°F.	35 to 40
Veal				
Leg	5 to 8	300°–325°F.	170°F.	25 to 35
Loin	4 to 6	300°–325°F.	170°F.	30 to 35
Rib (rack)	3 to 5	300°–325°F.	170°F.	35 to 40
Rolled shoulder	4 to 6	300°–325°F.	170°F.	40 to 45
Pork, Fresh				
Loin				
Center	3 to 5	325°–350°F.	170°F.	30 to 35
Half	5 to 7	325°–350°F.	170°F.	35 to 40
Blade loin or sirloin	3 to 4	325°–350°F.	170°F.	40 to 45
Picnic shoulder	5 to 8	325°–350°F.	185°F.	30 to 35
Rolled	3 to 5	325°–350°F.	185°F.	40 to 45
Cushion style	3 to 5	325°–350°F.	185°F.	35 to 40
Boston Shoulder	4 to 6	325°–350°F.	185°F.	45 to 50
Leg (fresh ham)				
Whole (bone in)	10 to 14	325°–350°F.	185°F.	25 to 30
Whole (boneless)	7 to 10	325°–350°F.	185°F.	35 to 40
Half (bone in)	5 to 7	325°–350°F.	185°F.	40 to 45
Pork, Smoked				
Ham (to be cooked)				
Whole	10 to 14	300°–325°F.	160°F.	18 to 20
Half	5 to 7	300°–325°F.	160°F.	22 to 25
Shank or butt portion	3 to 4	300°–325°F.	160°F.	35 to 40
Ham (fully cooked)*				
Half	5 to 7	325°F.	130°F.	18 to 24
Picnic shoulder	5 to 8	300°–325°F.	170°F.	35
Shoulder roll	2 to 3	300°–325°F.	170°F.	35 to 40
Canadian style bacon	2 to 4	300°–325°F.	160°F.	35 to 40
Lamb				
Leg	5 to 8	300°–325°F.	175°–180°F.	30 to 35
Shoulder	4 to 6	300°–325°F.	175°–180°F.	30 to 35
Rolled	3 to 5	300°–325°F.	175°–180°F.	40 to 45
Cushion	3 to 5	300°–325°F.	175°–180°F.	30 to 35

* Allow approximately 15 minutes per pound for heating whole ham to serve hot.

TIME-TABLE FOR BROILING*

Cut	Weight	Approximate Total Cooking Time: Rare	Approximate Total Cooking Time: Medium
Beef	Pounds	Minutes	Minutes
Chuck steak (high quality)—1 in.	1½ to 2½	24	30
1½ in.	2 to 4	40	45
Rib steak—1 in.	1 to 1½	15	20
1½ in.	1½ to 2	25	30
2 in.	2 to 2½	35	45
Rib eye steak—1 in.	8 ozs.	15	20
1½ in.	12 ozs.	25	30
2 in.	16 ozs.	35	45
Club steak—1 in.	1 to 1½	15	20
1½ in.	1½ to 2	25	30
2 in.	2 to 2½	35	45
Sirloin steak—1 in.	1½ to 3	20	25
1½ in.	2¼ to 4	30	35
2 in.	3 to 5	40	45
Porterhouse steak—1 in.	1¼ to 2	20	25
1½ in.	2 to 3	30	35
2 in.	2½ to 3½	40	45
Ground beef patties 1 in. thick by 3 in.	4 ozs.	15	25
Pork—smoked			
Ham slice—tendered		Ham always	
½ in.	¾ to 1	cooked	10–12
1 in.	1½ to 2	well done	16–20
Canadian style bacon			
¼ in. slices			6–8
½ in. slices			8–10
Bacon			4–5
Lamb			
Shoulder chops—1 in.	5 to 8 ozs.	Lamb chops	12
1½ in.	8 to 10 ozs.	are not usually	18
2 in.	10 to 16 ozs.	served rare	22

* This time-table is based on broiling at a moderate temperature (350°F.). Rare steaks are broiled to an internal temperature of 140°F.; medium to 160°F.; well done to 170°F. Lamb chops are broiled from 170°F. to 175°F. Ham is cooked to 160°F. The time for broiling bacon is influenced by personal preference as to crispness.

TIME-TABLE FOR BROILING (*Continued*)

Cut	Weight	Approximate Total Cooking Time: Rare	Approximate Total Cooking Time: Medium
Lamb	Pounds	Minutes	Minutes
Rib chops—1 in.	3 to 5 ozs.		12
1½ in.	4 to 7 ozs.		18
2 in.	6 to 10 ozs.	Lamb chops	22
Loin chops—1 in.	4 to 7 ozs.	are not usually	12
1½ in.	6 to 10 ozs.	served rare	18
2 in.	8 to 14 ozs.		22
Ground lamb patties 1 in. by 3 in.	4 ozs.		18

TIME-TABLE FOR COOKING IN LIQUID

Cut	Average Weight	Approx. Time Per Pound	Approx. Total Cooking Time
Smoked ham (old style and country cured)	Pounds	Minutes	Hours
Large	12 to 16	20	
Small	10 to 12	25	
Half	5 to 8	30	
Smoked ham (tendered)			
Shank or butt half	5 to 8	20–25	
Smoked picnic shoulder	5 to 8	45	
Fresh or corned beef	4 to 6	40–50	
Beef for stew			2½–3½
Veal for stew			2–3
Lamb for stew			1½–2

TIME-TABLE FOR BRAISING

Cut	Average Weight or Thickness	Approximate Total Cooking Time
Beef		
Pot-Roast	3 to 5 pounds	3–4 hours
Swiss steak	1½ to 2½ inches	2–3 hours
Fricassee	2 inch cubes	1½–2½ hours
Beef birds	½ inch (x 2 in. x 4 in.)	1½–2½ hours
Short ribs	Pieces (2 in. x 2 in. x 4 in.)	1½–2½ hours
Round steak	¾ inch	1–1½ hours
Stuffed steak	½ to ¾ inch	1½ hours
Pork		
Chops	¾ to 1½ inches	45–60 minutes
Spareribs	2 to 3 pounds	1½ hours
Tenderloin		
Whole	¾ to 1 pound	45–60 minutes
Fillets	½ inch	30 minutes
Shoulder steaks	¾ inch	45–60 minutes
Lamb		
Breast—stuffed	2 to 3 pounds	1½–2 hours
Breast—rolled	1½ to 2 pounds	1½–2 hours
Neck slices	¾ inch	1 hour
Shanks	¾ to 1 pound each	1–1½ hours
Shoulder chops	¾ to 1 inch	45–60 minutes
Veal		
Breast—stuffed	3 to 4 pounds	1½–2½ hours
Breast—rolled	2 to 3 pounds	1½–2½ hours
Veal birds	½ inch (x 2 in. x 4 in.)	45–60 minutes
Chops	½ to ¾ inch	45–60 minutes
Steaks or cutlets	½ to ¾ inch	45–60 minutes
Shoulder chops	½ to ¾ inch	45–60 minutes
Shoulder cubes	1 to 2 inches	45–60 minutes

TIME-TABLE FOR COOKING VARIETY MEATS

Kind	Broiled	Braised	Cooked in Liquid
Liver			
Beef			
3- to 4-pound piece		2–2½ hrs.	
Sliced		20–25 mins.	
Veal (Calf), sliced	8–10 mins.		
Pork			
Whole (3 to 3½ pounds)		1½ to 2 hrs.	
Sliced		20–25 mins.	
Lamb, sliced	8–10 mins.		
Kidney			
Beef			1–1½ hrs.
Veal (Calf)	10–12 mins.		¾–1 hr.
Pork	10–12 mins.		¾–1 hr.
Lamb	10–12 mins.		¾–1 hr.
Heart			
Beef			
Whole		3–4 hrs.	3–4 hrs.
Sliced		1½–2 hrs.	
Veal (Calf)			
Whole		2½–3 hrs.	2½–3 hrs.
Pork		2½–3 hrs.	2½–3 hrs.
Lamb		2½–3 hrs.	2½–3 hrs.
Tongue			
Beef			3–4 hrs.
Veal (Calf)			2–3 hrs.
Pork, Lamb } usually sold ready-to-serve			
Tripe			
Beef	10–15 mins.*		1–1½ hrs.
Sweetbreads	10–15 mins.*	20–25 mins.	15–20 mins.
Brains	10–15 mins.*	20–25 mins.	15–20 mins.

* Time required after precooking in water.

POULTRY CHARTS

TIME-TABLE FOR ROASTED CHICKEN

Ready-to-Cook Weight	Oven Temperature	Guide to Total Cooking Time
1½ to 2 lb.	400° F	¾ to 1 hour
2 to 2½ lb.	400° F	1 to 1¼ hours
2½ to 3 lb.	375° F	1¼ to 1¾ hours
3 to 4 lb.	375° F	1¾ to 2¼ hours

TIME-TABLE FOR ROTISSERIED WHOLE CHICKEN

Ready-to-Cook Weight	Guide to Total Cooking Time
1½ to 2 lb.	¾ to 1¼ hours
2 to 2½ lb.	1¼ to 1½ hours
2½ to 3 lb.	1½ to 1¾ hours

TIME-TABLE FOR ROASTED TURKEY

Ready-to-Cook Weight Pounds	Approx. Time at 325°F. Hours	Internal Temp. When Done Degrees F.
6 to 8	3 to 3½	180–185
8 to 12	3½ to 4½	180–185
12 to 16	4½ to 5½	180–185
16 to 20	5½ to 6½	180–185
20 to 24	6½ to 7	180–185

TIME-TABLE FOR ROTISSERIED WHOLE TURKEY

READY-TO-COOK WEIGHT (LBS.)	APPROXIMATE TIME-HOURS	INTERNAL TEMP. WHEN DONE
4 to 6	2 to 3	DEGREES F.
6 to 8	3 to 3½	180–185
8 to 10	3½ to 4	180–185
10 to 12	4 to 5	180–185

FISH CHARTS

BROILING FISH STEAKS

TYPE OF STEAK	THICKNESS	TIME ON 1ST SIDE	TIME ON 2ND SIDE	EXTRA BASTINGS
Cod	½ inch	3 min.	5 min.	1
	1 inch	5 min.	5 min.	1
Salmon	½ inch	3 min.	3 min.	
	1 inch	3 min.	5 min.	
Swordfish	½ inch	3 min.	3 min.	
	1 inch	3 min.	5 min.	
Fresh Tuna	½ inch	3 min.	3 min.	
	1 inch	4 min.	5 min.	
Halibut	½ inch	3 min.	3 min.	1
	1 inch	4 min.	5 min.	1
Striped Bass	½ inch	3 min.	3 min.	1
	1 inch	4 min.	4 min.	1

BROILING WHOLE DRESSED FISH

Name of Fish	Distance from Source of Heat	Time on 1st Side	Time on 2nd Side
Bluefish	3 inches	4 min.	5 min.
Butterfish	3 inches	4 min.	5 min.
Carp (up to 3 lbs.)	6 inches	12 min.	14 min.
Cisco (Lake Herring)	6 inches	4 min.	5 min.
Croaker	6 inches	5 min.	8 min.
Flounder	3 inches	10 min.	White Side up—don't turn
Fluke	3 inches	8 min.	White Side up—don't turn
Mackerel	6 inches	3 min.	5 min.
Mullet	6 inches	5 min.	9 min.
Pike	6 inches	5 min.	8 min.
Porgy	3 inches	3 min.	6 min.
Sea Bass	6 inches	5 min.	6 min.
Swellfish Tails	3 inches	5 min.	6 min.
Weakfish	6 inches	3 min.	5 min.
Whitefish	6 inches	5 min.	8 min.
Whiting	6 inches	4 min.	5 min.

BROILING SPLIT FISH

Name of Fish	Distance from Source of Heat	Thickness of Fish	Broiling Time
Bluefish	3 in.	¾ in.	8 min.
Bonito Mackerel	3 in.	½ to 1½ in.	10 min.
Croaker	2 in.	¾ in.	8 min.
* Carp	6 in.	½ to 1½ in.	12–14 min.
Cisco (Lake Herring)	3 in.	¼ to 1 in.	9–11 min.
Hake	3 in.	1 in.	6–8 min.
Mackerel	2 in.	¾ to 1 in.	8–10 min.
Mullet	3 in.	¼ to 1 in.	10–12 min.
Porgy	3 in.	½ to 1 in.	6–8 min.
* Pike	3 in.	¼ to 1¼ in.	8–10 min.
Sea Bass	3 in.	½ to 1 in.	6–8 min.
Weakfish	2 in.	½ to ¾ in.	6–8 min.
Whitefish	3 in.	½ to 1½ in.	10–12 min.
Whiting	3 in.	¼ to ½ in.	6–8 min.

* Carp and Pike should be basted twice during the broiling period instead of the single basting recommended for the other varieties.

BROILING FISH FILLETS

Name of Fish	Thickness of Fillets Vary from	Baste During Broiling	Broiling Time
Bluefish	¼ to ¾ inch	Once	6 min.
Carp	¼ to 1¼ inch	Once	8–10 min.
Cisco (Lake Herring)	¼ to ½ inch	Once	5–7 min.
Cod	½ to 1 inch	Twice	8–10 min.
Flounder	¼ to ½ inch	Once	5–7 min.
Fluke	¼ to ⅔ inch	Twice	5–8 min.
Haddock	⅓ to ⅔ inch	Twice	5–8 min.
Hake	¼ to ½ inch	Twice	6–8 min.
Mackerel	¼ to 1¼ inch	Once	6–8 min.
Mullet	¼ to ¾ inch	Twice	6–8 min.
Pike	¼ to ⅔ inch	Once	6–8 min.
Pollock	½ to 1 inch	Twice	6–8 min.
Porgy	¼ to ⅝ inch	Twice	6 min.
Sea Bass	¼ to ½ inch	Twice	5 min.
Sole-Lemon	¼ to ¾ inch	Twice	5–8 min.
Sole-Gray	¼ inch usual thickness	Once	5 min.
Weakfish	¼ to ¾ inch	Twice	6 min.
Whitefish	¼ to ¾ inch	Once	6–8 min.
Whiting	¼ to ¾ inch	Twice	5 min.

BAKING FISH

Name of Fish	Thickness	Baking Time Head On	Baking Time Head Off
Small Fish:			
Bluefish	1½ in.	1½ min. per oz.	2 min. per oz.
Butterfish	½ in.	3 min. per oz.	....
Croaker	1½ in.	1½ min. per oz.	2 min. per oz.
Flounder	1 in.	2 min. per oz.	....
Herring	1 in.	1½ min. per oz.	2 min. per oz.
Mackerel	2½ in.	2 min. per oz.	1 min. per oz.
Pike	2¼ in.	1¼ min. per oz.	1 min. per oz.
Porgy	2 in.	1 min. per oz.	1¼ min. per oz.
Sea Bass	1½ in.	1⅔ min. per oz.	2 min. per oz.
Mullet	2 in.	1½ min. per oz.	2 min. per oz.
Weakfish	1½ in.	1⅔ min. per oz.	2 min. per oz.
Whiting	2 in.	1¼ min. per oz.	1½ min. per oz.
Large Fish or Pieces:			
Carp	2½ in.	12 min. per lb.	16 min. per lb.
Cod	2¾ in.	9 min. per lb.	12 min. per lb.
Florida Mackerel	2½ in.	17 min. per lb.	19 min. per lb.
Haddock	3¼ in.	10 min. per lb.	14 min. per lb.
Halibut	2¾ in.	....	11 min. per lb.
Salmon	2¼ in.	....	11 min. per lb.
Spotted Sea Trout	3½ in.	14 min. per lb.	15 min. per lb.
Striped Bass	2½ in.	12 min. per lb.	16 min. per lb.
Whitefish	1½ in.	15 min. per lb.	16 min. per lb.

LESSON IX

BASIC SHORT PASTE

or

Short Crust

Short paste or short crust is best known to us as the shell that contains and covers the pie filling, makes the lid on deep-dish pies, and wraps around turnovers. Although we use it constantly, we rarely see it as it should be, light, crisp, evenly colored, without large bubbles, blisters, or cracks.

Basic short paste is easily made. Once having learned to make it by either of the following methods, the doors will be wide open to a few hundred more recipes. You will be able to make:

1. Hot Appetizers: Small meat turnovers, sausage rolls, cheese sticks.

2. Pies: All types of pies, covered and uncovered, sweet and savory, fruit-filled, meat, and deep-dish pies.

3. Flans and Quiches: All the French specialties, from quiche Lorraine to flan d'apricots.

4. English Pasties: Cornish pastries and savories.

5. Dumplings: Fruits and fillings in pastry, Vienna's Apfel im Schlafrock (a marmalade-filled apple in its dressing gown).

6. Fruit Tarts and Small Pastries: Barquettes, bases, and cups.

7. Wrappers, Blankets, and Pastry Covers: Hams wrapped in crust,

short crust, nut, fruit, or meat strudels. Braids and cups for vegetables and creamed seafood.

There are certain basic rules to be applied in making short paste whether you use the following recipes or your own.

BASIC RULES FOR MAKING SHORT PASTE

Beginners should not double recipe quantities; make two small batches rather than one large one.

Work in the coolest part of the kitchen.

Use regular or plain flour, unless otherwise specified, and sift it well.

Add salt and sugar, if one or both are called for, while sifting. If sugar and an egg or egg yolk are called for, beat the sugar with the egg before incorporating it.

Use chilled or cold fat.

Either *cut* the fat into the flour with two knives or a pastry blender or *rub* it into the flour with the fingertips. Cut or rub the fat into the flour until the mixture resembles coarse meal or breadcrumbs.

Keep the mixture light and cool by working quickly. Lift it out of the bowl while working and let it fall back through the fingers. Do not grind fingers down into the mixture. If the cut-in method is preferred, try the rub-in method at least once to get the *feel* of the paste. The French recommend the rub-in method.

Add iced or very cold water and never use more than 2 tablespoons to 1 cup flour, unless recipe specifically calls for more. Sprinkle most of the water over the flour and fat mixture, then stir quickly with a knife.

Use reserved water to gather the dry crumbs that always remain in the bottom of the bowl. The dough should be dry enough to leave the sides of the bowl clean. When an egg is called for in the recipe, use little or no water.

Knead short paste as little as possible and shape it into a round disk. At this point the dough or paste can be wrapped in an air-tight plastic bag and stored in the refrigerator for three to four days. If it is to be used immediately, rest it under a bowl, covered with a kitchen towel, for 25 to 30 minutes, or chill for 15 minutes in refrigerator.

Use very little flour on pastry board and rolling pin. A pastry canvas and stockinette-covered rolling pin will help.

Flatten disk of dough into a round or oval, as needed, by pressing the rolling pin down across it in several places. Roll dough to desired thickness, usually ⅛ inch.

Roll it with the fewest possible short, light strokes of the rolling pin. All strokes should go in the same direction. Turn dough only if necessary but never turn it over. Brush off all superfluous flour with a pastry brush.

Bake short paste on, or in, ungreased tins unless otherwise specified.

BASIC SHORT PASTE I

A light and flaky short crust for pies, tarts, quiches.

2 cups flour
½ teaspoon salt
⅔ cup vegetable shortening
3 to 4 tablespoons cold water

Sift flour and salt into a bowl, cut in vegetable shortening with a pastry blender or 2 knives, or rub it in with fingertips until mixture resembles coarse meal or rough breadcrumbs. Sprinkle with water and stir with a knife until mixture starts to gather. Gather into a ball, leaving the bowl clean, place ball on lightly floured board, and knead gently until smooth. Do not knead more than absolutely necessary. Cover with a bowl and rest dough for ½ hour in a cool place before using. Or wrap in plastic and store in refrigerator up to 1 week.

SWEET CRUST

Prepare basic short paste I as above, omitting the water. When shortening has been cut into the flour and the mixture resembles breadcrumbs, set it aside. Beat 2 tablespoons sugar with 1 egg until sugar is dissolved. Pour over the dry mixture in the bowl and stir with a knife. Continue as for basic short paste I.

QUICK CRUST

Use same ingredients as basic short paste I. Sift flour and salt into a bowl. Take away 3 tablespoons of this flour and place in a second bowl with the vegetable shortening and water. Stir for 30 seconds, then add remaining flour, and stir into a dough. Place dough on lightly floured board and knead lightly until smooth. Do not knead more than absolutely necessary.

BASIC SHORT PASTE II

(*Sweetened*)

1 egg
2 tablespoons sugar
2 cups flour
½ teaspoon salt
½ cup, 8 tablespoons, cold butter, thinly sliced
3 tablespoons vegetable shortening

Beat egg and sugar in a cup and set aside. Sift flour and salt into a cool bowl. Cut in butter and vegetable shortening with 2 knives or a pastry blender, or rub in with the fingers until the mixture resembles breadcrumbs. Beat egg and sugar once more and pour over the mixture. Stir quickly with a knife until the crumbs gather into a rough dough. Gather it with the fingers, knead lightly, and shape into a ball. Cover ball with a kitchen towel and refrigerate for 45 minutes, or wrap in plastic and refrigerate up to 4 days. Bake an empty pie or tart shell in a 450°F. oven for about 12 minutes. Bake a filled tart for about 20 minutes or until edges are browned.

Variations

FOR 2-CRUST, 10-INCH PIE

Follow basic instructions for preparation, pages 190 and 191.

1. 3 cups flour sifted with:
   1½ teaspoons salt

18 tablespoons vegetable shortening
(1 cup and 2 tablespoons)
6 tablespoons ice water

2. 2 cups flour sifted with:
1 teaspoon salt
⅔ cup lard
4½ tablespoons ice water

3. 2½ cups flour sifted with:
1 teaspoon salt
6 tablespoons butter
6 tablespoons lard
4 tablespoons ice water

4. 2 cups flour sifted with:
1 teaspoon salt
2 tablespoons sugar
5 tablespoons butter
1 egg yolk
1½ tablespoons ice water

5. 2 cups flour sifted with:
¾ teaspoon salt and
¾ teaspoon baking powder
⅔ cup lard beaten into:
⅓ cup boiling water

When lard-water mixture is cool, sift flour mixture over it and stir, then knead into a smooth dough.

6. 2¼ cups flour sifted with:
½ teaspoon salt
10 tablespoons lard
5 to 6 tablespoons cold orange juice

7. 2½ cups flour sifted with:
½ teaspoon salt
¾ cup butter
2 egg yolks
2 tablespoons apple cider
2 tablespoons lemon juice

8. 1 cup flour
   ½ cup cold butter
   4-ounce package, room temperature, cream cheese
   Work into a smooth paste.

9. 1 cup flour
   ½ cup butter
   4-ounce package cream cheese
   1 egg yolk
   Work into a smooth paste.

10. Cheese crust for chicken, apple, or other pies.
    1⅔ cup flour stirred with:
    1 cup grated cheese
    ½ teaspoon salt, depending on saltiness of cheese
    ½ cup vegetable shortening
    4 tablespoons ice water
    ½ teaspoon paprika (optional)

11. Hot water crust for molded and raised pies. Can be unmolded. Use only for long-baked meat and pork pies.
    ⅔ cup flour sifted with:
    ½ teaspoon salt
    1 egg yolk, dropped into a well in the flour and covered with flour
    3 ounces vegetable shortening brought to a boil and melted in:
    ½ cup water
    Pour into flour, mix with a wooden spoon until smooth. Knead until smooth. Chill for 30 minutes.

Faults and How to Avoid Them

Tough pastry or hard and brittle crust. This is most often due to over-handling, over-kneading, or over-rolling. It can also be caused by too much water or too little fat.

Too soft or too much crumbing. Too much fat, too little water, or the wrong type of flour. Use plain flour, well sifted.

Too pale pastry is either not baked long enough or baked at too low a temperature.

Too dark pastry is baked too long or baked in too hot an oven.

When pastry sinks or shrinks it was either stretched too much in rolling or the filling is too moist. Sinking may also be due to too little filling, or when a chilled pie crust is placed over a hot filling.
Where sides of "blind" or empty pie shells fall in, the pastry was either too soft or the cherry pits or baking beans were not piled against the sides of the shell.
Undissolved sugar will make marks on a short crust, and too much sugar in the filling will make the crust soggy.

Hints for Successful Short Crust Pieces

1. When sealing edges, or adding decorations, brush egg only on one surface. Leave second surface dry.
2. Do not try to make ½ recipe short crust. If less than 1 recipe is needed, store the unneeded portion in refrigerator or bake a "blind" shell to store in freezer until needed.
3. Do not grease or butter tins in which or on which short crust will be baked.
4. Kneading short crust is done with fingertips, not with the heel of the hand, as in bread kneading.
5. Bake any small amount of leftover pastry.

Uses for Short Crust

Note: Roll short crust to about ⅛-inch thickness for tarts that will be removed from pan and to about ⅛-inch thickness for pies that will remain in pan.

BASIC UNCOOKED BERRY OR STEWED FRUIT TARTS

Roll out 1 recipe chilled short crust paste II on a lightly floured board. Cut into 36 2-inch rounds or 18 4-inch rounds with a fluted cookie cutter. Invert the rounds and line 18 2½-inch muffin tins or 36 1½-inch miniature muffin tins with them. Use "non-stick" tins if possible. Press paste into the tins with rounded handle of a kitchen spoon. If large tarts are preferred, divide paste in half and use it to line 2

8-inch spring forms or flan rings or layer cake pans with removable bottoms. Flute the edges and line tarts with waxpaper. Fill with cherry pits or baking beans, place on a baking sheet, and bake "blind" in a 450°F. oven for 15 minutes. Remove pits or beans and paper, reduce heat to 350°F. and bake 10 to 15 minutes longer or until lightly browned. Cool, take from tins or rings, and transfer gently to wire rack.

Fill cold tart shells with a ¼-inch deep layer of pastry cream, page 197, and arrange 1 to 1½ pounds fresh hulled strawberries with pointed ends up, or raspberries or blackberries with rounded ends up, on the pastry cream. Spoon 1 to 1½ cups melted, sieved strawberry, raspberry, or blackberry jam over the fruit. Cool, chill, and serve plain or with sweetened whipped cream piped onto the center of the tart.

Variations

1. Grape Tart: Substitute ripe green seedless grapes for the berries and spoon over a mixture of half melted apple and half red currant jelly.

2. Apricot (Flan d'Apricot), Peach, Plum, or Cherry Tarts: Line tart shells with pastry cream and cover with a layer of apricot, peach, or plum halves, placed cut side down on the cream. Pitted cherries should be placed rounded side up. Spoon melted apricot, peach, or plum jam or cherry jelly over them. For small tarts use individual half apricots or peaches. For large tarts arrange the fruit close together or overlapping or fill with overlapping sliced peaches.

3. Alternate Fruit Fillings: Start with a border of apricot halves, then a circle of pitted cherries, and a center of sliced peaches. Use any combination of fresh berries or stewed fruit.

4. Chestnut Tart: Spread baked tart shell with sweetened chestnut purée, canned or homemade, stirred until smooth with a little heavy cream and flavored with rum or brandy to taste. Pipe sweetened whipped cream on the top and decorate with whole or halved marrons glacé.

5. Pumpkin Pie: Cook in the top of a double boiler over boiling water until thick, 2 cups canned pumpkin, ⅓ cup sugar, ⅔ cup brown sugar, 1 tablespoon dark molasses, grated rind of 1 orange, ½ teaspoon ground cinnamon, 2 eggs, beaten, and 1 cup scalded light cream. Cool and beat in 1 tablespoon brandy. Pour mixture into large baked tart shell, chill, and decorate tops with pecan halves and rosettes of piped whipped cream.

OPEN CREAM TARTS OR PIES

Fill baked and cooled tart shells with any of the following custard-type cream fillings or cream combinations. After creams are chilled and set, decorate tops with short crust cutouts, baked on a separate baking sheet, or decorate with rosettes of piped whipped cream. For some cream tarts, beat the egg whites into a meringue, page 263, with 1 tablespoon sugar per egg white and pile or pipe it onto the cream filling. Brown the meringue lightly in a 325°F. oven for about 15 minutes.

BASIC CREAM FILLING FOR BAKED TART AND PIE SHELLS

FOR AN 8- TO 9-INCH PIE

1½ cups milk
⅓ cup flour
¼ teaspoon salt
9 tablespoons sugar
4 egg yolks
2 tablespoons butter
½ teaspoon vanilla or almond extract

FOR A 10- TO 11-INCH PIE

2¼ cups milk
½ cup flour
¼ teaspoon salt
¾ cup sugar
6 egg yolks
3 tablespoons butter
1 teaspoon vanilla or almond extract

Scald milk and gradually stir it into the flour and salt and ⅔ of the sugar in the top of a double boiler, over boiling water. Continue stirring until the mixture thickens. Cover and cook, stirring occasionally, 10 minutes longer. Beat egg yolks with remaining ⅓ of the sugar until light and creamy. Take milk mixture from heat and stir a little of it into the yolks. Gradually stir the yolk mixture back into the milk and set it back over the boiling water. Stir with a French wire whisk until smooth, thick, and light, about 3 to 4 minutes. Pour cream into a cool bowl and beat in butter and vanilla or other flavoring.

Use about 3 cups of any cream filling for an average 9-inch tart shell or pie shell.

Variations

1. Butterscotch Cream Filling: Substitute ⅔ cup dark brown sugar, tightly packed, for the 9 tablespoons sugar in the basic cream filling recipe for an 8- to 9-inch pie. Beat in 4 instead of 2 tablespoons butter.
2. Chocolate Cream Filling: Flavor basic cream tart or pie filling with 2 squares semisweet chocolate melted slowly over hot water. Add the melted chocolate to the scalded milk. Increase sugar to taste. Decorate top with whipped cream and shaved chocolate curls.
3. Coconut Cream Filling I: Add 1 cup shredded coconut to basic cream filling. If preferred, divide coconut in half, add half to the filling and sprinkle the other half on the cream. Broil the finished pie about 6 inches from heat unit until coconut turns brown, 2 to 3 minutes.
4. Coconut Cream Filling II: Divide as above, add half the coconut to the filling. Beat 4 egg whites stiff with 4 tablespoons sugar. Pile the meringue onto the pie, sprinkle over the remaining half of the coconut, and bake for 3 to 4 minutes in a 425°F. oven or until meringue and coconut are lightly browned.
5. Coffee Cream Filling: Flavor basic cream tart or pie filling with 2 tablespoons instant coffee stirred into the scalded milk. Increase sugar to taste. Decorate top with whipped cream and roasted coffee beans.

LEMON MERINGUE PIE FILLING

Prepare and bake a 9-inch pie shell and set it aside to cool.

½ cup cornstarch
⅓ cup cold water
1½ cups sugar
4 eggs, separated
½ cup lemon juice
grated rind of 2 lemons
¼ cup soft salt butter
¼ teaspoon salt
½ cup sugar

Stir cornstarch and water into a smooth paste. In a heavy saucepan, or upper section of a double boiler, boil sugar with 1½ cups water until sugar is melted. Reduce heat to a slow boil and gradually stir in cornstarch paste. Continue stirring until mixture is thick and clear. Take from heat, beat egg yolks and lemon juice together, and gradually stir them into the cornstarch. Set saucepan over boiling water or over lower section of double boiler over boiling water and stir constantly until mixture is thickened and smooth. Stir in lemon rind, butter, and salt and cool. Beat egg whites until half stiff. Gradually add the sugar and continue to beat until stiff. Pour lemon filling into baked crust. Spread the meringue over the cooled filling, spreading it up to the edges, and bake in a 325°F. oven until lightly browned, about 15 minutes.

BASIC CHIFFON CREAM FILLING FOR TARTS AND PIES

1½ cups milk or light cream, scalded
1 envelope gelatin
¼ cup liquid—fruit juice, sherry, milk, or water
3 eggs, separated
½ cup sugar
1 teaspoon flavoring, coffee extract, vanilla, or almond extract
¾ cup heavy cream, whipped

Scald milk in top of double boiler over boiling water. Stir gelatin into the ¼ cup liquid and set it aside to soften for 15 minutes. Beat yolks with sugar until light and creamy. Gradually beat a part of the hot scalded milk or cream into the yolk mixture, then stir the yolk mixture back into the milk and set it back over the boiling water. Add the lump of gelatin and stir until it is dissolved and the cream is thickened. Take from heat, add flavoring, and cool. When it is cold, but before the gelatin starts to set, fold in the 3 stiffly beaten egg whites and the whipped cream. Pour the mixture into a 9-inch baked tart or pie shell. Chill and decorate the top with whipped cream.

BASIC LEMON CHIFFON CREAM FILLING

1 envelope gelatin
9 tablespoons lemon juice
1 cup sugar, or to taste
4 eggs, separated
1 teaspoon grated lemon rind
1 cup heavy cream, whipped

Stir gelatin into 4 tablespoons lemon juice and set aside for 15 minutes. Beat remaining lemon juice, sugar, and egg yolks in the top of a double boiler, off the heat, until light and creamy. Set in lower section of double boiler, over boiling water, and continue to stir until smooth and thickened. Stir in the lump of gelatin and grated rind until gelatin is dissolved. Take mixture from heat and cool. Fold in the stiffly beaten egg whites and the whipped cream. Pour into a 9-inch tart or pie shell and chill. When chiffon cream is set, decorate top with whipped cream, pastry cutouts, or diced candied lemon, orange, or grapefruit peel.

BASIC FRESH FRUIT AND BERRY PIES

Make 1 recipe short paste I. Prepare fruit. Heat oven to 425°F. and roll out a little more than half the paste to ⅛-inch thickness on a lightly floured board. Invert a 9-inch pie pan over the paste and cut the paste to a circle, about 1 inch larger than the pie pan. Lift the paste with the pan, turn it over and press it gently into the pan. Turn in the edge and chill the shell for at least 30 minutes.

When the chart calls for flour, sprinkle half of it into the chilled shell, cover it with half the fruit, and sprinkle over remaining flour and half the sugar and spices. Add remaining fruit and sprinkle over remaining sugar and spices. Dot with butter and sprinkle with about 1 tablespoon water for every ½ pound of fruit. Add any further ingredients, such as grated lemon rind. Roll out chilled top crust, transfer it to the pie, pinch the edges together firmly, and flute them attractively. Brush top with melted butter, milk, cream, or ice water; cut vents for steam to escape. If desired, sprinkle top with a little sugar. Set pan on a baking sheet and bake 10 minutes. Reduce heat to 350°F. and bake until brown and done, about 40 minutes longer. Serve warm or cold with cream, ice cream, or sharp cheese. Pies served with vanilla ice cream are called à la mode.

FRUIT AND BERRY PIES

Name	Crust	Fillings	Additions to Be Mixed with Fruit	Preparation of Filling	Sugar and Spices	Serve
Apple Pie I	Basic I Any Method	1½ pounds cooking apples	1½ tablespoons water, 1 teaspoon lemon juice, grated rind of 1 lemon	Peel, core, and cut apples into thick slices	6 tablespoons sugar	Warm with sharp cheese
Apple Pie II	Basic II Variation 4	8 tart apples, 4 paper-thin lemon slices	1½ tablespoons flour, 1½ tablespoons butter, 1 tablespoon water	Peel, core, and slice apples, combine with lemon slices	⅔ cup sugar, ⅛ teaspoon ground cinnamon	À la mode
Apple Pie III	Basic I	6 cooking apples, ¼ cup raisins, ¼ cup slivered almonds	2 tablespoons bread-crumbs, 1½ teaspoons butter, 1 tablespoon water	Peel, core and, slice apples. Soak raisins in water for 2 hours, drain before using.	¾ cup brown sugar	With heavy cream or whipped cream
Apricot Pie	Basic I Variation 9	4 cups quartered apricots. Almonds out of cracked apricot pits. Use nutcracker.	2 tablespoons flour, 1 tablespoon butter, 1 tablespoon water	Cut apricots down natural cleft, twist to open, take out pit. Cut halves in two.	¾ cup white or brown sugar	Cold with whipped cream
Blackberry Pie	Basic I	3 cups hulled blackberries	⅛ teaspoon salt, water to cover, 2 tablespoons flour, 1 tablespoon butter	Cook blackberries in water with salt for 15 minutes, drain, add flour, butter, and sugar as basic recipe.	½ cup	Warm or cold with clotted cream
Blueberry Pie	Basic I	3 cups blueberries	1 tablespoon flour, ⅛ teaspoon salt, 1 teaspoon butter, 1 teaspoon lemon juice	Pick over berries, remove stems.	½ cup	Warm, à la mode
Cherry Pie	Basic I Lattice Top	1 quart sour cherries	3 tablespoons flour, 1 tablespoon melted butter, 1 teaspoon lemon juice, ½ teaspoon almond extract	Pit cherries, retain all cherry juice, and add.	1¼ cups	Cold or warm

FRUIT AND BERRY PIES (*Continued*)

Name	Crust	Fillings	Additions to Be Mixed with Fruit	Preparation of Filling	Sugar and Spices	Serve
Cranberry Pie	Basic I Lattice Top	2 cups cranberries, ½ cup raisins, soaked in water for 2 hours and drained.	1½ tablespoons flour, ½ cup water	Cook cranberries with the sugar and flour in ½ cup water for 10 minutes. Cool, pour into chilled shell with drained raisins.	1 cup sugar	Warm, à la mode
Huckleberry Pie	Basic I	4 cups	2 tablespoons flour, 2 tablespoons water, 1 teaspoon butter	Pick over fruit	½ cup	À la mode
Peach Pie	Basic II	4 cups sliced peaches, almonds out of cracked peach pits. Use nutcracker.	1½ tablespoons flour, 2 tablespoons water, 1 teaspoon butter	Scald peaches, draw off skins, halve, remove stones, slice peaches.	¼ cup sugar, ¼ cup brown sugar	Warm or cold, à la mode
Plum Pie	Basic I	2 pounds ripe blue plums	1½ tablespoons flour, 2 tablespoons water, 2 tablespoons plum juice, 1 pinch salt, 1 teaspoon butter	Cut plums in half, remove pits, cut halves into quarters.	½ cup sugar, ⅛ teaspoon ground cinnamon	Warm or cold, with sweetened whipped sour cream
Quince and Apple Pie	Basic I	½ pound quinces, 1 pound apples	1½ tablespoons flour, 2 tablespoons water, 2 teaspoons orange juice	Peel and core quinces and apples. Slice	½ cup brown sugar	Warm with sharp cheese
Raspberry Pie	Basic I	1 pound raspberries or half raspberries and half currants	1 tablespoon flour 2 tablespoons raspberry juice or water 1 teaspoon butter	Pick over fruit	½ cup, more if currants are used	Cold with heavy cream
Rhubarb Pie	Basic I	4 cups ½-inch lengths cut rhubarb	1 cup rusk or breadcrumbs, 2 tablespoons butter, 1 beaten egg, grated rind of 1 lemon	Brown crumbs in butter, combine cut rhubarb with egg, add crumbs, sugar, and lemon rind	1 cup	Warm or cold

BASIC DRIED FRUIT AND MINCEMEAT FILLINGS FOR PIES

Dried fruits can be soaked in water to cover, drained, and used as pie fillings, or they can be simmered until softened before they are used. Others are used without soaking or simmering.

Prepare basic short crust paste for the shell as for fruit pies. Fill and cover with the top crust and bake as fruit pies, page 200.

DRIED FRUIT AND MINCEMEAT PIES

Name	Crust	Fillings	Additions to Be Mixed with Fruit	Preparation of Filling	Sugar and Spices	Serve
Dried Apricot Pie	Basic I	1 pound dried apricots		Prepare apricots according to package directions. Purée to obtain 3 cups.	Sugar to taste	Warm
Date Pie	Basic I	2 cups pitted, chopped dates	3 tablespoons orange juice, ½ cup cream, 1 tablespoon brandy or rum	Boil dates in water to cover until soft, drain and crush into a thick paste, add all ingredients.	¼ cup or to taste	Cold
Fig Pie	Basic I	1 pound dried figs, chopped	1 lemon peel, diced, 1 clove, 1 tablespoon lemon juice, 2 tablespoons brandy or rum	Boil figs with lemon peel and clove for 3 to 5 minutes. Mash with other ingredients.	¼ cup or to taste	Warm with whipped cream
Mince Pie	Basic I Variation Cheese	3 cups prepared mincemeat	½ cup prune or orange juice or cider, 1 jigger brandy	Stir mincemeat and liquid together		Warm with brandy hard sauce
Mince Pies (individual)	Basic I Variation 2, cut 24 fluted rounds, lattice tops	1½ pounds prepared mincemeat, drained		Fill mincemeat into individual tarts, put on cutouts or lattice tops, reduce baking time to half		Warm with brandy hard sauce
Prune Pie	Basic I	1 pound dried prunes	1 teaspoon grated lemon rind, 3 tablespoons apricot jam	Prepare according to package directions, purée to obtain 2 cups.	⅔ cup or to taste	Warm with sweetened whipped sour cream
Raisin Pie	Basic I Lattice Top	1½ cup raisins, ¼ cup chopped candied orange rind	3 tablespoons orange juice, 4 tablespoons flour, 1 beaten egg, 1 tablespoon grated lemon rind	Soak raisins in 2 cups cider or water for 3 hours. Add all other ingredients and cook over boiling water for 15 minutes.	¾ cup	Warm with orange-flavored hard sauce

BASIC OPEN BAKED PIE

Pour cooked or uncooked filling into chilled pie shell, bake as pecan pie.

PECAN PIE FILLING

½ cup brown sugar
1 tablespoon flour
1 cup dark corn syrup
3 eggs
¼ teaspoon salt
1 tablespoon melted butter
1 teaspoon vanilla
1 cup roughly chopped pecans
½ cup pecan halves

Line a 9-inch pie pan with basic short crust pastry, brush bottom of shell with egg white, and chill for 30 minutes. Mix sugar, flour, corn syrup, eggs, salt, and melted butter. Flavor with vanilla and add roughly chopped pecans. Pour mixture into the chilled shell and sprinkle top with pecan halves. Bake in a 450°F. oven for 10 minutes, reduce heat to 350°F., and bake 35 minutes longer. Serve warm or cold with whipped cream.

BASIC DEEP DISH PIES

Fill a very well buttered deep baking dish with fresh fruit or cooked dried fruit. Either mix sugar to taste with the fruit or mix sugar with 1 tablespoon cornstarch and dissolve it in ½ cup fruit juice or water and mix it with the fruit. Roll out ½ recipe basic short crust pastry I. Cut large vents in the center, moisten the edge of the baking dish, and press the pastry well down onto it. Fold back the ½-inch edge and flute it against the edge. Bake in 450°F. oven for 10 minutes, reduce heat to 350°F., and bake 35 minutes longer. Place a funnel in one of the vents and pour ½ cup heavy cream into the pie.

TURNOVERS, TRIANGLES, RINGS, AND DUMPLINGS

Follow basic recipe for short crusts and fruit fillings or use sliced or whole apples. Do not use fillings that are too moist or liquid. Roll out pastry, cut it in squares, triangles, rounds, or oblongs and fill with whole fruit, thick jams or marmalades, mincemeat, or any thick puréed fruit. Moisten one edge of the paste with water, fold over the other half, and press together firmly to form triangles, half rounds, or any desired shape. Brush the top with egg white, cream, or ice water, cut small vents and bake on a baking sheet in a 375°F. oven for about 14 to 21 minutes. Serve with hard sauce, whipped cream, or à la mode.

APPLE DUMPLINGS

(*Wiener Apfel im Schlafrock*)

Prepare 1 recipe short crust pastry and divide into 3 equal pieces. Roll out each piece to as large a round as possible and cut the round in half. Arrange 6 small peeled and cored apples on the 6 half-rounds, placing them just in from the center of the long cut edge. Fill the core of the apples with orange marmalade, raisins, and almonds and fold the pastry around them. Pinch the edges firmly, seal with egg white, and top with a scalloped round of paste cut from the scraps. Brush with egg white, milk, or ice water, sprinkle with sugar, and bake in a 400°F. oven for 25 to 35 minutes. Serve with hard sauce or heavy cream.

BASIC CHICKEN PIE

Simmer quartered broilers for 20 to 25 minutes, as for basic boiled chicken, page 37. Boil small white onions and quartered carrots until they are half soft, about 10 minutes, depending on size. Hardcook eggs, make a white sauce of the chicken stock, page 49, and prepare basic short crust pastry I, variation 12 with cheddar cheese. Draw skin from broilers and remove the largest bones. Arrange the pieces in a wide, shallow baking dish with onions and carrots between. Slice or quarter the hardcooked eggs but hold them intact; do not separate the pieces. Lay them between the chicken pieces in such a way that they cannot spread open. This is to prevent the yolk from boiling into the sauce. Pour over the white sauce. Cover with a layer of cheese crust, rolled out to a little more than ¼-inch thickness. Cut rounds and petal shapes from scraps and attach them to the crust with egg white. Cut vents and brush top with beaten egg. Bake in a 425°F. oven for 10 minutes. Reduce heat to 375°F. and bake until crust is golden, 35 to 45 minutes longer.

BEEF AND KIDNEY PIE

Prepare 1 recipe short crust paste and chill until needed. Combine and place in a deep pie dish, or cook in a kettle and then pour into a pie dish, 2 pounds steak, cut into thick strips, and about 6 ounces beef kidney, trimmed and cubed. Add 1 medium onion, chopped, ¼ pound mushrooms, quartered, and enough strong beef stock to half cover. Cover the kettle or pie dish closely and bake in a 350°F. oven for 1½ hours. Take from heat and cool. Drain off any remaining liquid and use it in making 1 recipe basic brown sauce. Add bouillon to obtain the necessary amount of liquid. Transfer the beef and half the brown sauce to a deep pie dish, if it was cooked in a kettle, and cover with the pastry, rolled out to ¼-inch thickness. Cut a hole in the center, cut decorations out of the trimmings, brush them with beaten egg, and press them on the surface of the pie. Brush pie with egg and bake in a 375°F. oven for 45 minutes until golden. Serve with additional brown sauce.

Variations

1. The pie can be stretched into a buffet party pie by the addition of small white onions, green peas, more mushrooms, and minced parsley.
2. Chunks of cooked ham and strips of veal can be substituted for the steak and kidneys.

CHEESE STICKS

Prepare and roll out short crust paste I, variation 12, and sprinkle half the paste with ¼ cup grated Parmesan cheese, fold over as puff paste, page 213, chill, and roll out again. Cut into strips with a pastry wheel and brush with beaten egg. Sprinkle again with cheese and salt and bake in a 375°F. oven for 9 to 11 minutes until browned.

QUICHE LORRAINE

Line an 8- to 8½-inch layer cake pan with basic short crust paste I, variation 3. Chill for at least 30 minutes or up to 24 hours. Cut 6 slices chilled bacon into small dice with kitchen scissors. Fry dice over medium heat until transparent and lightly browned. Drain on absorbent paper. Cut 6 slices imported Swiss cheese into dice and spread them over bottom of chilled pastry shell. Spread drained bacon evenly over the cheese. Beat 4 eggs, 2 tablespoons flour, 1 teaspoon salt, and 2 cups heavy cream until smooth, pour into the shell, and bake in a 375°F. oven for about 20 minutes. Reduce heat to 325°F. and bake until quiche is puffed and brown and custard is set, about 30 minutes longer.

Variations

1. Onion and Mushroom Quiche: Follow above directions substituting 6 white onions, thinly sliced and separated into rings, for the cheese and 2 cups finely sliced mushrooms for the bacon. Sauté onions in 2 tablespoons butter for 5 minutes until transparent. Transfer them to the chilled shell with a slotted spoon. Sauté mushrooms in the same butter until glossy and lightly browned. Transfer them to the shell and pour over them the cream-and-egg mixture.
2. Shrimp Quiche: Cook 1 pound shelled and deveined shrimp in salted water for 3 minutes. Drain well and cool. Spread them in the chilled shell with ¼ cup sliced stuffed olives, 2 tablespoons chopped onion, and 2 tablespoons chopped chives or parsley. Pour over the cream-and-egg mixture.
3. Crabmeat Quiche: Fill chilled shell with 1 pound picked-over crabmeat, ¼ cup diced tomatoes, 2 tablespoons each diced green pepper, pimento, parsley, and onion.

LESSON X

BASIC FLAKY PASTRY, PUFF PASTRY, AND YEAST BAKING

Constructing flaky pastry and puff pastry is an architectural problem. The thinnest possible layers of dough should enclose minimum layers of fat and the maximum amount of air. The layers have to be crisp and the pastry should rise from a modest one-third or one-half inch to an imposing three inches. It should not only rise, it should rise straight up into the air without being tilted or lopsided. On top of all that, it should be evenly browned, glossy, and dry inside. It may not shrink, run, lean, sog, or harden. Also, it should not burn on the bottom.

There are excellent recipes for making it, but no amount of written directions can produce that perfect croissant the first time. Flaky pastry and puff pastry have to be *seen* and not just *read* about. We give you another one of those written recipes, but we accompany it with what every young architect needs, a detailed blueprint, a working drawing. If you have a flexible metal rule or yardstick, a free afternoon and the blueprint, you can make napoleons, pigs' ears or palmiers, vol-au-vent shells, cream horns, and croissants. More important, you can roll out a thin sheet of puff pastry to wrap around a filet of beef and produce that filet Wellington as it really should be.

We may call it flaky pastry and puff pastry but what it really is, is an achievement.

BASIC FLAKY PASTRY

2 cups fat—vegetable shortening, or butter
5⅓ cups flour
1 teaspoon salt
18 tablespoons ice water
1 teaspoon brandy, or all water

Divide fat into 4 equal parts of ¼ cup or 4 tablespoons each and chill.

Sift flour and salt into a bowl and cut in or rub in (see basic short paste recipe, page 191) a quarter section of the fat until the mixture resembles coarse meal or breadcrumbs.

Add water and brandy, all at once, and stir in quickly with a knife blade into a rough paste.

Knead, on a very lightly floured board, until smooth. Wrap in a cloth and rest in a cool place, or in warmest part of refrigerator, for 20 minutes. Roll dough out, away from you, on a lightly floured board into a rectangle ¼-inch thick. Follow dimensions Figure 1 in "Blueprint" 1, Method I. Page 211.

Mark the dough across with lightest possible lines, dividing it into 3 even pieces, see Figure 2 in "Blueprint" 1, Method I. Brush off all excess flour.

Dot the second ¼ section of the fat over the center and bottom thirds of the dough, leaving a margin of ¾ inch of plain dough on all sides. See Figure 3 in "Blueprint" 1, Method I.

Fold the plain top third of the dough down over the center third and fold the bottom third up over the top. Making three layers of dough and 2 layers of fat. Press the edges down firmly to seal in the fat and air. The uncut edge, called the *fold,* will be facing you, see Figures 2 through 5 in "Blueprint" 1, Method I. Wrap dough again without bending it and chill for 20 minutes.

Return dough to lightly floured board and give it a half turn in a clockwise direction. This means that the *uncut* fold A which was facing you when you finished the first folding should now be at your left hand, Figures 5 and 6.

Roll dough out away from you again and dot again with the third ¼ section of fat, repeating Figures 1 through 5. Fold and seal as previously and wrap and chill for 20 minutes.

Return dough to lightly floured board and give it a half turn. The *fold* should now be opposite you. Figures 6 through 11 illustrate the clockwise turns. Dot dough again with the fourth and last ¼ section of fat. Fold and seal as previously and wrap and chill for 20 minutes.

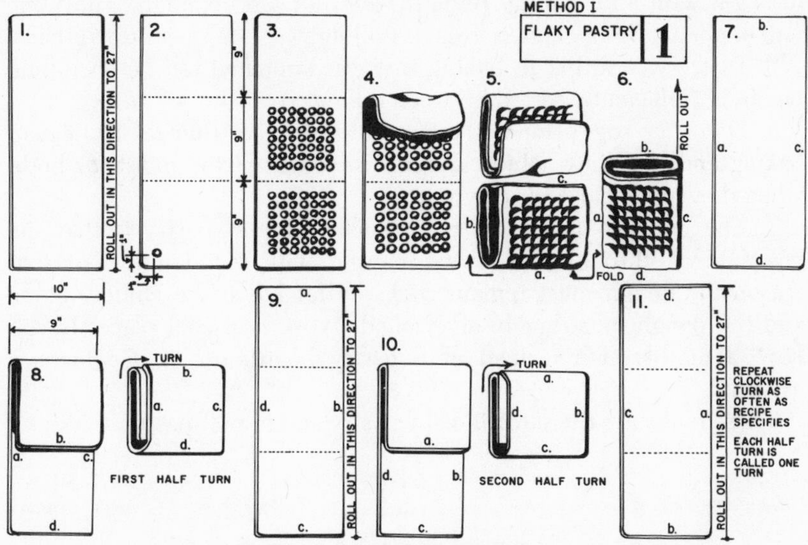

The last *turn* and *fold* is a dry operation. The *fold* should now be on your right. Roll out the dough, fold, seal, and chill it again. The dough is now ready to cut out and use as needed. It can be rolled to any required thinness, but it cannot be *balled*. You have created a structure of 81 layers of fat and 80 layers of air, carefully sealed in. If you were to roll up the dough into a ball, all your work would be for nothing. Even the scraps must remain unballed and can be rolled out for cheese sticks and other appetizers.

Avoid Possible Faults

To avoid faults, follow the recipe carefully and understand that certain steps are essential, while they sound unimportant.

1. Do not work additional flour into the dough by overflouring the board. Brush off all surplus flour and use as little as possible to begin with.

2. Too much liquid or overkneading the dough makes the pastry hard and tough.

3. If the sides of the dough are not carefully sealed, the fat will run out during baking. Leave a wide enough edge for sealing and seal with *firm* pressure. The fat will also run out if oven is not hot enough.

4. Pastry will lack flakiness and crispness if fat was not cold enough

to begin with and chilling periods were not long enough. The same will happen if dough is over-rolled. Roll lightly; don't bear down hard.

5. Pastry will shrink in baking if it was stretched too far in rolling out and insufficiently rested between rolling.

6. Damp or soggy inner sections of pastry are due to insufficient baking and to fillings which are either too hot or too moist, or both, when they are enclosed in the pastry.

7. The greatest danger in making flaky or puff pastry is that the layers break through and butter merges with the dough. For that reason the dough must remain cool, the fat has to be chilled again, and the dough must not be overrolled. Work in a cool place. If you have a marble slab instead of a pastry board, use it. Coolness is essential.

These faults are the same in flaky pastry and in puff pastry.

BASIC PUFF PASTRY

Puff pastry is a refinement of flaky pastry. The butter is wrapped in the dough instead of being dotted over it and it is rolled and turned 6 times instead of 4. All other rules are approximately the same.

BASIC PUFF PASTRY

8 cups flour
2 tablespoons salt
4 tablespoons fresh, unsalted butter
2 tablespoons kirsch or rum
1¾ cups water, approximately
¾ cup flour
3½ cups fresh, unsalted butter

Sift 8 cups flour onto a marble slab or pastry board in coolest part of kitchen, preferably on a cool day. Make a well in the center, add salt, 4 tablespoons butter, and the kirsch or rum. Start working the butter and kirsch into the flour with your fingers, and gradually add the water until a smooth paste is obtained. Shape it into a ball and slash it across top with a knife in two deep cuts to form a cross, See Fig. 1 in

"Blueprint" 2, Method II. Pull the four corners of the paste, which are created by the crosscuts, out to the four sides to shape a pointed square. Cover it with a dampened kitchen towel and let it rest for 30 minutes. Knead the remaining flour into the remaining butter until smooth and shape it into a square slab. Chill the slab just long enough to "stiffen" it. Roll out the paste to a cross, Figure 2. Place the slab of butter in the center and fold over the 4 flaps. Press very lightly with a rolling pin, "Blueprint" 2, Figure 3. Let paste rest for 10 minutes, then make the first double turn. This means rolling out the paste and folding it into 4 layers as shown on "Blueprint" 2, Figures 4 to 6. Chill paste for 20 minutes, lay it with the open fold at the bottom, "Blueprint" 2, Figure 7, and roll it out again (away from you) to the same dimensions as the first time and fold it again in a double turn. Refrigerate again for 20 minutes and repeat, making 4 double turns in all for various pastries and 5 turns in all for vol-au-vent shells. Chill between each turn. Chilling time may be decreased to 10 minutes in winter, and use as little flour in handling the paste as possible.

Cut out the paste immediately after the last chilling in the refrigerator. Arrange the strips or pieces on a pastry sheet previously sprinkled with water. Brush top with an egg wash of 2 eggs beaten with salt or sugar to taste, depending on whether the puff pastry is intended for a

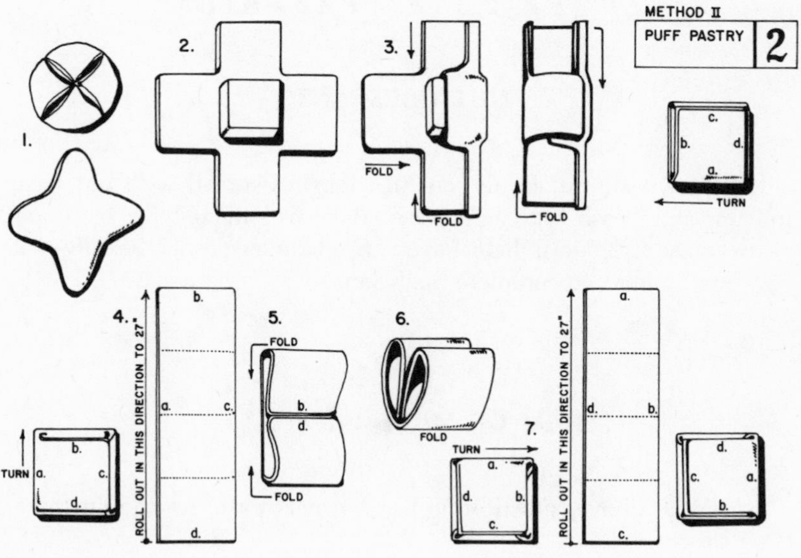

savory or a sweet. Do not let the egg wash run down the side of the paste as this may prevent it from rising properly. Bake in a 430° to 465°F. oven.

Refrigerate unused puff paste in pieces or layers as they are left over after cutting. Do not ball the scraps or remnants as the layers will be destroyed and the paste unusable.

BLITZ PUFF PASTRY

8¾ cups flour
2¾ cups cold unsalted butter
2 tablespoons salt or sugar
Ice water as needed

Chill butter, chop it into small cubes, and mix it with the flour. Make a well in the center, add salt or sugar and just enough cold water to gather the ingredients into a paste, leaving the butter cubes intact. Chill for 10 minutes, then roll out and give the paste 4 rapid single turns in succession, without any rest periods between. Cut out immediately and bake as regular puff pastry.

PUFF PASTE PASTRIES

NUT CRESCENTS

Roll puff paste out thinly, cut in triangles, spread with nut paste, roll up, and brush with egg wash. Bake as directed for basic puff paste, page 212, until half baked. Sprinkle crescents heavily with powdered sugar and complete the baking.

HAM OR MEAT CRESCENTS

Prepare as above, substituting ham or meat paste for the nut paste. Omit sugar.

OVALS OR SHOE SOLES

Roll puff paste to ⅛-inch thickness on a sugared slab or board. Cut out in ovals or in long ovals as large as a shoe sole and bake on a water-sprinkled pastry sheet with the sugared side up. If a waffled rolling pin is available, roll a waffle pattern over the sugared side and sprinkle with a little powdered sugar.

JAM TURNOVERS

Roll puff paste very thin. Cut with a large scalloped round cutter. Place jam filling in center, moisten edges, and turn one half over on the other. Crimp together firmly. Use back of a smaller cutter to press down against the paste to seal it inside the crimped edge.

PALM LEAVES

(*Palmiers*)

Sprinkle pastry board evenly with sugar. Roll out puff paste into a long rectangle. Fold in from each side to make layers that meet in the center. Fold center, Figure 6, "Blueprint" 2, page 213. Cut into slices, sugar tops, and bake in a hot oven. Turn palmiers when half baked.

CHEESE STICKS

Sprinkle thinly rolled puff paste with grated Parmesan cheese. Cut into long narrow strips, twist the strips, and press ends lightly onto baking sheet to prevent them from uncurling.

NAPOLEONS

Place 3 or 4 long strips of puff paste on a water-sprinkled baking sheet. Prick with a fork and cover with buttered underside of a second baking sheet. Bake in a 450°F. oven for about 15 minutes until crisp and browned. As soon as the strips are cool, sandwich them together with thick pastry cream, page 261, and spread the top with vanilla sugar icing, page 259. Dribble with cross lines of melted chocolate and draw a wooden pick down the length of the pastry in opposite directions to create the traditional chevron design.

VOL-AU-VENT SHELLS

Cut thinly rolled puff paste into 2½-inch even rounds and leave as many solid rounds as shells required. Cut remaining rounds into rings by cutting out the centers with a smaller cutter, but leave them in the rings. Place 2 or 3 of these cut layers on the solid rounds, moistening each layer around the edge with beaten egg to make it adhere. Always reverse the rings so that the underside becomes the top side. Brush top layer with egg wash. When the shells are puffed and brown, let them cool. Lift out the demarked center of the top to use as a lid and scoop out and discard the lower centers so that an empty shell is formed. Fill with creamed meat, poultry, fish, or shellfish and serve hot. The shells can be reheated slightly after they are emptied.

Use puff pastry for fruit dumplings, turnovers, lattice top pies, open pie shells, rolls and horns, and small pastries.

BASIC YEAST PUFF PASTRY FOR DANISH PASTRIES AND CRESCENTS

The yeast is incorporated into the paste, which is prepared without kneading. The butter is not chilled—instead it is brought to the same consistency as the paste. The butter is spread over two-thirds of the paste as for puff paste, Blueprint 2, Method II. The procedure is the same until after the last turn. The dough is then refrigerated for 30 minutes. The pieces are shaped and set on a baking sheet, covered, and allowed to rise. In order that the butter does not run out of the paste the pieces should be set to rise in a cool place. Some of the pieces can be left to rise in the warmest part of the refrigerator overnight. For this reason the rising takes much longer than it would under ordinary circumstances.

BASIC DANISH PASTRY PASTE

2 cakes compressed yeast or packages active dry yeast
4 tablespoons sugar
¾ cup lukewarm milk
2 eggs
4 cups flour
½ teaspoon salt
1½ cups butter to fold into paste

In a large bowl, dissolve yeast and sugar in milk. Add eggs and stir until smooth. Add the flour and salt gradually and work by hand into a smooth paste. Roll out the paste on a lightly floured surface and follow Blueprint 1 for all directions for rolling out and incorporating the butter. Chill the finished paste for 30 minutes, roll out, and shape as desired. Bake in a hot 450°F. oven for a few minutes, reduce heat to 350° to 375°F., and continue baking until golden. Count from 15 to 20 minutes baking time for small pieces, 20 to 35 minutes for large ones.

Shaping Danish Paste

Coffee cakes and braids: Roll out, fill, and shape as for basic sweet dough, page 224.

Turnovers: Follow directions for turnovers on page 206. Fill with jam, nut or almond paste, or cream cheese.

Snails, cock's combs, and unfilled rolls: Roll basic Danish pastry paste out and cut into strips and twist or braid into individual rolls. Use melted butter or butter and sugar and cinnamon and nuts between the layers, as on page 224. Bend strips of plain Danish pastry paste by cutting incisions along one side. As they are bent the cuts open to resemble cock's combs.

However the paste is shaped, the process remains the same. Use your own inventiveness. In Denmark the homemaker shapes the paste into initials, pretzels, Christmas trees, nests for Easter eggs, and anything that fits the holiday or pleases her children.

BASIC YEAST PUFF PASTRY FOR FRENCH CROISSANTS

METHOD III

2 cakes compressed yeast or 2 envelopes active dry yeast
¼ cup lukewarm water or milk
4 cups flour
1 teaspoon salt
1½ tablespoons sugar
1¼ cups milk
¾ pound sweet butter
1 egg, beaten

Dissolve yeast in water or milk in a small bowl, add 1 cup of the flour, and stir into a ball of dough. Cut a cross on the top of the ball and place it in a large bowl of warm water. Leave it for about 30 minutes or until it rises to the surface of the water and has doubled in bulk. Sift remaining flour, salt, and sugar onto a pastry board, make a well in the center, and work in the milk. Work and beat the dough until smooth and elastic. Drain the small ball of "sponge" well and work it into the dough by cutting and folding until smooth. Put in a floured bowl, cover, and rest for 10 minutes.

Roll out dough to about ½-inch thickness and fold in the butter as for puff pastry, Blueprint 3, Method III, page 219. Give the dough 4 to 5 turns, following basic puff pastry recipe, page 212. Chill dough in refrigerator overnight.

Roll out dough to ⅛-inch thickness, cut in 5-inch wide strips, and cut strips into triangles as on Blueprint 3, Figure 2, page 219. Roll up the triangles, starting at the wide base and ending with the tip under the roll. Draw the two ends forward to form a crescent. Place crescents on a floured baking sheet, cover, and let rise 20 to 30 minutes, or until doubled in bulk. Brush with beaten egg and bake in a 425°F. oven until golden, about 10 minutes.

FRENCH CROISSANTS
METHOD IV

2 cakes compressed yeast
1 tablespoon sugar
1 pinch salt
4 cups flour
2 tablespoons butter, cut into thin flakes
3 bars or 1½ cups fresh, unsalted butter

Stir yeast and sugar into a paste with the salt. Sift flour into a large

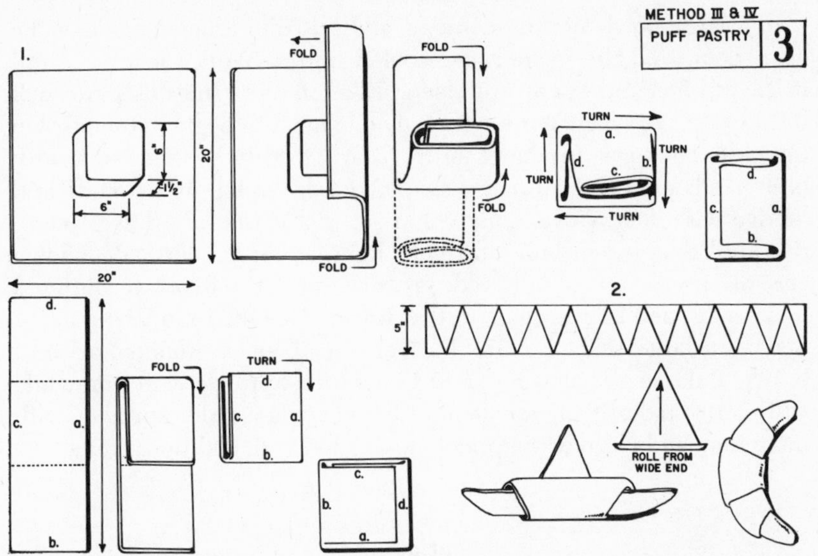

bowl, make a well in the center, and add the yeast paste and butter flakes. Work by hand into a smooth paste. Rest paste for 30 minutes. Roll out according to Chart 1, above. Dot with butter and fold. Follow all directions for Method I, refrigerating paste for 15 minutes between each turn. Turn 4 times then rest paste for several hours or overnight.

Roll out paste ¼-inch thick in a long 5-inch-wide strip. Cut into triangles, Blueprint 3, Method III, Figure 2, and rest triangles in refrigerator for 20 minutes. Flatten each triangle slightly with a rolling pin to a triangle of approximately 3-inch base and 5- to 6-inch length. Roll up from wide end, catching the tip under the roll. Bend into crescents. Place on a lightly greased baking sheet. Cover and let rise until double in bulk. Bake in a 400°F. oven until crisp and golden, 15 to 17 minutes. Serve warm with cold butter.

BASIC BABA OR SAVARIN PASTE

2 cakes compressed yeast
3 tablespoons sugar
¼ teaspoon salt
3 eggs
3 cups and 2 tablespoons flour, sifted
6 tablespoons butter, melted
1 tablespoon flour for dredging

In a large bowl, stir yeast, sugar, and salt into a paste. Beat in the eggs, flour, and the melted and cooled butter. Work the paste until it leaves bowl and hands are clean. Take off your rings as paste will be very sticky at first. Work with only one hand to begin with and slap the paste back into the bowl until it starts to cohere, then work with both hands until a clean ball is shaped. Gash the top with a knife and dredge with flour. Cover snugly and set in a warm, draftless place to rise until doubled in bulk and very light, about 2 hours. Slap down and fill paste into a buttered savarin ring or individual buttered baba molds and let rise again in that warm place for 1½ to 2 hours.

Bake a large ring in a 375°F. oven for about 35 minutes or until brown. Bake small babas for 16 to 18 minutes. Sprinkle with rum while still warm and still in the mold. Unmold when cold, sprinkle with more rum, and glaze with apricot jam melted with additional rum.

Variations

1. Add raisins and slivered, scalded almonds to paste.
2. Substitute kirsch, curacao, or brandy for the rum.
3. Fill center of ring with brandied or fresh fruits and whipped cream.
4. Sprinkle top of glazed babas with chopped pistacchio nuts.
5. Saturate savarin ring in mold like a plum pudding, with a little more rum each day for 3 to 5 days. Serve flaming. This method has to be served at once as the softened savarin has not got the strength to stand for long.

BASIC WHITE BREAD

4 LOAVES

2 cups milk, scalded
5 tablespoons sugar
1½ tablespoons salt
¾ cup shortening
2 cups warm water
2 packages active dry yeast or 2 cakes compressed yeast
12 cups sifted flour, 3 pounds

Stir sugar, salt, and shortening into hot milk. Allow to cool to lukewarm. Sprinkle active dry yeast over 2 cups warm water in a large bowl or crumble compressed yeast over 2 cups lukewarm water in a large bowl. Stir until dissolved, then stir in milk mixture. Beat in until smooth 6 cups sifted flour, work in 6 more cups, and turn the dough out onto a floured pastry board. Knead until smooth and elastic. Place dough in a bowl, brush with melted shortening, and turn dough until all sides of bowl are lightly greased. Brush top of dough again, cover with a kitchen towel, and set in a warm, draftless place until doubled in bulk, about 1 hour.

Punch down the dough, turn it out on the board and divide into 4 equal parts. Cover and let dough rest for 20 minutes. Shape into 4 loaves and place in 4 greased bread pans 9 × 5 × 3 inches. Cover and return the pans to the warm, draftless place and let rise a second time for about 1 hour, or until center of loaves has risen slightly above the edge of the pan. Bake in a 400°F. oven for 50 minutes.

Storing: Cool bread, wrap in airtight, moisture-proof material and store in freezer or freezing compartment up to 3 or 4 weeks.

For immediate use: Wrap bread in wax paper, store in a ventilated bread box at room temperature for several days. Bread stored in refrigerator is more apt to stale than in the bread box.

BASIC ROLL DOUGH

Prepare basic bread dough, altering the proportions as follows:

¾ cup milk
¼ cup sugar
2 teaspoons salt
4½ tablespoons shortening or butter

¾ cup warm water
2 packages active dry yeast or 2 cakes compressed yeast
4½ cups sifted flour

Follow all instructions for basic bread dough allowing the roll dough to rise about 40 minutes in the bowl. After the rolls are shaped, allow 30 to 35 minutes for the second rising and bake in a 375°F. to 400°F. oven for 15 to 20 minutes, according to times following the shaping instructions.

Shaping Rolls

Rolls are shaped after the dough is punched down and before it rises for the second time.

Pan rolls or round dinner rolls: Roll basic roll dough into 2 long sausages, about 12 inches long, cut into 1-inch lengths. Smooth into round balls and place in 2 greased layer cake pans, allowing about ¼ inch between rolls for expansion. Cover, let rise, as in basic recipe, for about 30 minutes, brush lightly with melted butter, and bake in a 375°F. oven for about 20 minutes.

Clover leaf rolls: Prepare dough as above but cut into 18 slices and shape each slice into 3 even rounds. Grease standard muffin pans and place 3 balls in each pan. Cover and let rise 30 minutes. Brush tops lightly with melted butter and bake in a 400°F. oven for about 18 minutes.

Parker House rolls: Roll dough out to about ⅝-inch thickness. Cut into 18 rounds with a 2½-inch cookie cutter. Mark each round a little to the left of the center with the back of a knife. Brush with butter and bend over at this indentation mark, folding the larger part over the smaller one. Place on a greased baking sheet, about 1 inch apart. Cover and let rise for 30 minutes. Brush lightly with melted butter and bake in a 400°F. oven for 15 minutes, or until golden.

Fantans: Roll dough to a rectangle, about 27 × 11 inches. Brush with melted butter and cut the long way into 7 1½-inch wide strips. Lay on top of each other, butter-side-up. Cut into 18 1½-inch lengths and lay them, cutside down into 18 standard, greased muffin tins. Cover and let rise for 30 minutes. Brush with melted butter and pull sections apart slightly at top. Bake in a 400°F. oven for about 20 minutes, until golden, and loose in the pans. Serve hot.

BASIC BRIOCHE DOUGH

(*Makes 16*)

- ½ cup milk, scalded
- ½ cup butter
- 5 tablespoons sugar
- ½ teaspoon salt
- ¼ cup warm water
- 1 package active dry yeast or 1 cake compressed yeast
- 3 eggs
- 1 egg yolk
- 3¼ to 3½ cups sifted flour
- 1 egg white beaten with:
- 1 tablespoon sugar
- 2 drops yellow food color (optional)

Make dough the day before needed.

Scald milk and cool. Cream butter in large bowl, gradually add sugar and salt. Sprinkle active dry yeast over ¼ cup warm water in small bowl or crumble compressed yeast over lukewarm water in a small bowl. Stir until dissolved. Add the lukewarm milk and the dissolved yeast to the creamed butter in the large bowl, add eggs, egg yolk, and flour. Beat vigorously for about 2 minutes with a wooden spoon. Cover with a kitchen towel and let rise in a warm, draftless place until more than doubled in bulk, about 2 hours. Beat down thoroughly, cover tightly with foil, and refrigerate overnight.

Stir down and turn out on a lightly floured board. Divide in 2 pieces of ¾ and ¼ the dough. Roll large piece in 16 evenly sized balls and place them in 16 well-greased brioche or muffin tins. Roll small piece into 16 evenly sized balls. Make deep indentations in the large balls in the tins, brush lightly with cold water and press a small ball into each indentation. Cover with a kitchen towel and let rise in warm, draftless place until doubled in bulk, about 1 hour.

Bruch brioches with a glaze of egg white beaten with sugar. Bake in a 375°F. oven for 20 to 22 minutes.

Variations

The same brioche dough can be used for a single large or 2 medium brioches or it can be shaped into oblong finger rolls and glazed and baked on a baking sheet.

BASIC SWEET DOUGH FOR BREADS AND ROLLS

1 cup milk, scalded
1 cup sugar
1 tablespoon salt
½ cup shortening
1 cup warm water
4 packages active dry yeast or 4 cakes compressed yeast
4 eggs, beaten
10 cups sifted flour

Stir sugar, salt, and shortening into hot milk, cool to lukewarm.

Sprinkle active dry yeast over 1 cup warm water in a large bowl or crumble compressed yeast over 1 cup lukewarm water in a large bowl. Stir until dissolved, then stir in milk mixture. Stir in eggs and 6 cups flour until smooth. Stir in about 4 more cups flour and turn dough out on a lightly floured pastry board. Knead until smooth and elastic. Place in bowl, brush top with melted shortening, and turn dough until all sides of bowl are lightly greased. Brush top of dough again, cover with a kitchen towel, and let rise in a warm, draftless place until doubled in bulk, about 1 hour. Punch the dough down, turn it out on a floured board, and cut it out or shape it for any of the following purposes. When dough is shaped and in pan or pans, cover again with a towel and let rise in the same warm, draftless place until doubled in bulk, about 1 hour. Bake rolls in a 350°F. oven for 35 to 45 minutes unless otherwise specified with shaping directions.

SHAPING BASIC SWEET DOUGH FOR BUNS, COFFEE CAKES, BRAIDS

Cinnamon Pecan Buns or Stickies: Roll out 1 recipe basic sweet dough to about 10 × 18 or 19 inches. Brush with melted butter and sprinkle with 1½ cups sugar, 1 to 2 teaspoons cinnamon to taste, ½ cup raisins and ½ cup slivered almonds, or 1 cup raisins. Roll up the short way to obtain an 18- or 19-inch long roll. Pinch the fold to seal. Cut roll into 18 equal slices and place, cut side up, in 2 buttered layer cake pans. Cover with a warm kitchen towel and let rise in a warm, draftless place for about 1 hour, or until doubled in bulk. Bake in a 350°F. oven for about 35 minutes. Ice top with plain sugar icing or serve plain.

Variations

1. Substitute 1 cup pecans for raisins and almonds and brush top with melted honey.

2. Use ⅔ cup brown sugar, ½ cup chopped nuts, and 2 teaspoons grated orange rind in place of basic filling.

3. Roll out and sprinkle dough with cinnamon, sugar, and ½ cup broken pecan meats. Melt ⅓ cup butter in each layer cake pan. Add ½ cup brown sugar to each pan and ½ cup pecan halves. Turn the pecans

so that the cut side is up. Arrange the cut slices of dough on the nuts. Let rise as for basic buns. Bake in a 375°F. oven for 35 minutes or until browned and done. Invert onto a shallow dish. Do not remove baking pan for 5 minutes. Remove baking pan and let buns cool until sugar syrup is partly set. Serve warm with butter.

4. Tube Bun Cake: Follow recipe for plain cinnamon and raisin buns. Stack them at random in a well-buttered tube pan, always facing a cut edge out. Sprinkle each layer with butter and broken walnuts, using ½ cup butter and 1 cup nuts. Cover, let rise for about 1 hour until doubled in bulk. Bake in a 375°F. oven for about 45 minutes or until brown and loosened from pan.

KUGELHUPF

¾ cup raisins
½ cup sherry or brandy
¾ cup sugar
½ teaspoon salt
6 tablespoons butter
¾ cup milk, scalded
1½ packages active dry yeast or 1½ cakes compressed yeast
6 tablespoons warm water
3 eggs, beaten
3 cups flour
3 tablespoons breadcrumbs
½ cup shaved, blanched almonds
grated rind of 1 lemon

Soak raisins in sherry or brandy for 3 hours. Stir sugar, salt, and butter into hot milk and cool to lukewarm. Sprinkle dry yeast over warm water in warm bowl, or crumble compressed yeast over lukewarm water in warm bowl. Stir until dissolved, and add warm milk mixture. Beat in eggs and flour for about 5 minutes. Cover with a kitchen towel and let rise in a warm, draftless place until doubled in bulk, at least 1½ hours. Butter a large tube pan well, sprinkle with breadcrumbs, tapping the mold to distribute them evenly, and sprinkle shaved almonds around the top and outside wall of the mold. Beat down batter, add drained raisins and lemon rind, and pour batter into the mold without disturbing the almonds and crumbs. Cover and let rise again in warm, draftless place until doubled in bulk, about 1 hour. Bake in a 350°F. oven for about 60 minutes. Cool, unmold, and sprinkle with powdered sugar. Makes 1 large tube-form cake.

LESSON XI

CREAM PUFF PASTE—CHOUX PASTE—PÂTE À CHOU

The hostess who wants to make some of those smart little Carolines, cheese-filled cocktail puffs, or coffee éclairs should know that here again is a single basic recipe that can also be used for choux paste, fritters, soufflés, puddings, gnocchi, Potatoes Dauphine, and cream puffs. The same recipe makes those tiny golden bubbles, or "peas," that the French float on their clear soaps, and without the slightest change, except in quantity, it makes that towering showpiece, the mighty Croquembouche. Between these poles-apart extremes the same paste makes everything from Profiteroles to Religieuse, Gâteau Saint-Honoré, and Paris-Brest. Furthermore, it makes all the chocolate and coffee and vanilla éclairs, the humbler Carolines, the sinister Othellos, and the various minor and major cream buns and puffs. When the same paste is fried in deep fat it turns into those beautiful beignets soufflés and Pets de Nonne that come floating to your table in the finest and most expensive restaurants.

The French name choux, cabbages, undoubtedly springs from the fact that a small ball of the paste explodes into a large, rough, cabbage-like round when it is baked in a hot oven or fried in hot fat. Unlike the cabbage, choux paste is hollow, dry, and crisp. The name is as typically French as the pastry itself, and most of the descendant recipes, with the exception of Italian gnocchi and American cream puffs, also come from France. In German it is called Brandteig, burned dough, because it is actually cooked before it is baked.

There is no other single pastry recipe that increases the cook's repertoire as quickly or as impressively. Choux paste is just another one of those simple basic recipes, but it is the one that produces the most dramatic results. A Croquembouche is, after all, the master chef's masterpiece. Actually it is just a lot of cream puffs assembled with wooden picks, and if you want to cheat you can use a paper cone in the center. No one will ever know, because no one has ever actually eaten a Croquembouche.

GENERAL RULES FOR MAKING CHOUX PASTE

Arrange shelf in center of oven and preheat oven to 400°F. Butter and flour a baking sheet and set it aside. Use a heavy metal saucepan with deep sides and a flat bottom. If necessary a number 4 iron frying pan, which measures seven inches across the top, will just hold one recipe choux paste. Avoid copper, which would discolor the eggs.

Choux paste requires a strong gluten flour. Use bread flour if possible, and never use self-rising flour. (See basic recipe, page 230.)

Bring water, butter, and salt to a boil in the heavy pan over medium heat. As soon as the butter is melted, add sifted flour, all at once. Stir vigorously with a wooden spoon (if you are using a low-sided frying pan, stir vigorously but carefully) until the mixture forms a smooth paste and gathers into a ball, leaving the sides of the pan completely clean. The stirring has to continue just long enough to make sure there are no hidden pockets of uncooked flour in the center of the ball of paste. The stirring-in of the flour should take at least 1½ minutes. Take pan from heat, prod the paste apart with the wooden spoon to cool it slightly and to allow air to escape from it. The French have a word for this stirring and cooking process, they "désecher" the paste. Some cookbooks advise taking the saucepan from the heat while stirring in the flour and then returning it to low heat. This again is a matter of choice. Actually the pan can remain over medium heat at all times, but the stirring must be constant to prevent the paste from scorching while it is being cooked. If flour is added off the heat, paste has to be cooked a little longer when it is returned to heat.

After paste has cooled for 2 minutes, beat in the room-temperature eggs, one at a time. Beat each egg until it is completely incorporated before adding the next one. This takes much more muscular strength than you would expect and there is a point at which you will despair but keep on beating, the paste does finally absorb each egg. All this can be done in an electric beater at low speed, but results are much better when the eggs are beaten in by hand with a wooden spoon. The paste should be soft, smooth, and glossy and it should hold any indentation made by the spoon. It should drop heavily from the spoon and hold its shape where it has fallen; it should also stand in a slight peak when it is dropped from the spoon. Be sure to do all the dropping tests onto a piece of wax paper so that the paste can be returned to the saucepan. As the size of eggs varies, it is better to omit one egg than to have a "runny" paste. If the paste is too stiff it will result in small, heavy puffs. It must be soft but not liquid.

Moisten a pastry bag with water and wring it out well. Adjust a ½-inch plain tube and fill the paste, which will be sticky, into the bag. Pipe the paste onto the prepared baking sheet and press down the peak left by the tube with a moistened finger. Keep the mounds of paste well apart to allow for their expansion. For beignets, fried in deep fat, or if you have no pastry bag and tube, shape the paste with two spoons. To facilitate shaping the sticky paste, dip the spoons into hot melted fat or water before using them and again whenever the paste becomes difficult to handle.

Place pan in center of preheated oven and bake for 20 minutes. Reduce heat to 350°F. and bake 10 minutes longer. Reduce heat to 325°F. and bake 10 minutes longer or until the puffs are brown, crisp, and dry. If puffs are not firm to the touch, bake 5 minutes longer at 350°F. The sides of the Choux Puffs have to be as crisp and dry as the top, otherwise they will sag when they are cool. Turn off the oven, open the oven door slightly and allow puffs to dry for another 5 minutes.

Baking times vary with size of pieces, follow individual variation recipes for proper baking times as well as temperatures for deep fat frying. Also follow directions on page 233 and individual recipes for filling choux paste pieces. If a split puff or éclair has any remaining soft paste in the center, scrape it out with a spoon; this happens to the best of chefs.

Faults and How to Avoid Them

Oven-baked choux paste:

1. Spreading, mixture too soft, resulting in soggy pastries which do not have a hollow core. This is due to insufficient cooking of paste or insufficient beating when eggs were added.

2. Sagging or sinking of puffs after cooling is due to insufficient baking.

3. When there is no rising or explosion, when puffs are pale, the oven was not hot enough.

4. When puffs are too dark in color before they are done, the oven was too hot.

Deep-fat-fried choux paste:

5. If puffs turn too brown when frying choux paste, and center is uncooked, the deep fat was too hot. When puffs are soggy and too pale in color, fat was not hot enough.

6. When paste does not explode, it was either insufficiently beaten when eggs were added, or fat was too hot. There may also have been too many puffs in the fryer at the same time.

7. Pale and soggy gnocchi (*Simmered Choux Paste Gnocchi*) are the result of insufficient cooking. Tough gnocchi are overcooked.

BASIC CHOUX PASTE RECIPE

(*Cream Puffs*)

1 cup water
¼ pound butter
½ teaspoon salt
1¼ cups bread flour, or plain flour, sifted
4 eggs

Read general directions for making choux paste. Preheat oven to 400°F. Butter and flour a baking sheet. Bring water, butter, and salt to a boil in a heavy saucepan over medium heat. Add flour all at once and stir with a wooden spoon until mixture gathers in a soft ball and leaves the sides of the pan. Work it well to make sure there are no lumps of uncooked flour in the paste. Take pan from heat, spread paste a little with the spoon, and cool for 2 minutes. Beat in eggs, one at a time. Beat thoroughly until each egg is completely absorbed into the paste before adding the next one. When paste is properly completed, according to tests on page 229, it is ready for use.

SWEETENED CHOUX PASTE

Beat 2 teaspoons sugar, and ½ teaspoon vanilla extract into the basic choux paste recipe after the paste is cooked, before adding the eggs.

SWEETENED CHOUX PASTE MADE WITH MILK

Bring 1 cup milk to a boil with ¼ pound butter, 1 teaspoon sugar, and 1 pinch salt. Boil until butter and sugar are melted, add 1 cup bread flour and continue as for basic choux paste. Beat in 4 large eggs.

CHEESE-FLAVORED CHOUX PASTE

Prepare 1 recipe basic choux paste and beat in ¼ cup grated Parmesan cheese, or any dry grated cheese, after the eggs have been added.

Holding or Storing

If choux paste is not going to be used immediately, cover the saucepan with moistened and wrung-out butcher's paper and cover the paper with a tight-fitting lid. The paste can be held at room temperature for several hours. The tight covering is essential to keep the paste from drying out.

Unfilled choux pastry, éclairs, profiteroles, or other small pieces can be baked ahead. Store them as soon as they have cooled out in airtight tins. Do not attempt to store a Paris-Brest or large piece.

Filled choux pastry, éclairs, profiteroles, and large pieces may be finished, covered well, and stored in the refrigerator for several hours until they are served for dessert. If filled with whipped cream they will not hold as long as when they are filled with pastry cream.

When Profiteroles are filled with ice cream, they may be stored in the freezer for several hours. In that case, transfer them to the refrigerator about 30 to 45 minutes before serving, depending on their size, and serve with hot chocolate sauce. The sauce will soften them further if they are still too hard.

HOW TO PIPE OR SHAPE CHOUX PASTE

ÉCLAIRS

Butter and flour a baking sheet, tilt it in all directions, and tap it lightly to spread the flour evenly over the butter. Shake off any superfluous flour. With back of a wooden spoon mark straight lines in the flour. Make them 4 inches long and keep them 3 inches apart. Fill choux paste into moistened pastry bag fitted with a plain ½-inch tube. Pipe the paste along the 4-inch lines and cut the end off sharply with a wet knife. 1 recipe choux paste will make 28 to 30 éclairs.

CREAM PUFFS, PROFITEROLES, CAROLINES, COCKTAIL PUFFS

Prepare a baking sheet as for éclairs, above, and mark it with little x's, about 6 inches apart. Fill choux paste into moistened pastry bag fitted with a plain ½-inch tube. Pipe paste onto the x's on the prepared baking sheet in high mounds. Smooth out point left by pastry tube with moistened finger. If pastry bag and tube are not available, shape choux paste with 2 teaspoons, for small pieces, and 2 tablespoons for large pieces. Dip spoons into water before using to facilitate sliding paste onto baking sheet. Continue dipping the spoons into water when paste becomes hard to handle. One recipe choux paste should make 20 or 21 rounds. Bake at once. For small cocktail puffs, pipe rounds the size of a hazelnut or large cherry. For small profiteroles or cream puffs, pipe rounds the size of a large walnut. For large cream puffs and Othellos, pipe rounds the size of golf balls.

BEIGNETS SOUFFLÉ (*French Fritters*)

Heat shortening as described on page 151. Dip two tablespoons into the hot shortening. Take up a heaping tablespoon of choux paste in one of the spoons and shape it into a round with the help of the second spoon. Do the shaping over the deep-fat fryer and drop the round into the hot fat the moment the shape is right. Continue in the same way until the fryer is sparsely filled, take out the first beignets as soon as they are golden, drain and sugar them at once, and serve 2 to a portion. For a party it is wise either to have two fryers going or to have such appreciative guests that they will take their beignets one at a time.

TO SHAPE GNOCCHI

Fill choux paste into a pastry bag fitted with a ½-inch plain tube. Hold bag over simmering water and cut 1-inch lengths of paste, letting them drop into the water as they are pressed from the bag. As this can result in some of the gnocchi being underdone while others are overdone, work just as quickly as possible. If preferred, shape the gnocchi by taking up just one heaping teaspoon of paste at a time and dropping it into the water. The spoon has to be dipped into the water before each gnocchi is shaped to facilitate the sliding.

HOW TO FILL CHOUX PASTE PIECES

LARGE PROFITEROLES, CREAM PUFFS, ÉCLAIRS, AND THEIR VARIATIONS

With a sharp knife, cut a slit in the sides or bottoms of choux pastry pieces. Fill with pastry cream, whipped cream, or ice cream. Pipe the filling into the puffs or fill them with a spoon. Use any of the pastry cream variations or any preferred ice cream flavor.

LARGE PIECES, PARIS-BREST, GÂTEAUX SAINT-HONORÉ, RINGS

Split cooled choux pastry ring by cutting through with a long sharp knife. Lift off top, pipe filling into lower part, and pipe it high enough to show at least ¾-inch of filling when the top is returned to the cake.

SMALL COCKTAIL PUFFS, CAROLINES, PROFITEROLES, AND SOUP GARNISHES

Place filling in a pastry bag fitted with a pointed tube or with a nozzle-type tube made especially for filling pastries. Jab the pointed tube or the pointed end of the nozzle tube into the bottom of small cocktail puffs, profiteroles, or puffs intended for soup garnish, and press the filling into the puff. When the pointed tube is withdrawn the hole closes and the filling is sealed in. To all but initiated cooks these cocktail puffs are a mystery, and so they should remain.

Needless to say the nicest filling of all is some ice-cold caviar, which has to be filled in with a small spoon. Precede it with just a little heading of whipped sour cream piped in before the caviar is added . . . but anchovy butter or curried cream cheese can be made to do.

GÂTEAU SAINT-HONORÉ

Preheat oven to 425°F. Butter and flour 1 of 2 baking sheets. Roll out ½ recipe short crust, page 191, to ¼-inch thickness and cut it into a nine-inch round. Transfer it to the center of the unbuttered baking sheet, prick it with a fork, and set it aside. Prepare 1 recipe choux paste, page 230, and fill it into a moistened pastry bag equipped with a plain ½- to ¾-inch tube. Pipe the choux paste in a ring about ½ inch in from the edge of the short crust round. Pipe the remaining choux paste onto the prepared baking sheet into 14 rounds, the size of small walnuts. Bake both baking sheets for 15 minutes. Reduce heat to 375°F. and bake 15 minutes longer. Open oven, inspect choux puffs, and border. If oven bakes unevenly turn the sheets around. Bake approximately 15 minutes longer or until crisp and brown. The puffs may be done before the ring is done. Dry further for 5 minutes with heat turned off and oven door ajar. Cool puffs and choux ring on a wire rack.

Boil sugar glaze, page 235, and quickly pour a border of it around the top of the ring. Dip the puffs into the sugar and immediately stick them around the top of the ring like a crown. Arrange the crown on a serving platter and fill the center with 2 recipes pastry cream, page 262, with whipped cream folded into it. Pipe the cream through a fluted tube to make it doubly pretty. The cake and puffs can be baked the day before, stored in an airtight tin and assembled and filled an hour or two before dinner. Cover and chill until served.

SUGAR GLAZE FOR GÂTEAU SAINT-HONORÉ, GLAZED PUFFS, AND CROQUEMBOUCHE

½ cup sugar
1 cup water

Bring sugar and water to a boil in a heavy pan, stirring until sugar is dissolved. Continue to boil the sugar syrup, without stirring, until it is a rich golden brown color, 290° to 300°F. on candy thermometer. Dip puffs into glaze or pour it in a stream over pastry that is to be glazed. Do not attempt to spread it with a knife.

Variations

Flavor pastry cream with curaçao or Grand Marnier and fold skinned and drained orange sections into the cream.

PROFITEROLES WITH CHOCOLATE SAUCE

(*Choux au Chocolat*)

Prepare 1 recipe choux paste, adding ½ teaspoon vanilla and 2 teaspoons sugar to the boiling water just before the flour is added. Let paste cool, then pipe or shape it with two spoons into 28 rounds on 2 prepared baking sheets. Bake in a 400°F. preheated oven for 20 minutes, reduce heat to 350°F., and bake 10 minutes longer. Reduce heat to 325°F. for the last 10 minutes of baking. Turn off heat, open oven door slightly, and let profiteroles dry for 5 minutes longer. Cool on a wire rack. Cut a slit on the side of each with a sharp knife and pipe or spoon pastry cream filling, page 261, into the cold puffs. Serve in shallow crystal bowls with a sauce of softened milk chocolate bars beaten with heavy cream to taste.

Variations: Fillings and Sauces

Fill puffs with chocolate- or coffee-flavored pastry cream, with purée of chestnuts, or fill with vanilla, coffee, or chocolate ice cream. Flavor chocolate sauce with coffee essence or a dash of curaçao.

1. Miniature puffs: Shape choux paste on baking sheet as large as hazelnuts or large cherries. Bake. When they are cold pipe in fillings from the bottom according to directions for filling on page 234. Use any of the above fillings. Serve each guest with 6 or 7 profiteroles and pour over a sauce made of 1 part whipped cream folded into 2 parts soft, whipped chocolate, coffee, or vanilla ice cream.

2. Othellos: Fill large puffs with chocolate-flavored pastry cream, page 262, and frost tops with chocolate fondant icing.

3. Carolines: Pipe sweetened or unsweetened choux paste onto baking sheets in small rounds the size of a cherry. Fill sweetened puffs from the bottom, see page 234, with any of the above fillings and dip into fondant icing, page 259. Fill unsweetened puffs with any of the following.

Roquefort cheese mixed to a smooth paste with sour cream, seasoning, and a little brandy or sherry to taste.

Cream cheese mixed to a smooth paste with sour cream and anchovy paste to taste.

Ice-cold caviar with a little whipped sour cream.

Crabmeat bound with mayonnaise, sweet pickle relish and seasoning to taste.

Egg salad with chopped watercress, seasoned with dry mustard.

PARIS-BREST

Prepare choux paste and pipe it through a ½- to ¾-inch plain tube onto a buttered baking sheet in a nine-inch circle or crown. Large pastry tubes are available for piping potato borders.

Brush the top of the crown with a well-beaten egg and dust it with ½ package scalded, shaved almonds. Bake as directed in the basic recipe, until golden and the almonds are lightly browned. Increase the drying time slightly, until the crown feels crisp. Cool and cut the crown in half crosswise. Fill the interior with crème Saint-Honoré, piping it through a star tube to come at least ½ inch higher than the lower half of the crown. Return the lid or cover that was cut from the Paris-Brest and be sure that the piped filling shows. Sprinkle with powdered sugar and serve. The crème Saint-Honoré may be replaced by coffee-flavored sweetened whipped cream or pastry cream.

ÉCLAIRS

Pipe basic choux paste through a ½-inch plain tube onto a buttered baking sheet in 4-inch fingers. Bake as directed and cool. Make a slit on the side, fill éclairs with pastry cream or whipped cream and dip top into chocolate fondant icing. Éclairs may also be filled with coffee, vanilla, or chocolate-flavored pastry cream and iced with chocolate, mocha, or vanilla fondant icing. For miniature éclairs, cut 2 inches long and cut baking time to about half. The finished éclair should be golden brown, dry, and crisp.

RELIGIEUSE

Prepare 12 éclairs and 8 1½-inch rounds of choux paste. Fill them with whipped cream and ice half with chocolate and half with coffee icing, page 259. Bake a 7-inch shell of sugar paste, page 266, with a ¼-inch border. When shell is cold, pipe a pyramid of pastry cream in the center and lean the 12 éclairs upright against it. Top with a pyramid of rounds and pipe lines of coffee butter cream between the éclairs and the puffs.

CROQUEMBOUCHE

A croquembouche is a 9- to 11-tier-high pyramid of 1½-inch choux pastry puffs, filled with pastry cream and dipped in sugar syrup boiled to the crack stage, 290°F. on candy thermometer. The puffs are assembled on a base of sugar pastry or nougat and are built up against a pointed cone. A heavy paper cone may be substituted. The bottom row usually starts with 14 to 18 puffs and the top ends with a single one. The caramel sugar holds them together and wooden picks are sometimes used to support the structure. It is a show piece and should, in theory, be built up of a solid cone of puffs. A 9-tier edifice on a cone takes about 75 puffs.

CORN FRITTERS

(*Made with choux paste*)

1 cup cooked or fresh corn kernels cut from cob
1 teaspoon salt
½ teaspoon sugar
¼ cup finely minced green pepper
salt and pepper
12 slices of bacon, fried crisp

BATTER

1 cup water or milk
4 tablespoons butter
1 cup flour
1 teaspoon salt
3 eggs

Heat milk or water with butter and salt. Add the flour when the mixture is boiling and stir very vigorously until the paste leaves the sides of the pan. Take from heat, cool for 2 or 3 minutes, and add the eggs one by one, beating well after each addition until the egg is completely incorporated.

Mix the corn with the green pepper. Add salt and sugar, mix with the batter, and drop into deep fat by spoonfuls. Fry at 375°F. until golden. Drain and surround with curls of crisp bacon. Serve with tomato sauce.

CHOUX PASTE FRITTERS

Prepare ½ recipe basic unsweetened choux paste and increase salt to taste. Clean and dry medium-sized mushrooms and cut stems even with heads. Press a mushroom into a large spoonful of the paste, shape into a fritter with 2 spoons dipped in hot fat, and fry in deep fat heated to 370°F. until brown, about 6 minutes. Be careful not to shape too much paste around each mushroom. Drain the finished fritters and serve as hot as possible with ice-cold tartar sauce.

Substitute boiled shrimp, asparagus tips, cauliflower flowerets, or boiled chestnuts for the mushrooms. Apple slices, half peaches, whole apricots, or pitted cherries may also be substituted for the mushrooms, in which case the salt is reduced to a pinch and 2 tablespoons sugar are added to the choux paste.

CHOCOLATE PUDDING

Prepare 1½ recipes sweetened choux paste, with 2 additional eggs. Add ½ cup grated chocolate and 1 teaspoon vanilla and pour into a well-buttered pudding form. Cover and boil for 1 hour in a covered kettle of water, making sure that the water reaches three-fourths of the way up the mold. Boiling water should be added, if necessary, to maintain the same level. Serve with sweetened whipped cream or Sabayon sauce.

CHEESE PUDDING

To 2 recipes basic choux paste made with milk, add 2 extra eggs, 1 cup grated Parmesan cheese, ½ cup breadcrumbs, and 3 tablespoons minced chives or parsley. Butter a tube pudding mold well, sprinkle with crumbs, and shake to distribute crumbs evenly. Pour batter into mold and set into a covered kettle of boiling water. The water should reach three-quarters of the way up the mold. Boiling water should be added if necessary to maintain the same level. Boil pudding for 1 hour. Unmold by loosening edges with a knife. Arrange on a platter surrounded by sliced tomatoes marinated in French dressing. Serve hot browned butter separately.

The pudding mold may be left open and set in a shallow pan of boiling water. Pan and pudding should then be set in a 375°F. oven and baked for 1 hour.

CHEESE SOUFFLÉ

Prepare the same mixture as for cheese pudding, but separate the eggs. Beat the yolks into the dough. Beat the whites stiff and fold into the paste. As the paste is stiff the eggs do not fold in easily. Pour into a buttered soufflé dish set into a pan of boiling water and bake in a 375°F. oven for 1 hour.

POTATOES DAUPHINE

Rice 1 pound hot boiled potatoes, beat in 2 egg yolks, 1 tablespoon butter, and a pinch of salt. Combine 1 recipe choux paste. Correct seasoning and shape into marble-sized balls. Fry in deep hot fat at 350°F. for 3 or 4 minutes. Increase heat to 370°F. Fry until golden brown, drain well, and serve garnished with parsley.

Puff Garnishes For Soup

1. Prepare ½ recipe unsweetened choux paste. Pipe through ¼-inch plain tube onto a buttered baking sheet, cutting the piped dough in ⅓-inch lengths with a wet knife. Bake until puffed and brown and serve hot from the oven with plain or cream soups. Depending on the size of the little puffs, baking time will be approximately 6 to 8 minutes. Increase the quantity of salt in the recipe to taste and add minced herbs, if desired.

2. Prepare slightly larger soup puffs and fill with any desired filling that will accent the soup. Serve only two or three to each guest. Fillings can be cheese, minced mushrooms, anchovy butter, minced herbs, or creamed minced chicken.

3. Prepare choux paste as above, increase salt to taste, stir in ¼ cup minced chives, and pipe small dumplings into simmering soup. Continue to cook until the dumplings are firm. Serve at once.

GNOCCHIS

Prepare 1 basic choux paste recipe with milk, adding salt and 2 tablespoons minced parsley. Force mixture through a pastry bag with a plain ½-inch tube and cut into small sections as the paste comes through the tube. Let sections drop directly into simmering water. Simmer gently until set and firm. Transfer gnocchis to pie plate, dot with 6 tablespoons butter, and sprinkle with ½ cup grated cheese. Place under preheated broiler until cheese is brown. If preferred, a cup of béchamel sauce may be poured over the gnocchis before cheese is sprinkled on the top.

LESSON XII

BASIC CAKE BATTERS AND QUICK BREADS

There are six basic types of cake batters and hundreds of variations on each of them.

1. Light sponge cake or biscuit is the most commonly used cake batter. It is usually a combination of yolks, sugar, and flour with stiffly beaten egg whites folded in just before baking. This type of batter is used for layer cakes, torten, shortcakes, open fruit cakes, and for *sheets* of dough which are cut into petits fours and slices. With more egg whites added, the sheets are used for nut, chocolate, and jelly rolls. Cocoa, grated chocolate or nuts, praline powder, spices, or flavorings are added to the basic batter to make a long list of variations.

2. Heavy sponge cake, pound cake or Sandtorte is a heavier and more solid version of light sponge cake. Eggs are sometimes used whole, sometimes separated and beaten. There is usually more flour in proportion to the eggs, and creamed or melted butter is used in the batter. Heavy sponge or sand cake batters are suitable for loaf and tube cakes, for raisin, nut, and fruit cakes and the types of cakes that can be thinly sliced to accompany afternoon tea or fruit desserts. Pound cake bases are also used for various desserts.

3. Butter sponge cake or Genoise is a lighter and finer cake batter, used for the most beautiful French and Italian gâteaux and Austrian

torten. It is made by the warm sponge method, which means that whole eggs are beaten over warm water until they expand. The flour is then gently folded into the warm egg mixture. Genoise batter is also baked in sheets and cut for slices and bases for fruit cakes and desserts.

4. Meringue or Vacherin batters consist of egg whites and sugar or a combination of ingredients in which stiffly beaten egg whites and sugar predominate. They are used for thin layers and cake shells for elaborate Torten and Gâteau. In some cases thin meringue layers alternate with sponge layers to make a crisper cake. Meringue-type layers are used for seven layer cakes and Dobos Torte.

5. Linzer torten batters are more elaborate short pastes made with grated nuts and sometimes with spices or even chocolate added. The batters do not rise and are Torten in name rather than in fact.

6. Yeast cake batters for Babas, Savarins, Panettone, and Kügelhupf are traditional French, Italian, and German cake batters. The basic recipes appear in Lesson X with breads and all basic yeast baking.

TESTS FOR DONENESS

The nicest directions for testing a sponge cake for doneness are in chef Franz Ruhm's *Wiener Kuche* (Viennese Cookery). He writes, "The cake is done when the light pressure of your hand calls forth a whispered response." It sounds better than "when a straw tests done," and it is actually the proper way of testing all light sponge cakes. The pastry chef's method is to press his hand gently on the golden surface of the cake. When the impression of his hand is pushed out and disappears because of the springiness of the cake, it is done. It should come out of the oven and be removed from the pan immediately. Invert it onto a wire rack, or if it is a large sheet of cake, onto wax paper. All lining papers should be stripped off as quickly as possible.

Sponge cake should always be an even golden brown and it should shrink slightly away from the sides of the pan. When all three tests—color, shrinkage, and the hand- or finger-pressure test—are positive, the cake is done. Approximate baking times follow the basic recipes, but for a delicate cake, all tests should be applied. Use the hand test even if the time schedule is right for your conditions, if for no other reason than to get your cake to whisper to you.

BASIC LIGHT SPONGE CAKE BISCUIT COLD METHOD

8 eggs, separated
½ cup sugar
Grated rind of 1 lemon
½ teaspoon vanilla extract
3 tablespoons powdered sugar
1 cup sifted flour
1 pinch salt
2 tablespoons melted and cooked butter

Preheat oven to 325°F. Butter, line with brown paper, and butter the surface of the paper in one shallow 11 × 17 × ⅞-inch baking pan or 2 8-inch layer cake pans.

Beat egg yolks with sugar, lemon rind, and vanilla until thick, creamy, and light. Beat egg whites until nearly stiff. Gradually add powdered sugar and beat until stiff. Fold egg whites into egg yolks very gently, while sifting over the flour and salt. Stir in the butter carefully and pour the batter into the prepared pans. Bake approximately 30 minutes or until it tests done.

BASIC LIGHT SPONGE CAKE FOR BISCUIT ROLLS AND YULE LOGS COLD METHOD

4 eggs, separated
7½ tablespoons sugar
10 tablespoons flour
½ teaspoon vanilla

Beat yolks with half the sugar until light and thick. Whip whites until half stiff. Add remaining sugar while continuing to whip until stiff. Fold whites into yolks while sifting over the flour, little by little. Add vanilla, or if preferred, add vanilla to yolks before beating. Pour batter into a buttered, paper-lined and rebuttered 8 × 15 inch cookie pan. Bake in a 375°F. oven for about 12 minutes. If edges of cake are brittle, trim them off. Spread cake quickly with filling while it is still in the pan. Roll it up tightly, stripping off the paper clinging to the reverse side. Wrap roll tightly in a long strip of wax paper. Secure the two ends of the paper with a twist and chill until ready to frost, glaze, or ice.

The sheet of batter may be cut into rounds or small heart shapes to be filled and made into a small, festive cake. For a larger baking sheet, increase quantities in the same proportions.

BASIC MOCHA CAKE

½ cup butter
½ cup vegetable shortening
1 cup sugar
1 egg
3 egg yolks
1 tablespoon coffee essence
4 tablespoons finely ground almonds or walnuts
1¼ cups flour
2 teaspoons baking powder
½ cup milk
3 stiffly beaten egg whites

Preheat oven to 350°F.

Cream butter and shortening with sugar until pale and foamy. Stir in egg and yolks. Stir in coffee essence, almonds, and flour sifted with baking powder and milk. Fold in stiffly beaten egg whites and bake in a prepared spring form or on a baking sheet until cake tests done. Spring form will take about 45 minutes, the sheet will take about 15 minutes.

BASIC HEAVY SPONGE CAKE

For loaf and tube cakes to be served with tea, coffee, or with fruit or cream desserts.

1 cup butter, at room temperature
1½ cups sugar
1 teaspoon grated lemon rind
1 teaspoon vanilla
6 eggs, separated
1½ cups milk
2 tablespoons brandy (optional)
4 cups cake flour, sifted with:
2 teaspoons baking powder

Cream butter with 1 cup sugar, lemon rind, and vanilla. Stir in yolks, one at a time, until light and creamy. Stir in milk and brandy. Beat whites until half stiff. Gradually add the remaining ½ cup sugar and continue to beat until stiff whites do not slide when bowl is inverted. Fold whites into butter-and-yolk mixture. Sift flour and baking powder gradually over the egg mixture and stir it in slowly and carefully. Bake in a prepared loaf or tube pan in a 350°F. oven for about 60 minutes or until golden, and a straw tests done.

BASIC BUTTER SPONGE CAKE

(*Genoise*)

WARM METHOD

6 whole eggs, large
¾ cup sugar
½ teaspoon grated lemon rind
½ teaspoon vanilla extract
1½ cups cake flour, sifted three times
3 tablespoons melted butter

Preheat oven to 325°F. for thick layers or loaf cakes. Preheat oven to 300°F. for thin layers or sheets.

Place water in lower section of double boiler and heat to just under boiling. Place upper section over the hot water and in it beat the eggs, sugar, lemon rind, and vanilla until light, foamy, and doubled in volume. When beater is lifted, the batter will flow in a "ribbon." It will also stand in a peak for an instant. This will take about 7 minutes with an electric hand beater and about 14 minutes with a rotary egg beater or French wire whisk. Take mixture from heat and continue to beat slowly until it is cold. (If time is short, the upper section of the double boiler may be set over ice water or ice cubes to speed the cooling, while beating slowly.) When mixture is cold, sift or sieve the flour over it, a little at a time, folding it in carefully and gently. Add warm butter, alternating with the flour, in a thin stream. Be sure the folding in is very gentle. Do not stir. Pour immediately into lightly buttered, or buttered and paper-lined, pans and bake until cake tests done. See preparation of pans and tests for doneness, page 244. A thin sheet of batter will bake approximately 12 to 14 minutes, a layer will take about 30 to 35 minutes, and a deep layer or loaf will take from 45 minutes to 1 hour.

It is impossible to give absolutely accurate baking time in minutes for sponge cakes, as much depends on thickness and depth of pans. The tests are completely reliable and easy to follow. Watch the cake carefully, take it out of the oven when it tests done, and immediately invert it onto a wire rack. Let it cool completely. If the batter was baked in a sheet to be used for a jelly roll or similar sponge roulade, invert it onto wax paper, draw off the brown paper liner, and cut off the brittle edges quickly. Spread with jelly or filling and roll up tightly while cake is warm. Roll into wax paper or foil to hold its shape while it cools. If whipped cream, ice cream, or butter cream is being used for the filling, roll after the sheet is cold. See page 245.

The following batters are all prepared in the same way as basic butter sponge cake I. Any slight change in method is noted below the ingredients.

CHOCOLATE BUTTER SPONGE CAKE

WARM METHOD

5 whole eggs, large
¾ cup sugar
½ teaspoon grated orange rind
1 teaspoon vanilla
1¼ cups cake flour
½ cup dark unsweetened cocoa powder
2½ tablespoons melted butter

Sift flour and cocoa powder together 3 times.

FILBERT OR HAZELNUT SPONGE CAKE

WARM METHOD

4 whole eggs, large
½ cup sugar
1½ cups toasted filberts,* ground
14 tablespoons cake flour (⅞ cup), sifted
7 tablespoons stale cake crumbs
1½ tablespoons melted butter

Sift flour 3 times, stir in ground nuts and cake crumbs, and add to egg mixture as in basic butter sponge cake I.

* Parched filberts may be washed to remove salt, oven-dried, and ground if there is no time to toast fresh ones.

WALNUT BUTTER SPONGE CAKE

WARM METHOD

6 whole eggs, large
⅔ cup sugar
¼ teaspoon vanilla
1½ cups cake flour, sifted
½ cup walnuts, ground
3 tablespoons melted butter

Sift flour 3 times, stir in walnuts.

COFFEE BUTTER SPONGE CAKE

WARM METHOD

6 whole eggs, large
¾ cup sugar
1 teaspoon instant coffee
½ teaspoon coffee extract; if unavailable, use 1½ teaspoons instant coffee
1¼ cups cake flour, sifted 3 times
3 tablespoons melted butter

Beat coffee with eggs and sugar.

Variations

1. Use 1 teaspoon grated orange rind and 1 tablespoon orange juice or extract in the batter for orange cakes.
2. Use 1 teaspoon grated lemon rind and 1 tablespoon lemon juice or extract in the batter for lemon cakes.

For directions for using cake layers or sheets for the traditional cakes, gâteaux, and torten, see page 254.

BASIC NUT OR FRUIT CAKE

1 cup flour
2 tablespoons baking powder
1¾ cups sugar
1 cup butter, at room temperature
4 eggs
1 cup milk
1 cup nuts, raisins, candied fruits, or combination of them
1 tablespoon vanilla

Preheat oven to 375°F.

Sift flour with baking powder and ¼ cup of the sugar. Cream butter with remaining sugar and beat in eggs one by one. Add the dry ingredients, alternating with the milk and vanilla, beginning and ending with dry ingredients. Add nuts or fruits and pour batter into a buttered, paper-lined and buttered large loaf pan, or 2 small loaf pans. Bake approximately 45 minutes or until a straw tests done.

BASIC LIGHT FRUIT CAKE

1 cup butter
¾ cup sugar
4 eggs
¼ cup almonds, blanched and slivered
¼ cup Brazil nuts, chopped
2⅔ cups cake flour
1 teaspoon baking powder
½ teaspoon salt
1 cup raisins
1 cup currants
¼ cup candied orange peel, chopped
¼ cup candied lemon peel, chopped
¼ cup citron, chopped
¼ cup candied cherries, chopped
¼ cup orange juice

Cream butter, beat in sugar, beat in eggs, one by one, beating well before adding the next. Stir in nuts. Sift flour, baking powder, and salt into a bowl, add all the fruits and juice, and stir well. Add the butter-and-egg mixture and pour into 3 loaf pans, buttered, and lined with brown paper and rebuttered. Bake in a 275°F. oven for about 1 hour and 20 minutes.

Variations

1. Decorate top of cakes with whole blanched almonds, candied cherries, and citron.

2. Fruits and proportion of fruits and nuts can be varied according to taste.

3. Bishop's bread: Add 1 package chocolate bits and use ½ cup almonds instead of Brazil nuts. Omit citron and candied cherries.

Do not attempt to cut fruit cake until the second day, preferably longer.

BASIC DARK FRUIT CAKE

½ cup butter
¾ cup brown sugar
2 eggs
1 teaspoon grated lemon rind
1¾ cups flour
½ teaspoon baking soda
½ teaspoon salt
½ teaspoon cinnamon
¼ teaspoon ground cloves
½ cup light cream
½ cup molasses
3 tablespoons brandy
½ cup chopped raisins
½ cup chopped currants
½ cup chopped nuts
¼ cup flour

In a large bowl, cream butter, beat in sugar, eggs, and lemon rind as for light fruit cake, page 250. Sift flour with soda, salt, and spices and set aside. Stir cream, molasses, and brandy together and beat into the butter-and-egg mixture alternating with the dry ingredients. Dredge fruit and nuts with flour. Pour a thin layer of batter into a large buttered paper-lined and buttered ring or cake pan. Sprinkle with some of the flour-dredged fruit, then add batter. Continue in layers until all the ingredients are used. End with a thin layer of batter.

Bake in a 325°F. oven for about 1¼ hours. After half the baking time has elapsed, cover the cake with foil or paper to keep it from becoming too brown. Pour a little brandy over the warm cake. Cover it and let it ripen for several days.

BASIC QUICK BREADS

Bake the day before using.

WALNUT BREAD

(*using baking powder*)

2 cups flour
2 teaspoons baking powder
1 teaspoon salt
½ cup sugar
1 large egg yolk
1 cup milk
2 tablespoons melted butter
⅔ cup shelled walnuts

Sift flour, baking powder, salt, and sugar into a bowl. Beat in yolk, milk, and butter. Sprinkle nuts with a little flour and beat them into the batter. Butter 2 miniature loaf pans, sprinkle with flour, and divide the batter between them. Set them aside for 25 minutes. Bake in a 350°F. oven for about 45 minutes or until bread is brown and has pulled away slightly from the sides of the pans. Cool on wire racks. Wrap and place in a ventilated breadbox until the following day.

Variations

1. Substitute pecans, filberts, or toasted almonds for the walnuts.
2. Substitute diced dates or diced candied orange peel for the walnuts.
3. Substitute ⅔ cup peanut butter for the walnuts. Omit butter and use 1 whole egg. Bake about 10 minutes longer.
4. Orange Pecan Bread: Substitute ½ cup orange marmalade for the sugar. Add 2 teaspoons grated orange rind and reduce milk to ⅔ cup.

PECAN DATE BREAD

(*using baking soda*)

¾ cup boiling water or cranberry juice
1 cup dates, pitted and diced
¾ cup sugar
¼ cup melted butter
1 egg, beaten
1¾ cups flour combined with:
1 cup chopped pecans
1 teaspoon soda
½ teaspoon salt

Pour boiling water over dates, sugar, and melted butter in a large bowl. Set aside until cold. Beat in eggs, the combined flour and nuts, soda, and salt. Fill into 3 buttered and floured miniature bread tins. Bake in a 350°F. oven for 45 to 55 minutes until brown and slightly shrunken from sides of pan.

Variations

Banana Bread: Sift 2 cups flour with 1 teaspoon each baking soda and salt and ¾ cup sugar. Stir in 2 beaten eggs, 4 mashed bananas, and ½ cup chopped pecans. Bake 55 to 60 minutes.

BASIC CHOCOLATE CAKE

2 cups cake flour
1 teaspoon baking soda
½ teaspoon salt
4 squares (4 ounces) semisweet chocolate
½ cup cream
1½ cups sugar
½ cup butter
3 eggs
⅔ cup milk
1 teaspoon rum or vanilla

Sift flour, soda, and salt together and set aside. Melt chocolate slowly in top of double boiler, over boiling water, with the cream. Beat until smooth. Add ½ cup sugar and beat 3 minutes longer, set aside.

In a large bowl, cream butter slowly with remaining sugar, add eggs, one by one, and beat well after each addition. Beat in part of the sifted flour, add milk and remaining flour alternately, a little at a time, ending with flour. Add chocolate mixture and rum. Bake in 2 8-inch buttered layer cake pans in a 350°F. oven for about 45 minutes or until a straw tests done. Cool layers on a wire rack. Do not assemble until later in the day or the following day.

BASIC DOBOS TORTE AND 7-LAYER CAKE BATTER

1¼ cups flour
1 pinch salt
4 eggs
1⅓ cups sifted confectioners sugar

Prepare baking sheets or cookie tins by brushing them lightly with melted butter or oil. Dust lightly with flour and tap to distribute flour evenly. Use a 7½-inch plate as a guide, or use a 7½-inch diameter paper circle, and trace 7 circles on the floured tins. Set them aside. Sift flour and salt and set aside. Whisk eggs and sugar in the top of a double boiler over simmering water until thick and light in color. Take from heat and continue whisking (or beat with an electric hand beater) until cold. Fold the flour lightly into the egg mixture. Divide the batter into 7 parts and spread them evenly on the prepared sheets or tins. Bake in a 350°F. oven for about 7 minutes, until lightly browned. Trim layers while they are still warm on the baking sheet. Lift them up carefully with a spatula and cool on racks. For dobos torte, select the underside of the best layer to use as the top. Lay it on a lightly oiled slab and pour over the liquid caramel in a wide stream to cover the entire top. Cool slightly, then mark in portions with an oiled knife, as the caramel will splinter if it is cut after it is cold. For seven-layer cake, pour chocolate fondant icing on the top layer. Fill both cakes with a double portion of basic butter cream, page 257. Assemble the cake and spread the sides with butter cream. Small rosettes of butter cream can be piped around the outside edge of the top.

CARAMEL GLAZE

5 ounces lump sugar
6 tablespoons water

Melt sugar in water in a heavy pan over low heat. When it is completely dissolved into a clear syrup, increase heat to boil and boil rapidly, undisturbed, until a rich brown color is reached. Pour at once on top layer of dobos torte.

THE TRADITIONAL CAKES: GÂTEAUX AND TORTEN

The English word "cake" has come to mean the plainer loaf, sponge, and layer cakes, while *Gâteaux* is the French and *Torten* is the German word for more elaborate cakes. The name usually depends on the filling or predominant flavor of the cake or on the person or occasion for which the cake was named.

CHOCOLATE CAKES

GÂTEAU AU CHOCOLAT

Chocolate-base layers filled with chocolate-flavored pastry cream and iced with chocolate butter cream. Decorated with a border of piped chocolate butter cream rosettes. The center is filled with mounded chocolate shavings.

GÂTEAU MEXICAIN

Chocolate-base layers filled with chocolate butter cream. It is iced with chocolate fondant icing over apricot glaze. This is a layer cake. Sacher torte is similar but is not a filled layer cake.

OTHELLO TORTE

Prepare as seven-layer cake. Press shaved chocolate against the butter cream sides and pipe large chocolate butter cream rosettes around the edge of the top. Set a small baked meringue round into each rosette.

SACHER TORTE

Chocolate batter baked in a spring form. The cake is not cut in layers. Cake covered with apricot glaze and heavily iced with chocolate fondant icing. Serve with whipped cream.

GÂTEAU PRALINE

A genoise base filled with vanilla butter cream mixed with praline powder. Iced with white fondant or butter cream icing. Sides dusted with praline powder.

GÂTEAU CENDRILLON

A coffee-flavored genoise base filled with coffee-flavored butter cream. Top and sides are covered with coffee fondant or butter cream. Decorated with coffee butter cream rosettes with a toasted filbert pressed into each.

GÂTEAU AU MOCHA; MOCHA TORTE

As above, with sides covered with chopped toasted almonds, and almonds substituted for the filberts on top.

ESTERHAZY TORTE

Nut-base layers filled with rum-flavored pastry cream. Iced with a chocolate butter cream top and vanilla butter cream sides. Chocolate butter cream rosettes around the base and lines of chocolate butter cream on the vanilla sides.

BASIC LAYER CAKE OR TORTE

Assembling, Filling, Icing, and Decorating

Cake layers are baked out of the various batters in four ways. The customary American way is to bake two or three separate layers in layer cake pans. This means that a three-layer cake has six crusts. In Europe the batter is usually baked in a deep spring form or in a deep tin with a removable bottom and cut into layers after it is cold. Since the European cake has only a firm top and bottom crust, the filling is apt to saturate the cake when it stands too long before cutting. Another method is to bake the batter in large sheets and cut out the layers after the sheet has cooled. The wasted corners of cake can be used for petits fours. Thin cake layers for seven-layer cake are either done by the sheet method or the batter is spread thinly on the backs of cake pans. The layers then resemble thin disks. A combination of the first and second method is to bake 2 or even 3 layers and split them into 4 or 6 layers before assembling the cake.

When the cake layers are cold, trim them evenly, turn them, and select the best for the top. Always use them with the underside up. Brush off any crumbs and spread filling or butter cream on all but the top layer. Assemble the layers. If the cake is high and shows any inclination to slide, secure it with a long, thin skewer. Chill the filled cake until it is set. Carefully withdraw the skewer and set the cake on four or more wedges of wax paper on the platter from which it will be served. The purpose is to catch the icing that runs down from the cake on the wax paper. A single sheet of wax paper could not be drawn out after the icing has set, but the separate wedges can be pulled out without disturbing the cake.

Soft icings or prepared icing mixes are usually swirled onto cakes with a palette knife or spatula. Butter cream is spread more thinly and evenly. Torten or European cakes are either covered with glossy fondant icing or a thin layer of butter cream. The tops of the cakes are then decorated with rosettes and swirls of piped butter cream. Fondant is usually poured over the cake after it has been spread with a film of apricot glaze to even all irregularities and prevent crumbs from marring the surface. The top of the fondant is either left plain or decorated with butter cream. Many torten have fondant tops and the sides are spread with butter cream. Shaved or chopped nuts or macaroon crumbs are lightly pressed against the butter cream.

Cake layers or cakes iced with simple sugar frosting can be frozen as long as three or four months. Freeze cake, then wrap tightly, and thaw in the wrapper. Cake sheets or layers freeze more successfully than filled or iced cakes.

BASIC BUTTER CREAM I

SMALL CAKE	LARGE CAKE
¾ cup butter	1¼ cups butter
¾ cup superfine powdered sugar	1¼ cups superfine powdered sugar
3 small eggs	5 small eggs
1 teaspoon vanilla	2 teaspoons vanilla

Cream butter, gradually adding half the sugar. Beat eggs with remaining sugar until creamy and light. Combine both mixtures, add vanilla, and beat only until well combined.

For all butter cream or custard butter cream cake fillings, use butter at room temperature and do not overbeat. Butter cannot absorb much moisture, so do not try to flavor butter cream fillings with very liquid flavorings, such as too much orange or lemon juice, or coffee. Use concentrated flavorings such as instant coffee or coffee extract. Cocoa powder, strong liqueurs, thick flavorings such as melted chocolate, puréed chestnuts or fruits, or praline powder are easily incorporated. Omit one egg when adding purées.

BASIC BUTTER CREAM II

(*Crème au Beurre*)

3 tablespoons granulated sugar
¼ cup water
2 egg yolks
¾ cup unsalted butter

In a heavy saucepan, bring sugar and water to a boil over medium heat. Let it boil undisturbed until the syrup reaches the "thread" stage or 216° to 218°F. on a candy thermometer. Take from heat immediately and pour the syrup in a thin stream over the egg yolks, while whisking or beating steadily with a hand electric beater until the mixture is thick. Cream the butter and gradually beat the yolk-and-sugar mixture into it. (For dobos torte and seven-layer cake, stir in 4 ounces semi-sweet chocolate, melted and cooled.)

BASIC FRENCH BUTTER CREAM FILLING AND FROSTING

8 egg yolks
2½ cups sugar
1 pound soft butter
½ cup melted chocolate, extra-strength coffee, strained fruit pulp, or fruit juice
2 teaspoons vanilla or suitable flavoring

Beat yolks and sugar until creamy and thick. Beat in the soft butter with an electric beater and add flavorings last. Do not overbeat.

BASIC FONDANT ICING

Fondant requires three pieces of equipment. It should be worked on a marble slab, which may mean you will have to make it on your coffee table. Do not attempt it on metal, which turns the Fondant an unattractive shade of gray, or on wood. A wide enameled surface can be used if necessary. To avoid making a sugar test, use a candy thermometer and work the fondant icing with a wide spatula.

2½ cups sugar
¼ cup glucose, from the pharmacy
1 cup water

Place all ingredients in a heavy enameled saucepan and boil into a clear syrup until candy thermometer registers 240°F. Pour syrup onto a wet marble slab or enamel surface and allow to cool until the surface seems to film slightly. With the spatula, work the Fondant as you would work putty with a putty knife, until it becomes opaque and white but not hard. Do *not* work it until it granulates. Watch carefully. Pour it into a jar, cover, and store in a cool place until needed. Before using, warm the fondant in the top of a double boiler over boiling water, until it reaches pouring but not running consistency. If necessary stir in a little light corn syrup to bring it just to the right stage.

Chocolate Fondant Icing: When fondant is being heated in top of double boiler, add melted unsweetened chocolate. Add enough to turn the fondant to a rich, deep brown color.

Coffee Fondant Icing: Add coffee extract or essence, to taste, to the heating fondant.

Vanilla Icing: Add vanilla extract, to taste, to the heating fondant.

Variations

Add fruit flavors, liqueur flavors, and a few drops of food color to heating fondant.

Application

Before the fondant has been brought to the proper flowing consistency, arrange filled cake, individual cakes, or petits fours on a wire rack set over an enamel pan. Europeans spread large cakes with a thin film of strained jam before applying the icing. This prevents cake crumbs from marring the mirror-like surface. Pour fondant icing in a wide stream over the top of the cake in such a way that it will flow over the entire top surface without the help of a knife. Never spread fondant icing in any way except to tilt the cake to make it flow in all directions. Start with a generous flow to begin with (double or triple the recipe for a very large cake). The flow should cover the top and run down over the sides in one perfect stream. Any fondant icing that does not cling to the cake drops into the pan under the rack and can be reheated and reused.

Petits fours can be given a second coat of fondant icing. It is wise to start with small pieces and do a large cake after you have experience in handling it.

When the perfect mirror-like surface is accomplished it is rarely broken with any other form of decoration. The famous sacher torte stays perfectly plain. Petits fours are decorated with a modest candied Violet, a little Silver Shot, or a sliver of Angelica. Some large cakes are coated with fondant icing on top (which is a good way to start learning) and spread with butter cream on the side. The butter cream is covered with chopped or flaked nuts and the outside edge of the top is decorated with piped butter cream.

Many specialty shops carry canned fondant that has only to be heated and flavored.

Note: Fondant is also used for filling chocolate candies and peppermint drops. Flavor with mint extract and drop on wax paper.

BASIC BLENDER BUTTER CREAM

3 cups confectioners sugar, sifted
¼ cup melted chocolate, strong coffee, orange or fruit juice
⅓ cup butter
1 teaspoon vanilla, coffee, almond, or maple extract, or liqueur best suited to the flavor of the cream

Blend 1 cup sugar with melted chocolate or liquid for 1 minute. Scrape sides of container down into mixture. Add butter and flavoring and ½ cup sugar; blend for a few seconds. Pour the mixture into a bowl and beat in remaining sugar.

Makes enough for 1 layer cake or 28 cup cakes.

CRÈME SAINT-HONORÉ

5 egg yolks
½ cup sugar
½ cup flour
1½ cups milk
½ tablespoon gelatin
¼ cup cold water
10 egg whites

Beat yolks and sugar until light and creamy, add the flour gradually and stir well. Bring milk to a boil, add it to mixture and stir well. Set over medium heat, stir, and bring back to boiling. Stir in gelatin previously softened for 15 minutes in water and stir until dissolved. Take from heat, cool and fold in the stiffly beaten egg whites.

BASIC CUSTARD CREAM FILLING I
PASTRY CREAM (*Crème Patisserie*)

½ cup sugar
3 egg yolks
6 tablespoons flour
1 cup boiling milk
½ teaspoon vanilla
1 teaspoon sweet butter

Beat sugar and egg yolks for about 3 minutes until light in color and creamy in texture. Raise the beater, and when the mixture that clings to it runs back into the bowl in the form of a ribbon, it is sufficiently beaten. Beat in flour and gradually beat in the milk in a very thin stream. Pour the mixture into a round-bottomed, heavy saucepan and set it over medium heat. Bring it slowly to a boil, stirring constantly with a French wire whisk, this should take about 3 minutes. Reduce heat and continue to cook, stirring for 3 more minutes. If the custard has any lumps beat it vigorously until it is smooth. Take from heat and beat in vanilla or any called for flavoring and the butter.

There is no change in proportions if recipe is doubled.

Butter the top of créme patisserie if it has to be stored, as for velouté sauce, page 53. Store in refrigerator up to 1 week.

Makes about 1¼ cups, sufficient to fill 1 small or 6 individual fruit tarts, or 6 medium cream puffs.

BASIC CUSTARD CREAM FILLING WITH STIFF EGG WHITES, II
CRÈME SAINT-HONORÉ

1 recipe basic custard cream filling I
6 egg whites
1 tablespoon sugar

After completing the basic custard cream filling I, set it aside. Beat egg whites until they are about half beaten. Gradually add the sugar while continuing to beat until they stand in soft peaks and do not move when bowl is tilted. Fold the stiff egg whites into the warm basic custard cream filling and serve at once or chill and serve cold.

Makes about 3 cups, sufficient for 6 large cream puffs, 12 small profiteroles or 8 medium éclairs. Double quantity for 1 Gâteau Saint-Honoré or 1 Paris-Brest.

Variations

1. Almond Custard Cream Filling: Add ½ cup blanched almonds, grated, to 1 recipe basic custard cream filling I or II and add ¼ teaspoon almond extract.
2. Chocolate Custard Cream Filling, Crème Au Chocolat: Add 2 squares semisweet chocolate, melted, and 1 tablespoon heavy rum to 1 recipe basic custard cream filling I or II.
3. Coffee Custard Cream Filling: Add 2 tablespoons instant coffee or coffee extract to 1 recipe basic custard cream filling I or II.
4. Macaroon Custard Cream Filling: Crush stale or oven-dried macaroons to obtain ⅔ cup crumbs. Combine crumbs with 1 recipe basic custard cream filling I or II and add ¼ teaspoon almond extract.
5. Praline Custard Cream Filling, Crème Pralinée: Add ⅔ cup finely crushed praline candies to a double recipe basic custard cream filling I or II. Use to fill 1 Paris-Brest, 12 profiteroles, or as filling for 1 layer cake. Pralines can be purchased in gourmet or candy shops.
6. Rum Custard Cream Filling: Add 2 tablespoons heavy rum to 1 recipe basic custard cream filling I or II.

Combinations

Grated almonds, praline powder, or crushed macaroons may be

added to chocolate or coffee custard cream filling in the same proportions as shown above.

BASIC MERINGUE FOR TORTEN AND SHELLS

(*Vacherin*)

5 large egg whites
1½ cups sugar

Use eggs or egg whites that are a few days old. Beat egg whites half stiff, gradually adding half the sugar while beating stiff. Fold in remaining sugar.

MERINGUE TORTE

(*Gâteaux Vacherin*)

Fill this meringue into a rinsed pastry bag and pipe through a plain tube onto a piece of floured parchment paper on a baking sheet. Start in a spiral from the center and pipe around and around until you have a 9-inch disk. Pipe 2 disks and bake in a low oven until dried, cream colored, and brittle. Peel paper off carefully, and set in a "warm" oven to dry further. Pipe the remaining meringue through a fluted tube into a 9-inch circle of adjoining rosettes. Pipe an arabesque in the center if you like. Bake and subsequently dry in a "warm" oven as for the previous layers. Assemble the layers with whipped cream, add crushed raspberries or any preferred fruit if wanted, top with the rosette layer, and serve.

Use the same recipe for meringue shells and small rosettes.

AUSTRIAN MERINGUE CAKE

(*Spanische Wind Torte*)

The Austrian meringue cake is another version of France's vacherin. The meringue has to be made in 2 or 3 batches depending on available oven space. The bottom layer and top layer should be piped and baked like vacherin, except that the top has more elaborate rosettes and curlicues. It has to be baroque and festive. After, or while these are baking, pipe 2 or 3 hollow rings in the same size as the base and bake them with or after the base and lid. When rings are cold, whip up the second batch of meringue. Assemble the rings on the base and use the fresh meringue to smooth the sides, so that a hollow, fairly smooth meringue shell is obtained. Bake it until it is dry, like vacherin. Before serving, fill the interior with raspberries or strawberries and whipped cream and cover with the prepared lid. Serve each guest with part of the meringue and berries and cream.

SALZBURGER NOCKERDLN

Prepare all ingredients and place them within easy reach. The preparations cannot be delayed after they are started.

4 egg yolks
1 tablespoon flour
Grated rind of 1 lemon
3 tablespoons milk
3 tablespoons sweet butter
½ cup powdered sugar, sifted
8 large egg whites

Beat yolks with flour and lemon rind until creamy. Set them aside. Heat milk, butter, and 2 tablespoons of the sugar in a shallow, heatproof pan measuring about 7½ × 11½ inches, until butter has melted. Do not scald the milk, only warm it. Take from oven and increase oven heat to 450°F. If there are two ovens available, do these two steps simultaneously. Beat the egg whites until stiff, incorporating the sugar gradually after they are half stiff. Fold yolk mixture gently and quickly into the whites and scoop up 6 big sections of the meringue with a wide piece of cardboard. Float them on the warm milk in the prepared pan. Bake in the 450°F. oven for about 5 minutes or until puffed and golden. Serve faster than immediately.

BASIC LINZER PASTE FOR TORTE AND TARTS

1⅓ cups shelled almonds or hazelnuts (filberts)
3 large egg yolks, beaten
Grated rind of 1 lemon

2 cups flour
½ cup sugar
1¾ bars cold butter (14 tablespoons)
1 12-ounce jar or 1 cup strawberry jam
Vanilla sugar for top

Parch almonds or filberts in a wide pan in a 250°F. oven for 30 minutes. Shake every 10 minutes. Grate them through a fine nut grinder into a large bowl. Add flour and sugar. Cut butter into the dry ingredients with a pastry blender until mixture resembles small peas. Stir in egg yolks and lemon rind. Work into a smooth dough with your hands. The dough will not gather until the warmth of your hands has softened the butter. Do not overwork; the dough should not become oily. Chill it while preparing pan.

Butter a 9-inch low spring-form layer cake pan, or flan ring, lay brown paper on the bottom, and butter the brown paper. (If a flan ring is used, butter a small baking sheet, cover with brown paper, butter the paper, and set the buttered flan ring on it.) Divide paste in half, press one half evenly into the pan with a raised ¼-inch rim around the edge. Roll remaining paste into pencil-thick rolls. It may be necessary to chill dough again as the nuts make the paste crumble easily. If rolls are not very long, patch them together. Fill the shallow base of paste with strawberry jam. Lay a lattice over it, but do not attempt to interlace it. Use the last lengths of rolls around the edge to cover the ends of the lattice strips. Press it down firmly, especially where it is pieced.

Bake in a 375°F. oven for 45 minutes or until brown. Watch it after 30 minutes. Take from oven, sieve vanilla sugar over the hot cake. Remove from spring form or flan ring when it is cold. Set aside for a day or two, when it will slice easily. Sprinkle with vanilla sugar before serving.

Variations

Fill with apricot jam, or add to the paste cinnamon and ground cloves to taste.

LINZER TARTS

Roll or pat out paste to ⅛-inch thickness, cut it into 3½-inch rounds, and cut a 1¼-inch round out of the center of half of them. When all paste is used up, transfer them to a buttered baking sheet and bake in a 375°F. oven for about 18 minutes, until golden and loosened from the baking sheet. Transfer at once with a spatula to a piece of wax paper. When rounds are cool, spread the solid ones carefully and thinly with apricot or sieved raspberry jam and sandwich a "ring" on top of each. Fill a little more jam in the centers, sprinkle with vanilla sugar, and serve with tea or with fruit or ice cream desserts.

BASIC COOKIE PASTE WITH HARDCOOKED EGG YOLKS
BROWN SUGAR COOKIES

6 hardcooked egg yolks
1 cup butter
1⅓ cups sifted brown sugar, packed
½ teaspoon cinnamon powder (optional)
2 cups sifted flour
1 egg white, lightly beaten with:
1 tablespoon water
½ cup shaved almonds

Preheat oven to 350°F.

Press yolks through a coarse sieve and cream them with butter until smooth. Work in sugar, cinnamon, and flour until smooth. Chill paste for 30 minutes. Roll out on a very lightly floured pastry canvas or on a sugared pastry canvas and cut out in desired shapes with a 2-inch cookie cutter, or shape into a roll, and slice. Arrange on a buttered cookie sheet and brush tops with egg white, sprinkle with almonds, and bake for about 10 minutes. Lift from cookie sheet with a spatula; cookies stiffen as they cool. Makes about 80 cookies.

BASIC SUGAR PASTE
FOR TART SHELLS, BASES, AND COOKIES

2 cups flour
4 egg yolks
4½ tablespoons sugar
½ cup butter, thinly sliced
¼ teaspoon vanilla extract

Sift flour onto pastry board, make a well in the center, and put egg yolks, sugar, butter, and vanilla into it. Stir center ingredients into a paste and quickly work flour into the paste to obtain a smooth dough. In warm weather, chill for a few minutes and roll out to a little thicker than ⅛ inch. Carefully move the paste to a flan ring on a heavy cookie sheet, or to a straight-sided layer cake pan, and line the ring or pan with it. Trim off the edges and chill before baking. Bake in a 400°F. oven for 30 to 35 minutes or until golden. Cool before filling.

Roll out trimmings to ¼ inch, cut into heart shapes, rounds, rings, or any attractive shape and chill. Bake on a lightly buttered cookie sheet in a 375°F. oven for about 10 minutes or until golden. Take from sheet with a spatula and cool. Lay cutout on the tart after it is filled with any cream or mousse filling.

Variations

1. Flavor with ½ teaspoon cinnamon and ⅛ teaspoon ground cloves or nutmeg.
2. Substitute almond extract for vanilla extract and decorate cookies or tarts with scalded almonds.

Index